Table of Contents

Introduction 12
Sous Vide Breakfast Recipes 13
    Cinnamon Toast 13
    Cheesy Eggs Mix 13
    Shallot Scramble 13
    Ham and Eggs 13
    Crab and Eggs Mix 14
    Lime Coconut Jars 14
    Berry Coconut Mix 14
    Parmesan Eggs 14
    Scrambled Eggs 15
    Pesto Eggs 15
    Spinach Scramble 15
    Herbed Ricotta Cheese 15
    Cinnamon Rice Pudding 16
    Asparagus, Spinach and Eggs Mix 16
    Coconut Eggs 16
    Pepper Eggs Mix 16
    Sausage Ramekins 17
    Eggs, Green Beans and Mushrooms 17
    Cream Cheese and Spinach Eggs 17
    Smoked Salmon, Avocado and Eggs Mix 17
    Lime Eggs, Tomato and Avocado Mix 18
    Zucchini and Eggs 18
    Ground Beef and Eggs Ramekins 18
    Tomato Ramekins 18
    Coconut Leeks Mix 19
    Almond Oats 19
    Lemon Eggs 19
    Oregano Scramble 19
    Bacon and Radish Scramble 20
    Brussels Sprouts Salad 20
    Seeds Porridge 20
    Cinnamon Eggs 20
    Chicken and Eggs 21
    Lime and Chia Eggs 21
    Broccoli Eggs 21
    Ginger Tomatoes Eggs 21
    Bok Choy and Veggies Bowls 22
    Bok Choy and Eggs 22
    Greens and Eggs 22
    Eggs and Asparagus 23
    Zucchini Bowls 23
    Tomato Sausage Salad 23
    Sausages and Mushrooms Mix 23
    Kale, Sausage and Eggs 24
    Eggs, Cheese and Sun-dried Tomatoes Mix 24
    Shrimp, Eggs and Mushrooms 24
    Enchilada Eggs Mix 25
    Italian Squash and Olives Bowls 25
    Prosciutto and Zucchini Eggs 25
    Green Beans, Kale and Eggs 26
    Oregano Eggs 26
    Quinoa and Berries Bowls 26

Eggplant Bowls 26
Banana Oatmeal 27
Cheddar Eggs 27
Spinach Frittata 27
Mushroom Oatmeal 27
Strawberry Bowls...28
Sweet Potato Mix 28
Walnut and Berries Bowls...28
Chives Avocado Quinoa 28
Balsamic Avocado and Tomato Salad 29
Apple Salad...29
Pesto Zucchini Ramekins 29
Chickpeas Breakfast Spread 29

Sous Vide Lunch Recipes 30
Lemon Shrimp and Avocado Bowls 30
Mustard Salmon Steaks 30
Shrimp Salad...30
Balsamic Calamari and Tomatoes 30
BBQ Cod Mix 31
Cod Salsa 31
Calamari, Salmon and Shrimp Bowls..31
Mustard Salmon Mix 32
Creamy Calamari..32
Lime Lobster 32
Chicken, Shrimp and Rice...32
Vanilla and Butter Shrimp 33
Pork and Blueberries Mix 33
BBQ and Paprika Ribs...33
Herbed Pork and Sun dried Tomatoes..33
Buttery Pork Tenderloin..34
Garlic and Nutmeg Pork 34
Thyme Pork and Carrots 34
Thyme Pork Chops...35
Lamb Rack and Cherry Tomatoes Mix 35
Lamb and Pomegranate Mix 35
Lamb, Leeks and Mushroom Mix 35
Coriander Leg Of Lamb...36
Lamb Fillets and Olives...36
Rack of Lamb and Baby Cauliflower Mix 36
Garlic and Peppercorns Lamb Chops..36
Sage Cajun Turkey..37
Ginger and Shallot Duck 37
Curry Chicken Thighs..37
Provence Chicken Breast 37
Turkey Breast and Cranberries 38
Chili Chicken 38
Spring Onion and Soy Chicken 38
Beet Cream Soup...38
Chicken Soup..39
Cauliflower Soup 39
Zucchini Cream..39
Roasted Pork and Apples..40
Pork Chops and Mushrooms 40
Lemony and Parsley Beef..40
Cranberry Beef..40

Maple Pork Chops ... 41
Pork Roast and Olives Salsa ... 41
Lamb and Spinach Salad ... 41
Harrisa Lamb Mix ... 41
Lamb with Fennel and Tomatoes ... 42
Beef and Yogurt Mix ... 42
Chili and Paprika Pork ... 42
Greek Rosemary Lamb Chops ... 43
Curry and Coconut Pork Chops ... 43
Tomato and Eggplant Stew ... 43
Lentils Stew ... 43
Turmeric Veggies and Rice ... 44
Pork Bowls ... 44
Shrimp and Sweet Potato Bowls ... 44
Chicken and Eggplants ... 45
Turkey Hash ... 45
Eggplant Stew ... 45
Turmeric Shrimp Mix ... 46
Beef and Tomato Mix ... 46
Lentils and Quinoa Stew ... 46
Chickpeas Stew ... 47
Peppers Stew ... 47
Potato Stew ... 47
Green Beans Salad ... 47

Sous Vide Side Dish Recipes ... 48

Cauliflower Salad ... 48
Spinach and Pear Salad ... 48
Balsamic Beet Salad ... 48
Glazed Beets ... 48
Orange Green Beans ... 49
Lime Brussels Sprouts ... 49
Buttery Squash Mix ... 49
Parmesan Fennel ... 49
Soy Mushrooms ... 50
Balsamic Carrots and Parsnips ... 50
Thai Eggplant Mix ... 50
Peppers and Eggplant Mix ... 50
Peppers and Seeds Mix ... 51
Parsley Asparagus ... 51
Olives and Cauliflower ... 51
Tarragon Mushrooms ... 51
Creamy Spinach ... 52
Parsley Cauliflower ... 52
Mushroom and Broccoli Mix ... 52
Cumin Okra ... 52
Eggplant and Okra Mix ... 53
Lemony Okra ... 53
Cheesy Broccoli ... 53
Tomato and Okra Mix ... 53
Italian Tomatoes ... 54
Mushroom Salad ... 54
Coriander Tomato and Spinach Mix ... 54
Tomato and Mango Salsa ... 55
Balsamic Tomato and Pineapple Mix ... 55
Eggplant and Pearl Onion Mix ... 55

Spicy Beets and Okra 55
Coconut Endives and Radish 56
Cabbage and Carrots Mix 56
Kale and Spring Onions Mix 56
Simple Cabbage and Avocado Mix 57
Green Beans and Walnuts Mix 57
Lemon Olives and Radish Mix 57
Cauliflower and Chard Mix 58
Ginger Broccoli and Radish Mix 58
Apple and Zucchini Mix 58
Creamy Garlic Spinach and Corn 59
Lemon Greens Mix 59
Spicy Collards Greens 59
Spinach, Mango and Tomatoes 60
Mustard Greens, Olives and Kale Salad 60
Greens and Shallots Mix 60
Jalapeno Greens Mix 61
Sprouts Salad 61
Mango and Radishes Mix 61
Creamy Radish and Corn Mix 61
Balsamic Carrots 62
Creamy Corn 62
Rosemary Broccoli Mix 62
Creamy Tomatoes 62
Hot Cauliflower 63
Ginger Green Beans 63
Dill Eggplant 63
Chives Potatoes 64
Black Beans Mix 64
Dill Peas 64

Sous Vide Snack and Appetizer Recipes 65
Turkey Meatballs 65
Pearl Onions Bowls 65
Thyme Shrimp Platter 65
Cauliflower Spread 65
Coconut Cheese Dip 66
Shrimp and Pineapple Bowls 66
Peppers Salsa 66
Radish Chips 67
Zucchini Salsa 67
Crab Dip 67
Olives Balls 68
Spinach Dip 68
Stuffed Mushrooms 68
Spicy Meatballs 69
Parmesan Chicken Wings 69
Cauliflower Bowls 69
Artichoke Dip 70
Shrimp Bites 70
Lemon Oysters 70
Parsley Calamari Bites 71
Salmon Salsa 71
Tuna Bites 71
Shrimp and Cucumber Salad 72
Lemon Mussels 72

Squid Salad 72
Calamari and Radish Salad 73
Octopus and Mango Salad 73
Clam Bowls 73
Italian Shrimp Salad 74
Cod Salsa 74
Apple and Shrimp Salsa 74
Shrimp and Pico De Gallo 75
Scallops and Radish Salad 75
Tuna Salad 75
Tuna Bites and Mint Sauce 76
Bbq Chicken Meatballs 76
Creamy Corn Dip 76
Chicken Salad 77
Duck and Spinach Salad 77
Stuffed Peppers 77
Chicken Dip 78
Chinese Beef Bites 78
Mushroom Dip 78
Shrimp Meatballs 79
Sausage Bites 79
Radish Dip 79
Sriracha Turkey Bites 80
Beet Salsa 80
Fennel and Shrimp Salad 80
Pesto Radish and Corn Dip 81
Balsamic Salmon Bites 81
Spicy Lentils Bowls 81
Eggplant Dip 81
Chickpeas Spread 82
Garlic Chicken Bites 82
Coconut Dip 82
Pesto Dip 82
Shrimp and Olives Bowls 83
Mussels Bowls 83
Walnuts Bowls 83

Sous Vide Fish and Seafood Recipes 84
Lemon Salmon 84
Chili Tuna 84
Shrimp and Tomatoes Mix 84
Paprika Cod 84
Shrimp and Spinach 85
Cod and Green Beans 85
Turmeric Tuna 85
Salmon and Avocado Mix 85
Shrimp and Corn 86
Lemon Cod and Peas 86
Ginger Cod 86
Salmon and Olives 86
Curry Shrimp 87
Chives Shrimp Mix 87
Pesto Sea Bass 87
Shrimp and Pineapple Bowls 87
Garlic Sea Bass 88
Shrimp and Broccoli 88

Tuna and Brussels Sprouts 88
Mackerel and Avocado Mix 89
Tuna and Asparagus 89
Cod and Carrots 89
Chili Cod 90
Balsamic Salmon and Beans 90
Lemon Trout and Cabbage 90
Lime and Chili Mussels 91
Chives Cod 91
Tuna Bites with Pineapple 91
Sea Bass and Avocado 91
Smoked Salmon and Chives 92
Shrimp and Eggplant 92
Garlic Mackerel 92
Coconut Cod 92
Shrimp and Peas 93
Italian Mackerel 93
Honey Cod 93
Basil Shrimp 93
Curry Sea Bass 94
Calamari and Mushrooms 94
Curry Trout and Green Beans 94
Coriander Shrimp Mix 94
Shrimp and Mustard Sauce 95
Shrimp and Quinoa 95
Shrimp and Rice 95
Parsley Cod 96
Cod, Olives and Zucchinis 96
Creamy Salmon Mix 96
Trout and Capers Mix 97
Balsamic Sea Bass 97
Creole Calamari 97
Clams and Wine Sauce 97
Tarragon Trout 98
Shrimp, Corn and Tomato Bowls 98
Shrimp, Crab and Avocado Bowls 98
Salmon and Kale 99
Rosemary Calamari 99
Salmon and Sweet Potatoes 99
Creamy Cod and Zucchinis 99
Salmon with Quinoa and Rice 100
Lemon Sea Bass and Olives 100
Sous Vide Poultry Recipes 101
Lime Duck and Eggplant Mix 101
Pesto Turkey 101
Mustard Chicken and Capers 101
Orange Chicken Mix 102
Turkey with Sauce 102
Italian Turkey and Carrots 102
Chicken and Green Beans 103
Duck and Tomatoes 103
Garlic Chicken Mix 103
Chicken and Avocado 104
Turkey and Tomato Sauce 104
Turkey Medley 104

Chili Chicken	105
Chicken and Mango Mix	105
Ginger Turkey	105
Turkey and Potatoes	106
Chicken and Asparagus	106
Sage Turkey and Olives	106
Chicken with Brussels Sprouts Mix	107
Turkey and Fennel	107
Chicken with Endives	107
Balsamic Turkey	108
Chicken and Squash Mix	108
Paprika Turkey Mix	108
BBQ Chicken Wings	109
Chicken and Salsa	109
Coconut Turkey	109
Cumin Turkey	110
Chicken and Red Beans	110
Rosemary Chicken	110
Chicken and Peppers	110
Turkey and Quinoa	111
Spiced Chicken Wings	111
Turkey with Mushrooms	111
Turkey with Lime Sauce	111
Turkey with Lentils	112
Chicken and Leeks	112
Turmeric Duck	112
Chicken and Cauliflower	113
Chicken with Hot Red Chard	113
Creamy Chicken	113
Turkey with Chickpeas	114
Masala Turkey	114
Turkey with Pomegranate Mix	114
Chicken with Tomato and Kale	115
Ground Chicken and Veggies Mix	115
Chicken and Yogurt Sauce	115
Duck and Plums Mix	116
Chicken Wings and Tomato Sauce	116
Cayenne Turkey and Green Beans	116
Oregano Turkey	117
Allspice Turkey	117
Chicken with Okra	117
Cinnamon Chicken	118
Turkey Meatballs and Sauce	118
Chicken and Bulgur	118
Turkey and Tomatoes	119
Turkey with Spinach and Kale	119
Turkey and Spring Onions	119
Chicken and Lime Red Cabbage	119
Sous Vide Meat Recipes	**120**
Turmeric Pork Chops	120
Garlic Pork Chops	120
Creamy Pork	120
Italian Lamb Chops	120
Chives Lamb	121
Oregano Pork	121

Pork Chops and Green Beans ... 121
Basil Lamb ... 122
Hot Beef ... 122
Mint Lamb ... 122
Lamb and Zucchini Mix ... 122
Beef and Artichokes ... 123
Pork and Mushrooms ... 123
Pork and Tomatoes ... 123
Allspice Lamb ... 124
Pork and Fennel ... 124
Creamy Lamb ... 124
Paprika Lamb ... 125
Beef and Berries ... 125
Pesto Lamb ... 125
Pork and Lentils Mix ... 125
Lamb and Potatoes ... 126
Spiced Beef and Peppers ... 126
Rosemary Beef ... 126
Lamb and Corn ... 127
Sage Beef ... 127
Lemon Chops and Peas ... 127
Parsley Pork ... 127
Beef and Sprouts ... 128
Lamb and Avocado Mix ... 128
Beef and Corn ... 128
Pork and Olives ... 128
Lamb and Cucumber Mix ... 129
Ground Lamb and Carrots Mix ... 129
Lamb and Capers ... 129
Beef and Spicy Zucchinis ... 130
Pork with Tomatoes and Potatoes ... 130
Lamb and Savoy Cabbage Mix ... 130
Beef with Carrots and Cabbage ... 131
Orange Lamb ... 131
Ginger Pork ... 131
Beef and Swiss Chard ... 132
Nutmeg Pork Roast ... 132
Lamb with Ginger Artichokes ... 132
Balsamic Pork Chops ... 133
Pork and Creamy Scallions Sauce ... 133
Almond Beef ... 133
Pork, Capers and Green Beans ... 133
Beef and Beets ... 134
Lamb and Broccoli ... 134
Lamb and Radish Mix ... 134
Citrus Lamb Mix ... 135
Pork and Red Onions Mix ... 135
Pork and Walnuts Mix ... 135
Pork and Pumpkin Mix ... 136
Pork with Peppers and Avocado ... 136
Ground Beef with Beets and Radishes ... 136
Orange Pork and Veggies ... 137
Oregano and Chili Lamb ... 137
Pork and Pears Mix ... 137

Sous Vide Vegetable Recipes ... **138**

Lime Artichokes	138
Basil Green Beans	138
Buttery Leeks	138
Green Beans and Capers	138
Balsamic Tomatoes	139
Mustard Asparagus	139
Green Beans and Corn	139
Balsamic Radishes	139
Parsley Artichokes	140
Balsamic Zucchini Mix	140
Garlic Brussels Sprouts	140
Creamy Bell Peppers	140
Cayenne Broccoli	141
Nutmeg Brussels Sprouts	141
Garlic Kale	141
Chives Radish	141
Dill Tomatoes	142
Green Beans Sauté	142
Garlic Spinach	142
Creamy Zucchini	142
Spicy Eggplant	143
Pesto Tomato Mix	143
Cabbage Sauté	143
Zucchini and Tomato Mix	143
Paprika Okra	144
Chili Collard Greens	144
Beet and Radish Mix	144
Cilantro Hot Artichokes	144
Dill Endives	145
Lime Fennel	145
Paprika Olives Mix	145
Olives and Tomatoes	145
Eggplant and Okra Mix	146
Beets and Olives	146
Lemon Bok Choy	146
Ginger Bok Choy Mix	146
Spicy Cabbage with Kale	147
Mint Eggplant	147
Broccoli and Tomatoes	147
Balsamic Pearl Onions	147
Coconut Cabbage	148
Turmeric Brussels Sprouts	148
Lemon Cauliflower	148
Bok Choy and Cauliflower Mix	148
Nutmeg Fennel and Tomatoes	149
Green Beans and Avocado Mix	149
Green Beans and Pine Nuts Mix	149
Mustard Roasted Peppers	149
Peppers and Green Beans	150
Lemon Okra	150
Ginger Radish and Spring Onions	150
Broccoli and Zucchini Mix	150
Broccoli and Rice	151
Coconut Broccoli Mix	151
Balsamic Mushroom Mix	151

Mushroom and Tomatoes Sauté 151
Balsamic Walnuts and Radish Mix 152
Paprika Avocado and Mushrooms 152
Coconut Tomatoes and Spinach 152
Chili Okra and Radishes 152
Sous Vide Dessert Recipes 153
    Coffee Cream 153
    Turmeric and Lime Crème Brule 153
    Walnuts Pudding 153
    Cinnamon Apples 153
    Vanilla Pudding 154
    Grapes Bowls 154
    Grapes and Rice Pudding 154
    Raisins Pudding 154
    Orange Bowls 155
    Almond Cheesecake 155
    Cocoa Strawberries Cream 155
    Caramel Apples Mix 155
    Avocado and Strawberries Bowls 156
    Blackberries Cream 156
    Lemon Compote 156
    Apple Compote 156
    Orange Jam 157
    Avocado Cream 157
    Chocolate Cream Cheese Ramekins 157
    Coconut Raspberry Bowls 157
    Mascarpone and Plums Cream 158
    Maple and Plums Pudding 158
    Almond Blueberries Ramekins 158
    Carrot and Rice Pudding 158
    Cardamom Pudding 159
    Nuts Custard 159
    Creamy Berries Bowls 159
    Sweet Coconut Mix 159
    Carrot Custard 160
    Pears Jam 160
    Strawberries Compote 160
    Cinnamon Nectarines Bowls 160
    Rhubarb Compote 161
    Apples and Berries Compote 161
    Minty Apples Compote 161
    Figs and Grapes Compote 161
    Sweet Pumpkin Bowls 162
    Pecan Plums Bowls 162
    Blackberry and Rhubarb Jam 162
    Black Currant Marmalade 162
    Lime Jam 163
    Creamy Pears 163
    Peaches Bowls 163
    Avocado and Figs Bowls 163
    Peach Jelly 164
    Cocoa Berries Cream 164
    Dates and Cauliflower Rice Pudding 164
    Berry and Pumpkin Curd 164
    Peach Compote 165

Tomato Jam 165
  Dates Espresso Cream 165
  Mango Bowls 165
  Fruit Salad 166
  Nuts and Apples Bowls 166
  Plums and Peaches Bowls 166
  Yogurt and Berries Pudding 166
  Strawberries and Ginger Cream 167
  Cinnamon Cream 167
  Quinoa Pudding 167
  Avocado and Quinoa Bowls 167
Conclusion **168**
Recipe Index **169**

Introduction

Have you ever heard about sous vide cooking? You might think that this futuristic cooking method can only be handled by professional cooks but we are here to change this old concept.

Sous vide cooking has gained a lot of popularity over the last years and sous vide machines are now available everywhere. Anyone who's interested in having such a machine and cooking with it can purchase it.

The sous vide cooking method is a healthy way to cook incredible, rich, colored and textured meals for your friends and family. Cooking in sous vide actually refers to cooking in a temperature controlled water bath using vacuum sealed bags.

This cooking method never fails! You will get incredible and tasty meals each time whether we are talking about meat, seafood, veggies and even desserts. Cooking will seem much easier and a lot more fun if you decide to start using the sous vide machine and this cooking method.

If you are determined to give sous vide cooking a chance, then this great cooking journal is exactly what you need. This recipes collection shows you how to cook the best sous vide breakfasts, lunch, side dishes, snacks, appetizers, meat, poultry, seafood and of course desserts. You only need to follow the directions and you'll obtain some of the best dishes ever.

Does this sound amazing or what?

So, what are you still waiting for? You need to get your hands on a copy of this special cookbook right away and start using the sous vide machine to make some incredible and delightful meals.

Discover what sous vide cooking is all about! Start this amazing culinary trip and enjoy cooking in a new and interesting manner. Use the sous vide cooking method to make some of the tastiest dishes! Have fun in the kitchen cooking in such a different manner!

Sous Vide Breakfast Recipes

Cinnamon Toast

Preparation time: 10 minutes | Cooking time: 1 hour | Servings: 4

Ingredients:
- 4 bread slices
- 2 eggs, whisked
- ½ teaspoon cinnamon powder
- 1 tablespoon brown sugar
- ¼ cup ghee, melted

Directions:
In a bowl, mix the eggs with the cinnamon, sugar and the ghee and whisk. Dip the bread slices in this mix, place them in a sous vide bag, seal it, introduce in your sous vide machine and cook them at 147 degrees F for 1 hour. Serve right away for breakfast.

Nutrition: calories 172, fat 4, fiber 5, carbs 12, protein 5

Cheesy Eggs Mix

Preparation time: 10 minutes | Cooking time: 1 hour | Servings: 4

Ingredients:
- ½ cup heavy cream
- ½ cup mozzarella, shredded
- 4 eggs, whisked
- 1 tablespoon chives, chopped
- Salt and black pepper to the taste

Directions:
In a bowl, mix the cream with the eggs and the other ingredients, whisk well and pour this into a sous vide bag. Seal the bag, cook the eggs at 170 degrees F for 1 hour and serve them for breakfast.

Nutrition: calories 188, fat 4, fiber 7, carbs 12, protein 4

Shallot Scramble

Preparation time: 10 minutes | Cooking time: 1 hour | Servings: 4

Ingredients:
- 4 eggs, whisked
- ½ cup shallots, chopped
- 1 tablespoon chives, chopped
- Salt and black pepper to the taste
- ½ cup mozzarella, shredded
- 2 tablespoons heavy cream

Directions:
In a bowl, mix the eggs with the shallots and the other ingredients, whisk well and pour into a sous vide bag. Seal the bag, cook at 160 degrees F for 1 hour and serve for breakfast.

Nutrition: calories 200, fat 3, fiber 6, carbs 12, protein 4

Ham and Eggs

Preparation time: 10 minutes | Cooking time: 1 hour | Servings: 4

Ingredients:
- ½ cup bacon, chopped
- 4 eggs, whisked
- ½ cup heavy cream
- Salt and black pepper to the taste
- ½ teaspoon chili powder

Directions:
In a bowl, mix the eggs with the bacon and the other ingredients, whisk and pour into a sous vide bag. Seal the bag, submerge in preheated water oven and cook at 170 degrees F for 1 hour. Divide the mix between plates and serve.

Nutrition: calories 162, fat 3, fiber 6, carbs 12, protein 5.

Crab and Eggs Mix

Preparation time: 10 minutes | Cooking time: 25 minutes | Servings: 2

Ingredients:
- 1 tablespoon crab meat
- 2 eggs, whisked
- 1 tablespoon butter, melted
- Salt and black pepper to the taste
- 1 tablespoon chives, chopped
- 2 tablespoons cream cheese

Directions:

Put eggs whisked with the butter, crabmeat and the other ingredients in 2 sous vide bags, submerge in your sous vide machine and cook them for 25 minutes at 167 degrees F. Divide between plates and serve.

Nutrition: calories 172, fat 4, fiber 6, carbs 12, protein 5

Lime Coconut Jars

Preparation time: 10 minutes | Cooking time: 3 hours | Servings: 6

Ingredients:
- 1-quart almond milk, heated
- ½ cup coconut cream
- ½ tablespoon lime zest, grated
- 1 tablespoon brown sugar
- ½ tablespoon heavy cream
- ½ tablespoon lime juice

Directions:

In a bowl, combine the milk with the cream and the other ingredients, whisk well, pour into canning jars, put the lid on, introduce in your sous vide machine and cook for 3 hours and 120 degrees F. Serve for breakfast.

Nutrition: calories 134, fat 4, fiber 4, carbs 6, protein 3

Berry Coconut Mix

Preparation time: 10 minutes | Cooking time: 20 minutes | Servings: 2

Ingredients:
- 1 cup blackberries
- 1 cup heavy cream
- 2 tablespoons coconut flakes
- 2 tablespoons sugar
- ½ teaspoon vanilla extract
- Juice of 1 lemon

Directions:

In a bowl mix the berries with the cream and the other ingredients, toss, divide in canning jars, put the lid on, introduce in your sous vide machine and cook at 147 degrees F for 20 minutes. Divide into bowls and serve for breakfast.

Nutrition: calories 152, fat 3, fiber 3, carbs 6, protein 4

Parmesan Eggs

Preparation time: 10 minutes | Cooking time: 35 minutes | Servings: 4

Ingredients:
- 4 eggs
- 2 tablespoons chives, chopped
- ½ teaspoon sweet paprika
- ½ teaspoon cumin, ground
- ½ cup parmesan, grated
- Salt and black pepper to the taste
- 2 scallions, chopped

Directions:

Crack each egg in a sous vide bag, season with the chives, paprika and the other ingredients, seal the bags, submerge in the water oven and cook at 150 degrees F for 35 minutes. Divide between plates and serve for breakfast.

Nutrition: calories 162, fat 3, fiber 6, carbs 12, protein 5

Scrambled Eggs

Preparation time: 10 minutes | Cooking time: 30 minutes | Servings: 2

Ingredients:
- 4 eggs, whisked
- ½ teaspoon rosemary, dried
- ½ teaspoon sweet paprika
- ½ teaspoon chili powder
- ½ teaspoon cumin, ground
- Salt and black pepper to the taste
- 1 tablespoon chives, chopped

Directions:
In a bowl, mix the eggs with the paprika, rosemary and the other ingredients, whisk, transfer to a sous vide bag, seal it, introduce in your sous vide machine and cook at 160 degrees F for 30 minutes. Divide between plates and serve for breakfast.

Nutrition: calories 200, fat 3, fiber 6, carbs 12, protein 5

Pesto Eggs

Preparation time: 10 minutes | Cooking time: 30 minutes | Servings: 2

Ingredients:
- 4 eggs
- Salt and black pepper to the taste
- ½ teaspoon hot paprika
- 1 tomato, cubed
- 2 tablespoons basil pesto

Directions:
Place the eggs in your sous vide bath, cook at 150 degrees F for 30 minutes and crack them on plates Divide the pesto, tomato and sprinkle the paprika on each egg and serve for breakfast.

Nutrition: calories 177, fat 3, fiber 6, carbs 8, protein 7

Spinach Scramble

Preparation time: 10 minutes | Cooking time: 20 minutes | Servings: 2

Ingredients:
- 1 tablespoon parmesan, grated
- 1 tablespoon chives, minced
- ½ teaspoon rosemary, dried
- 4 eggs
- 1 ounce spinach, chopped
- Salt and black pepper to the taste
- A pinch of red pepper flakes, crushed

Directions:
In a bowl, mix eggs with salt, pepper, parmesan and the other ingredients, whisk, pour into a sous vide bag, introduce in your sous vide machine and cook at 140 degrees F for 20 minutes. Divide between plates and serve for breakfast.

Nutrition: calories 211, fat 3, fiber 6, carbs 8, protein 2

Herbed Ricotta Cheese

Preparation time: 10 minutes | Cooking time: 40 minutes | Servings: 12

Ingredients:
- 3 quarts almond milk
- 1 cup white vinegar
- 3 tablespoons chives, chopped
- 1 tablespoon oregano, chopped
- 1 tablespoon parsley, chopped

Directions:
Put the milk in a big sous vide bag, remove most of the air, seal, submerge in bath water and cook in your sous vide machine for 40 minutes at 172 degrees F. Add the vinegar, and the other ingredients, stir, open the bag, collect the curd, drain for a couple of hours and serve for breakfast.

Nutrition: calories 132, fat 3, fiber 3, carbs 7, protein 7

Cinnamon Rice Pudding

Preparation time: 10 minutes | Cooking time: 40 minutes | Servings: 4

Ingredients:
- 1 cup white rice
- 2 cups almond milk
- 3 tablespoons sugar
- 1 teaspoon cinnamon powder
- ½ teaspoon vanilla extract

Directions:

In a sous vide pouch, mix the rice with the milk and the other ingredients, whisk, seal, submerge in your sous vide machine and cook at 180 degrees F for 40 minutes. Divide the rice pudding into bowls and serve.

Nutrition: calories 141, fat 2, fiber 6, carbs 7, protein 5

Asparagus, Spinach and Eggs Mix

Preparation time: 10 minutes | Cooking time: 50 minutes | Servings: 4

Ingredients:
- 2 asparagus spears, chopped
- 4 eggs whisked
- ¼ cup parmesan, grated
- ½ cup heavy cream
- Cooking spray
- 1 teaspoon smoked paprika
- Salt and black pepper to the taste
- 1 teaspoon chives, chopped

Directions:

Grease 4 ramekins with the cooking spray, and divide the eggs mixed with the asparagus and the other ingredients in each. Preheat your water oven, place ramekins inside, cover them with tin foil and cook everything at 180 degrees F for 50 minutes. Serve for breakfast.

Nutrition: calories 211, fat 3, fiber 6, carbs 8, protein 5

Coconut Eggs

Preparation time: 10 minutes | Cooking time: 40 minutes | Servings: 4

Ingredients:
- 4 eggs, whisked
- 1 cup coconut cream
- ½ teaspoon nutmeg, ground
- 3 tablespoons sugar
- 2 tablespoons coconut milk

Directions:

In a bowl, mix the eggs with the cream and the other ingredients, whisk and divide into 4 ramekins. Put the ramekins in the water oven, add water halfway, and cook at 140 degrees F for 40 minutes. Serve for breakfast right away.

Nutrition: calories 165, fat 3, fiber 8, carbs 12, protein 6

Pepper Eggs Mix

Preparation time: 10 minutes | Cooking time: 40 minutes | Servings: 4

Ingredients:
- 1 tablespoon butter, melted
- 1 red bell pepper, chopped
- 1 green bell pepper, chopped
- 1 red onion, chopped
- 8 eggs, whisked
- Salt and black pepper to the taste
- 1 tomato, cubed
- ¼ teaspoon chili powder
- 1 tablespoon cilantro, chopped

Directions:

Heat up a pan with the butter over medium heat, add the onion, pepper and the other ingredients except the eggs, toss, cook for 10 minutes and take off the heat. In a bowl, mix the eggs with salt, pepper and the sautéed ingredients and whisk. Pour this mix into a ziplock bag, seal, submerge in the preheated water oven and cook at 167 degrees F for 30 minutes. Divide between plates and serve for breakfast.

Nutrition: calories 250, fat 12, fiber 5, carbs 12, protein 7

Sausage Ramekins

Preparation time: 10 minutes | Cooking time: 40 minutes | Servings: 4

Ingredients:
- Cooking spray
- 2 sausage links, chopped
- 6 eggs, whisked
- Salt and black pepper to the taste
- 1 red bell pepper, chopped
- 2 spring onions, chopped
- 1 tablespoon chives, chopped
- 1 tablespoon parsley, chopped
- ½ teaspoon sweet paprika

Directions:
Grease 4 ramekins with the cooking spray and divide the eggs mixed with the sausage, pepper and the other ingredients in each. Carefully place ramekins in the preheated water oven and cook at 170 degrees F for 40 minutes. Serve for breakfast right away.

Nutrition: calories 240, fat 6, fiber 4, carbs 12, protein 14

Eggs, Green Beans and Mushrooms

Preparation time: 10 minutes | Cooking time: 30 minutes | Servings: 2

Ingredients:
- 4 eggs, whisked
- 1 cup green beans, chopped
- ½ cup mushrooms, sliced
- 1 red onion, chopped
- ½ teaspoon sweet paprika
- Salt and black pepper to the taste
- 1 tablespoon avocado oil, melted

Directions:
Heat up a pan with the oil over medium heat, add the onion, mushrooms and the other ingredients except the eggs, toss and sauté for 5 minutes. In a bowl, mix eggs with sautéed mushroom mix and whisk. Pour this into a sous vide bag, seal, submerge in the water oven and cook at 167 degrees F for 25 minutes. Divide between plates and serve for breakfast.

Nutrition: calories 260, fat 13, fiber 6, carbs 15, protein 8

Cream Cheese and Spinach Eggs

Preparation time: 10 minutes | Cooking time: 30 minutes | Servings: 4

Ingredients:
- 1 cup baby spinach, torn
- ½ cup cream cheese, soft
- 4 eggs, whisked
- 2 garlic cloves, minced
- ½ teaspoon coriander, ground
- Salt and black pepper to the taste
- 2 tablespoons parmesan, grated

Directions:
In a bowl, mix the eggs with the spinach, cheese and the other ingredients and whisk well. Pour this into a sous vide bag, seal, submerge in the water oven and cook at 170 degrees F for 30 minutes. Divide the whole mix between plates and serve.

Nutrition: calories 248, fat 4, fiber 1, carbs 7, protein 18

Smoked Salmon, Avocado and Eggs Mix

Preparation time: 10 minutes | Cooking time: 30 minutes | Servings: 4

Ingredients:
- 4 eggs, whisked
- 1 avocado, peeled, pitted and cubed
- 1 tablespoon spring onions, chopped
- Salt and black pepper to the taste
- 4 ounces smoked salmon, skinless, boneless and flaked
- 1 teaspoon garlic powder
- Salt and black pepper to the taste
- 1 tablespoon lemon juice
- 1 tablespoon lemon zest, grated

Directions:
In a bowl, mix the eggs with the spring onions, avocado and the other ingredients, whisk well, transfer to a ziplock bag, seal, submerge in the water oven and cook at 165 degrees F for 30 minutes. Divide everything between plates and serve.

Nutrition: calories 220, fat 10, fiber 2, carbs 15, protein 8

Lime Eggs, Tomato and Avocado Mix

Preparation time: 10 minutes | *Cooking time:* 30 minutes | *Servings:* 4

Ingredients:
- 2 avocados, pitted, peeled and cubed
- ½ cup tomatoes, cubed
- ½ teaspoon rosemary, dried
- ½ teaspoon chili powder
- 1 tablespoon lime zest, grated
- 4 eggs, whisked
- Salt and black pepper to the taste
- 1 tablespoon chives, chopped

Directions:
In a bowl, mix the eggs with the avocados, tomatoes and the other ingredients, toss well, pour into a sous vide bag, seal, introduce in your sous vide water oven and cook at 165 degrees F for 30 minutes. Divide between plates and serve for breakfast.

Nutrition: calories 250, fat 6, fiber 7, carbs 13, protein 15

Zucchini and Eggs

Preparation time: 10 minutes | *Cooking time:* 40 minutes | *Servings:* 4

Ingredients:
- 8 eggs, whisked
- 2 zucchinis, grated
- ½ teaspoon rosemary, dried
- ½ teaspoon chili powder
- Salt and black pepper to the taste
- ½ teaspoon garlic powder
- ½ teaspoon basil, dried

Directions:
In a bowl, mix the eggs with the zucchinis and the other ingredients, and whisk well. Transfer this to a sous vide bag, seal, submerge in the water oven and cook at 170 degrees F for 40 minutes. Divide between plates and serve for breakfast.

Nutrition: calories 240, fat 15, fiber 2, carbs 13, protein 17

Ground Beef and Eggs Ramekins

Preparation time: 10 minutes | *Cooking time:* 30 minutes | *Servings:* 4

Ingredients:
- 8 eggs, whisked
- 1 pound beef stew meat, ground
- 1 tablespoon olive oil
- 4 mushrooms, sliced
- ½ teaspoon chili powder
- 1 yellow onion, chopped
- 1 cup baby spinach, torn
- Salt and black pepper to the taste

Directions:
Heat up a pan with the oil over medium heat, add the mushrooms and the onion and sauté for 5 minutes. Add the meat, brown for another 5 minutes and take off the heat. Divide the mix into 4 ramekins, add the eggs and the remaining ingredients as well, put the ramekins in the water oven, add water halfway and cook at 167 degrees F for 20 minutes. Divide between plates and serve right away.

Nutrition: calories 245, fat 7, fiber 6, carbs 14, protein 22

Tomato Ramekins

Preparation time: 10 minutes | *Cooking time:* 40 minutes | *Servings:* 6

Ingredients:
- 1 cup cherry tomatoes, cubed
- Salt and black pepper to the taste
- ½ teaspoon chili powder
- 2 tablespoons parsley, chopped
- 8 eggs, whisked
- 2 tablespoons parmesan, grated
- ½ teaspoon coriander, ground

Directions:
In a bowl, mix the eggs with the tomatoes and the other ingredients and whisk well. Pour this mix into ramekins, introduce them into your sous vide water oven, add water halfway and cook at 174 degrees F for 40 minutes. Divide between plates and serve for breakfast.

Nutrition: calories 340, fat 13, fiber 3, carbs 12, protein 17

Coconut Leeks Mix

Preparation time: 10 minutes | Cooking time: 40 minutes | Servings: 4

Ingredients:
- 2 leeks, chopped
- 8 eggs, whisked
- ¼ cup coconut milk
- ½ teaspoon rosemary, dried
- ½ teaspoon cumin, ground
- 1 tablespoon chives, chopped
- Salt and black pepper to the taste
- ¼ teaspoon garlic powder

Directions:
In a bowl, mix the eggs with the leeks, milk and the other ingredients, whisk well and divide into 4 ramekins. Place them in your sous vide machine, add water halfway and cook at 176 degrees F for 40 minutes. Divide between plates and serve for breakfast.

Nutrition: calories 340, fat 12, fiber 3, carbs 8, protein 13

Almond Oats

Preparation time: 10 minutes | Cooking time: 2 hours | Servings: 2

Ingredients:
- 1 teaspoon cinnamon powder
- 1 cup old fashioned oats
- ½ cup almonds, ground
- ½ teaspoon vanilla extract
- ½ cup almond milk
- ¾ cup coconut cream

Directions:
In a ziplock bag, mix the oats with the cream, milk and the other ingredients, toss, seal the bag, submerge in the water oven and cook at 180 degrees F for 2 hours. Divide into bowls and serve.

Nutrition: calories 260, fat 12, fiber 4, carbs 8, protein 16

Lemon Eggs

Preparation time: 10 minutes | Cooking time: 20 minutes | Servings: 4

Ingredients:
- ½ cup chives, chopped
- Juice of 1 lemon
- Salt and black pepper to the taste
- 4 eggs, whisked
- 2 teaspoons lemon thyme, chopped

Directions:
In a sous vide bag, mix the eggs with the lemon thyme, chives and the other ingredients, whisk and seal the bag. Submerge the bag into the water oven and cook at 167 degrees F for 20 minutes. Divide between plates and serve for breakfast.

Nutrition: calories 203, fat 7, fiber 2, carbs 11, protein 8

Oregano Scramble

Preparation time: 10 minutes | Cooking time: 20 minutes | Servings: 4

Ingredients:
- 8 eggs, whisked
- 1 tablespoon oregano, chopped
- 2 tablespoons butter, melted
- 2 tablespoons parmesan cheese, grated
- ½ teaspoon sweet paprika
- Salt and black pepper to the taste
- ½ cup heavy cream

Directions:
In a bowl, mix the eggs with the oregano, butter and the other ingredients, whisk well, pour into a ziplock bag, introduce in your sous vide machine in the water oven and cook at 167 degrees F for 20 minutes. Divide the mix between plates and serve.

Nutrition: calories 160, fat 3, fiber 2, carbs 6, protein 10

Bacon and Radish Scramble

Preparation time: 10 minutes | Cooking time: 30 minutes | Servings: 2

Ingredients:
- ½ cup bacon, chopped
- ½ cup radish, chopped
- 8 eggs, whisked
- Salt and black pepper to the taste
- 1 yellow onion, chopped
- 1 tablespoon chives, chopped

Directions:

In a bowl, mix the eggs with the radishes and the other ingredients, whisk, pour into a ziplock bag, seal, introduce in your sous vide machine and cook at 170 degrees F for 30 minutes. Divide everything between plates and serve.

Nutrition: calories 240, fat 7, fiber 3, carbs 12, protein 8

Brussels Sprouts Salad

Preparation time: 10 minutes | Cooking time: 30 minutes | Servings: 4

Ingredients:
- Salt and black pepper to the taste
- 1 tablespoon olive oil
- 1 cup cherry tomatoes, halved
- ½ cup black olives, pitted and halved
- 2 shallots, minced
- 12 ounces Brussels sprouts, halved
- 2 ounces bacon, cooked and chopped
- 1 tablespoon balsamic vinegar

Directions:

In a sous vide bag, mix the sprouts with the tomatoes and the other ingredients, toss, seal, introduce in your sous vide machine and cook at 170 degrees F for 30 minutes. Divide into bowls and serve for breakfast.

Nutrition: calories 240, fat 7, fiber 4, carbs 12, protein 12

Seeds Porridge

Preparation time: 3 minutes | Cooking time: 1 hour | Servings: 2

Ingredients:
- 1 cup almond milk
- 2 tablespoons flax seeds
- 1 tablespoon sunflower seeds
- ½ cup heavy cream
- ½ teaspoon cinnamon powder
- 1 tablespoon sugar
- ¾ teaspoon vanilla extract

Directions:

In a sous vide bag, mix the almond milk with the seeds and the other ingredients, seal the bag, introduce in your sous vide machine and cook at 180 degrees F for 1 hour Divide the porridge into bowls and serve for breakfast.

Nutrition: calories 230, fat 12, fiber 7, carbs 12, protein 13

Cinnamon Eggs

Preparation time: 10 minutes | Cooking time: 30 minutes | Servings: 2

Ingredients:
- 4 eggs, whisked
- 1 teaspoon ginger powder
- 2 tablespoons sugar
- 1/3 cup heavy cream
- ½ teaspoon cinnamon powder

Directions:

In a sous vide bag, combine the eggs with the sugar and the other ingredients, seal, introduce in your sous vide machine and cook at 167 degrees F for 30 minutes. Divide into bowls and serve.

Nutrition: calories 240, fat 12, fiber 6, carbs 12, protein 14

Chicken and Eggs

Preparation time: 10 minutes | *Cooking time:* 30 minutes | *Servings:* 2

Ingredients:
- 1 cup rotisserie chicken, cooked and shredded
- ½ cup black olives, pitted and halved
- 1 tomato, chopped
- 4 eggs, whisked
- 1 avocado, peeled, pitted and cubed
- Salt and black pepper to the taste

Directions:
In a sous vide bag, combine the meat with the eggs and the other ingredients, toss, seal the bag, introduce in your sous vide machine and cook at 170 degrees F for 30 minutes. Divide between plates and serve.

Nutrition: calories 260, fat 6, fiber 6, carbs 12, protein 25

Lime and Chia Eggs

Preparation time: 10 minutes | *Cooking time:* 20 minutes | *Servings:* 2

Ingredients:
- 4 eggs, whisked
- 1 tablespoon chia seeds
- 1 tablespoon lime juice
- ½ cup heavy cream
- 1 teaspoon sweet paprika
- Salt and black pepper to the taste

Directions:
In a sous vide bag, combine the eggs with the chia seeds and the other ingredients, toss, seal, introduce in your sous vide machine and cook in the water oven at 167 degrees F for 20 minutes. Divide the mix between plates and serve.

Nutrition: calories 260, fat 12, fiber 6, carbs 14, protein 14

Broccoli Eggs

Preparation time: 10 minutes | *Cooking time:* 30 minutes | *Servings:* 4

Ingredients:
- 1 cup broccoli florets
- ½ teaspoon sweet paprika
- ½ teaspoon coriander, ground
- Salt and black pepper to the taste
- 4 eggs, whisked
- 2 garlic cloves, minced
- 1 tablespoon chives, chopped
- ½ cup heavy cream

Directions:
In a sous vide bag, combine the eggs with the broccoli, paprika and the other ingredients, toss, seal, introduce in your sous vide machine and cook at 175 degrees F for 30 minutes. Divide everything between plates and serve for breakfast.

Nutrition: calories 230, fat 3, fiber 3, carbs 6, protein 10

Ginger Tomatoes Eggs

Preparation time: 10 minutes | *Cooking time:* 40 minutes | *Servings:* 4

Ingredients:
- 1 cup cherry tomatoes, cubed
- 1 tablespoon ginger, grated
- 4 eggs, whisked
- A drizzle of olive oil
- 1 red onion, chopped
- Salt and black pepper to the taste
- A pinch of red pepper, crushed
- 1 garlic clove, minced
- 1 tablespoon chives, chopped

Directions:
Heat up a pan with the oil over medium heat, add the ginger, onion and the other ingredients except the eggs, stir and cook for 10 minutes. In a bowl, combine the eggs with the ginger mix, stir, pour this into a sous vide bag, seal, submerge in the water oven and cook at 170 degrees F for 30 minutes. Divide everything between plates and serve for breakfast.

Nutrition: calories 210, fat 6, fiber 4, carbs 15, protein 12

Bok Choy and Veggies Bowls

Preparation time: 10 minutes | Cooking time: 30 minutes | Servings: 4

Ingredients:
- 1 red onion, chopped
- 1 bunch bok choy, chopped
- A drizzle of olive oil
- 1 cup white mushrooms, halved
- 1 cup cherry tomatoes, halved
- 1 cup kalamata olives, pitted and halved
- Salt and black pepper to the taste
- ½ tablespoon red pepper flakes
- 2 tablespoons balsamic vinegar
- 2 tablespoons Worcestershire sauce
- 2 tablespoons chives, chopped

Directions:
Heat up a pan with the oil over medium heat, add the mushrooms and onion and sauté for 10 minutes. In a sous vide bag, mix the bok choy with the tomatoes, mushroom mix and the remaining ingredients, seal, introduce in your sous vide machine and cook at 170 degrees F for 20 minutes. Divide the whole mix into bowls and serve for breakfast.

Nutrition: calories 100, fat 3, fiber 1, carbs 2, protein 6

Bok Choy and Eggs

Preparation time: 10 minutes | Cooking time: 20 minutes | Servings: 2

Ingredients:
- 2 garlic cloves, minced
- 4 eggs, whisked
- ½ teaspoon turmeric powder
- ½ teaspoon chili powder
- 2 bunches bok choy, chopped
- 2 bacon slices, chopped
- Salt and black pepper to the taste
- A drizzle of avocado oil

Directions:
In a sous vide bag, combine the eggs with the bok choy and the other ingredients, toss, seal, submerge in the water bath and cook at 170 degrees F for 20 minutes. Divide between plates and serve for breakfast

Nutrition: calories 120, fat 1, fiber 2, carbs 6, protein 6

Greens and Eggs

Preparation time: 10 minutes | Cooking time: 20 minutes | Servings: 4

Ingredients:
- 1 cup baby spinach
- 1 cup collard greens, chopped
- ¼ cup spring onions, chopped
- 1 tablespoon lime juice
- 8 eggs, whisked
- ½ teaspoon chili powder
- Salt and black pepper to the taste

Directions:
In a sous vide bag, combine the greens with the eggs and the other ingredients, seal the bag, introduce in your sous vide machine and cook at 170 degrees F for 20 minutes. Divide between plates and serve for breakfast.

Nutrition: calories 170, fat 8, fiber 1, carbs 7, protein 7

Eggs and Asparagus

Preparation time: 10 minutes | Cooking time: 25 minutes | Servings: 4

Ingredients:
- ¼ cup red onion, chopped
- 1 pound asparagus spears, chopped
- Salt and black pepper to the taste
- 4 eggs, whisked
- ½ teaspoon sweet paprika
- ½ teaspoon chili powder
- 1 cup cheddar cheese, grated

Directions:
In a sous vide bag, combine the eggs with the eggs and the other ingredients, toss, seal, introduce in your sous vide machine and cook at 168 degrees F for 20 minutes. Divide between plates and serve for breakfast.

Nutrition: calories 200, fat 12, fiber 2, carbs 7, protein 14

Zucchini Bowls

Preparation time: 10 minutes | Cooking time: 30 minutes | Servings: 4

Ingredients:
- 2 zucchinis, cubed
- 4 eggs, whisked
- Salt and black pepper to the taste
- 1 tablespoon butter, melted
- 1 teaspoon oregano, dried
- 2 spring onions, chopped
- 1 ounce parmesan, grated
- ¼ cup heavy cream

Directions:
Heat up a pan with butter over medium-high heat, add the spring onions and the zucchinis and sauté for 5 minutes. In a sous vide bag, combine the eggs with the zucchinis and the other ingredients, seal the bag, introduce in your sous vide machine and cook at 180 degrees F for 25 minutes. Divide into bowls and serve for breakfast.

Nutrition: calories 200, fat 4, fiber 2, carbs 6, protein 8

Tomato Sausage Salad

Preparation time: 10 minutes | Cooking time: 40 minutes | Servings: 4

Ingredients:
- 2 pork sausage links, sliced
- 1 cup cherry tomatoes, halved
- 1 cup baby spinach
- 1 tablespoon avocado oil
- 1 cup kalamata olives, pitted and halved
- 2 tablespoons lemon juice
- 2 tablespoons basil pesto
- Salt and black pepper to the taste

Directions:
In a sous vide bag, mix the sausage slices with the tomatoes, spinach and the other ingredients, seal the bag, submerge in the water bath, cook at 180 degrees F for 40 minutes, divide into bowls and serve for breakfast.

Nutrition: calories 250, fat 12, fiber 3, carbs 12, protein 18

Sausages and Mushrooms Mix

Preparation time: 10 minutes | Cooking time: 40 minutes | Servings: 4

Ingredients:
- 1 cup Italian pork sausage, chopped
- 1 cup white mushrooms, halved
- 1 cup baby spinach
- 1 cup cherry tomatoes, halved
- Salt and black pepper to the taste
- 2 sweet onions, chopped
- 1 tablespoon balsamic vinegar
- A drizzle of olive oil

Directions:
Heat up a pan with the oil over medium-high heat, add the sausage, mushrooms and the onions and sauté for 10 minutes. Put the mix in a sous vide bag, add the rest of the ingredients, seal the bag, submerge in the water oven and cook at 160 degrees F for 30 minutes. Divide the mix plates and serve for breakfast.

Nutrition: calories 230, fat 12, fiber 1, carbs 13, protein 9

Kale, Sausage and Eggs

Preparation time: 10 minutes | Cooking time: 45 minutes | Servings: 4

Ingredients:
- 1 red onion, chopped
- A drizzle of olive oil
- 1 cup Italian pork sausage, sliced
- 1 cup kale, torn
- 4 eggs, whisked
- ½ cup red bell pepper, chopped
- Salt and black pepper to the taste
- ½ cup kale, chopped
- 1 teaspoon garlic, minced
- ¼ cup red hot chili pepper, chopped
- 1 tablespoon chives, chopped

Directions:
Heat up a pan with the oil over medium-high heat, add onion, kale and sausage, stir and cook for 10 minutes. Transfer this to a sous vide bag, add the rest of the ingredients, stir, seal the bag, submerge in the water bath and cook at 180 degrees F for 35 minutes. Divide everything between plates and serve.

Nutrition: calories 200, fat 4, fiber 6, carbs 12, protein 12

Eggs, Cheese and Sun-dried Tomatoes Mix

Preparation time: 10 minutes | Cooking time: 45 minutes | Servings: 4

Ingredients:
- 8 eggs, whisked
- A drizzle of avocado oil
- 1 yellow onion, sliced
- ½ cup sun-dried tomatoes, thinly sliced
- Salt and black pepper to the taste
- ½ cup cheddar cheese, grated
- A pinch of red pepper flakes
- A handful parsley, chopped

Directions:
Heat up a pan with the oil over medium heat, add the onion and tomatoes, cook for 5 minutes and take off the heat. In a sous vide machine, combine the eggs with the onion and tomato mix and the other ingredients, seal, submerge in the water bath, cook at 187 degrees F for 40 minutes, divide between plates and serve for breakfast.

Nutrition: calories 200, fat 5, fiber 3, carbs 12, protein 14

Shrimp, Eggs and Mushrooms

Preparation time: 10 minutes | Cooking time: 30 minutes | Servings: 4

Ingredients:
- 1 cup mushrooms, sliced
- 4 eggs, whisked
- 1 cup shrimp, peeled and deveined
- 3 spring onions, chopped
- ½ teaspoon coriander, ground
- ½ teaspoon turmeric powder
- 4 bacon slices, chopped
- Salt and black pepper to the taste
- ½ cup coconut cream

Directions:
In a sous vide bag, combine the eggs with the mushrooms, shrimp and the other ingredients, seal, introduce in a sous vide machine and cook at 140 degrees F for 30 minutes. Divide between plates and serve for breakfast.

Nutrition: calories 340, fat 23, fiber 1, carbs 14, protein 17

Enchilada Eggs Mix

Preparation time: 10 minutes | Cooking time: 30 minutes | Servings: 4

Ingredients:

- ½ cup enchilada sauce
- Salt and black pepper to the taste
- 8 eggs, whisked
- 1 avocado, peeled, pitted and cubed
- ½ cup kalamata olives, pitted and sliced
- 1 tomato, chopped
- ½ cup red onion, chopped
- 1 tablespoon chives, chopped

Directions:

In a sous vide bag, combine the eggs with the sauce, avocado and the other ingredients, toss, seal, introduce in your sous vide machine and cook at 180 degrees F for 30 minutes. Divide between plates and serve.

Nutrition: calories 250, fat 32, fiber 4, carbs 7, protein 12

Italian Squash and Olives Bowls

Preparation time: 10 minutes | Cooking time: 40 minutes | Servings: 4

Ingredients:

- 1 tablespoon butter, melted
- 1 butternut squash, peeled and cubed
- 4 eggs, whisked
- 1 cup black olives, pitted and cubed
- Salt and black pepper to the taste
- ½ cup tomatoes, chopped
- 2 garlic cloves, minced
- ½ teaspoon Italian seasoning
- 3 ounces Italian salami, chopped
- 1 tablespoon oregano, chopped

Directions:

In a sous vide bag, mix the squash with the melted butter, eggs and the other ingredients, toss, seal, introduce in your sous vide machine and cook at 170 degrees F for 40 minutes. Divide everything between plates and serve.

Nutrition: calories 263, fat 23, fiber 4, carbs 12, protein 15

Prosciutto and Zucchini Eggs

Preparation time: 10 minutes | Cooking time: 30 minutes | Servings: 4

Ingredients:

- 8 eggs, whisked
- 4 prosciutto slices, chopped
- 1 teaspoon sweet paprika
- ½ teaspoon rosemary, dried
- 2 zucchinis, cubed
- Salt and black pepper to the taste
- ¼ cup chives, chopped

Directions:

In a sous vide bag, mix the eggs with the prosciutto, paprika and the other ingredients, seal, introduce in the sous vide machine and cook at 170 degrees F for 30 minutes. Divide between plates and serve for breakfast.

Nutrition: calories 200, fat 3, fiber 6, carbs 13, protein 10

Green Beans, Kale and Eggs

Preparation time: 10 minutes | *Cooking time:* 35 minutes | *Servings:* 4

Ingredients:
- 8 eggs, whisked
- 1 cup green beans, trimmed and roughly sliced
- 1 cup baby kale, chopped
- ½ teaspoon sweet paprika
- ½ teaspoon ginger, ground
- A pinch of salt and black pepper
- 1 tablespoon parmesan, grated

Directions:
In a sous vide bag, combine the eggs with the kale, green beans and the other ingredients, toss, seal, submerge in the water oven and cook at 170 degrees F for 35 minutes. Divide between plates serve for breakfast.

Nutrition: calories 200, fat 4, fiber 6, carbs 8, protein 5

Oregano Eggs

Preparation time: 10 minutes | *Cooking time:* 30 minutes | *Servings:* 2

Ingredients:
- 1 red bell pepper, chopped
- 2 shallots, chopped
- 4 eggs, whisked
- A pinch of salt and black pepper
- 1 tablespoon oregano, chopped
- ½ teaspoon chili powder
- ½ teaspoon sweet paprika

Directions:
In a bowl, mix the eggs with the pepper, shallots and the other ingredients, whisk and pour into a sous vide bag. Seal the bag, submerge in the water oven and cook at 170 degrees F for 30 minutes. Divide between plates and serve.

Nutrition: calories 331, fat 17.7, fiber 8.7, carbs 43.1, protein 7

Quinoa and Berries Bowls

Preparation time: 10 minutes | *Cooking time:* 30 minutes | *Servings:* 4

Ingredients:
- 1 cup quinoa
- 2 cups almond milk
- ½ cup blueberries
- ½ cup strawberries, halved
- 2 tablespoons sugar
- 1 teaspoon vanilla extract

Directions:
In a sous vide bag, mix the quinoa with the milk and the other ingredients, whisk and seal the bag. Submerge in preheated water oven and cook at 170 degrees F for 30 minutes. Divide the mix into bowls and serve.

Nutrition: calories 217, fat 10, fiber 5, carbs 15, protein 14

Eggplant Bowls

Preparation time: 10 minutes | *Cooking time:* 25 minutes | *Servings:* 2

Ingredients:
- 2 spring onions, chopped
- 1 pound eggplants, cubed
- 8 eggs, whisked
- 1 cup baby spinach
- ½ teaspoon basil, dried
- 1 tablespoon oregano, chopped
- A pinch of salt and black pepper
- 1 tablespoon chives, chopped

Directions:
In a bowl mix the eggs with the basil, oregano and the other ingredients, whisk and pour into a ziplock bag. Seal the bag, submerge in the water oven and cook at 170 degrees F for 25 minutes. Divide into bowls and serve.

Nutrition: calories 223, fat 12, fiber 5, carbs 15, protein 5

Banana Oatmeal

Preparation time: 10 minutes | Cooking time: 25 minutes | Servings: 4

Ingredients:
- 1 cup old fashioned oats
- 2 cups almond milk
- 2 bananas, peeled and mashed
- ½ teaspoon vanilla extract
- ½ teaspoon nutmeg, ground

Directions:

In a sous vide bag, mix the oats with the milk and the other ingredients, whisk, seal the bag, submerge in the water oven and cook at 167 degrees F for 25 minutes. Divide the oatmeal into bowls and serve.

Nutrition: calories 371, fat 12, fiber 2, carbs 5, protein 5

Cheddar Eggs

Preparation time: 10 minutes | Cooking time: 30 minutes | Servings: 4

Ingredients:
- 8 eggs, whisked
- ½ cup almond milk
- ½ cup cheddar cheese, shredded
- 2 spring onions, chopped
- ½ teaspoon sweet paprika
- A pinch of salt and black pepper
- 2 tablespoons chives, chopped

Directions:

In a bowl, mix the eggs with the milk and the other ingredients, whisk and divide into 4 ramekins. Put the ramekins in the water oven and cook at 165 degrees F for 25 minutes. Serve for breakfast.

Nutrition: calories 367, fat 13, fiber 3, carbs 15, protein 12

Spinach Frittata

Preparation time: 5 minutes | Cooking time: 30 minutes | Servings: 4

Ingredients:
- 8 eggs, whisked
- 1 cup baby spinach
- 2 spring onions, chopped
- ½ teaspoon sweet paprika
- A pinch of salt and black pepper
- ½ cup heavy cream

Directions:

In a bowl, mix the eggs with the spinach and the other ingredients, whisk and pour into a ziplock bag. Seal the bag, submerge in the water oven and cook at 168 degrees F for 30 minutes. Serve for breakfast.

Nutrition: calories 253, fat 4.9, fiber 2, carbs 26.4, protein 23.6

Mushroom Oatmeal

Preparation time: 10 minutes | Cooking time: 30 minutes | Servings: 4

Ingredients:
- ½ pound mushrooms, sliced
- 1 cup steel cut oats
- 2 cups coconut milk
- ½ teaspoon cumin, ground
- 1 red chili, minced
- A pinch of salt and black pepper
- 1 carrot, peeled and grated

Directions:

In a ziplock bag, mix the oats with the mushrooms and the other ingredients, whisk and seal the bag. Submerge in the water oven and cook at 170 degrees F for 30 minutes. Divide into bowls and serve.

Nutrition: calories 342, fat 12, fiber 5, carbs 16, protein 15

Strawberry Bowls

Preparation time: 10 minutes | Cooking time: 25 minutes | Servings: 4

Ingredients:
- 1 cup strawberries
- 1 cup coconut milk
- ¼ teaspoon raw honey
- ½ tablespoon lime juice
- 2 teaspoons vanilla extract

Directions:

In a sous vide bag, mix the berries with the honey and the other ingredients, toss gently, seal the bag and cook in the water oven for 25 minutes at 117 degrees F. Divide into bowls and serve for breakfast.

Nutrition: calories 197, fat 2, fiber 3, carbs 36, protein 6

Sweet Potato Mix

Preparation time: 10 minutes | Cooking time: 30 minutes | Servings: 4

Ingredients:
- ½ pound sweet potatoes, peeled, and cubed
- 4 eggs, whisked
- ½ teaspoon sweet paprika
- A pinch of salt and black pepper
- 3 tablespoons Greek yogurt
- 1 teaspoon oregano, dried
- 1 tablespoon chives, chopped

Directions:

In a bowl, mix the sweet potatoes with the eggs and the other ingredients, whisk and pour everything into a ziplock bag. Seal the bag, submerge in the water oven and cook at 165 degrees F for 30 minutes. Divide the mix into bowls and serve.

Nutrition: calories 438, fat 13, fiber 9, carbs 64, protein 26

Walnut and Berries Bowls

Preparation time: 10 minutes | Cooking time: 30 minutes | Servings: 4

Ingredients:
- 1 cup walnuts, chopped
- ½ cup old fashioned oats
- 1 cup blackberries
- 1 cup coconut cream
- 1 tablespoon raisins
- ½ teaspoon vanilla extract

Directions:

In a sous vide bag, mix the walnuts with the berries and the other ingredients, toss, seal the bag and cook in the water oven at 160 degrees F for 30 minutes. Divide into bowls and serve.

Nutrition: calories 224, fat 12, fiber 5, carbs 15, protein 5

Chives Avocado Quinoa

Preparation time: 10 minutes | Cooking time: 30 minutes | Servings: 4

Ingredients:
- 1 cup quinoa
- 2 cups veggie stock
- 1 avocado, peeled, pitted and cubed
- 1 tablespoon chives, chopped
- ½ teaspoon coriander, ground
- ½ teaspoon chili powder
- A pinch of salt and black pepper
- 1 teaspoon chili powder
- ½ teaspoon sweet paprika

Directions:

In a ziplock bag, mix the quinoa with the stock and the other ingredients, toss, seal the bag, submerge in the water oven and cook at 165 degrees F for 30 minutes. Divide into bowls and serve for breakfast.

Nutrition: calories 300, fat 12, fiber 6, carbs 16, protein 6

Balsamic Avocado and Tomato Salad

Preparation time: 10 minutes | *Cooking time:* 15 minutes | *Servings:* 4

Ingredients:
- ½ pound cherry tomatoes, halved
- 1 tablespoon avocado oil
- ½ teaspoon rosemary, dried
- ½ teaspoon chili powder
- 1 avocado, peeled, pitted and cubed
- 2 cucumbers, cubed
- 1 tablespoon balsamic vinegar
- A pinch of salt and black pepper
- 1 tablespoon chives, chopped

Directions:
In a sous vide bag, mix the tomatoes with the avocado oil, avocado and the other ingredients, toss, seal the bag and cook at 165 degrees F for 15 minutes. Divide into bowls and serve for breakfast.

Nutrition: calories 424, fat 23, fiber 12, carbs 42, protein 15

Apple Salad

Preparation time: 5 minutes | *Cooking time:* 20 minutes | *Servings:* 2

Ingredients:
- ½ pound apples, cored and cut into wedges
- ¼ cup almond milk
- 1 teaspoon cinnamon powder
- 2 teaspoons raw honey
- 1 teaspoon vanilla extract

Directions:
In a sous vide bag, mix the apples with the milk and the other ingredients, toss, seal the bag, submerge in the water oven and cook at 165 degrees F for 20 minutes. Divide the salad into bowls and serve for breakfast.

Nutrition: calories 305, fat 19, fiber 5, carbs 29, protein 8

Pesto Zucchini Ramekins

Preparation time: 10 minutes | *Cooking time:* 30 minutes | *Servings:* 4

Ingredients:
- Cooking spray
- 2 spring onions, chopped
- 2 tablespoons basil pesto
- ½ pound zucchinis, cubed
- 2 garlic cloves, minced
- 8 eggs, whisked
- ½ teaspoon oregano, dried
- ½ teaspoon chili powder
- A pinch of salt and black pepper
- 1 tablespoon dill, chopped

Directions:
In a bowl, mix the eggs with the zucchinis and the other ingredients except the cooking spray and whisk well. Grease 4 ramekins with the cooking spray, divide the zucchini mix, put the ramekins in the water oven and cook at 170 degrees F for 30 minutes. Serve the mix for breakfast.

Nutrition: calories 356, fat 29, fiber 2, carbs 3, protein 18

Chickpeas Breakfast Spread

Preparation time: 10 minutes | *Cooking time:* 20 minutes | *Servings:* 4

Ingredients:
- 2 cups canned chickpeas, drained and rinsed
- 1 cup heavy cream
- 2 spring onions, chopped
- 1 tablespoon avocado oil
- 1 tablespoon lemon juice
- 1 tablespoon lemon zest, grated
- 1 tablespoon tahini paste
- ¼ teaspoon sweet paprika
- A pinch of salt and black pepper
- 1 tablespoon chives, chopped

Directions:
In a sous vide bag, mix the chickpeas with the cream, spring onions and the other ingredients except the oil and the tahini paste, seal the bag, submerge in the water oven and cook at 165 degrees F for 20 minutes. Transfer the mix to a blender, add the remaining ingredients, pulse well, divide into bowls and serve for breakfast.

Nutrition: calories 203, fat 12, fiber 4, carbs 15, protein 4

Sous Vide Lunch Recipes
Lemon Shrimp and Avocado Bowls
Preparation time: *10 minutes* | ***Cooking time:*** *20 minutes* | ***Servings:*** *4*

Ingredients:
- 1 pound shrimp, peeled and deveined
- Juice of ½ lemon
- 1 avocado, peeled, pitted and cubed
- 1 cup baby spinach
- A pinch of salt and black pepper to the taste
- 2 tablespoons ghee, melted

Directions:
In s sous vide bag, mix the shrimp with the lemon juice and the other ingredients, toss, seal the bag, put it into your sous vide machine and cook everything at 126 degrees F for 20 minutes. Divide into bowls and serve for lunch.

Nutrition: calories 211, fat 5, fiber 6, carbs 12, protein 6

Mustard Salmon Steaks
Preparation time: *10 minutes* | ***Cooking time:*** *25 minutes* | ***Servings:*** *4*

Ingredients:
- 4 salmon steaks, bones removed
- 2 tablespoons mustard
- Salt and black pepper to the taste
- 1 tablespoon lemon juice
- 1 teaspoon chives, chopped
- 2 tablespoons olive oil

Directions:
In a bowl, mix the salmon with the mustard and the other ingredients, and toss well. Transfer the salmon steaks to sous vide bags, seal them, submerge in your sous vide machine and cook at 130 degrees F for 25 minutes. Divide steaks between plates and serve with a side salad.

Nutrition: calories 221, fat 4, fiber 6, carbs 12, protein 5

Shrimp Salad
Preparation time: *10 minutes* | ***Cooking time:*** *20 minutes* | ***Servings:*** *2*

Ingredients:
- 1 pound shrimp, peeled and deveined
- 1 cup cherry tomatoes, halved
- 1 cup baby spinach
- 1 cup kalamata olives, pitted and halved
- 1 tablespoon olive oil
- 1 tablespoon lemon juice
- 1 tablespoon balsamic vinegar
- 1 tablespoon chives, chopped

Directions:
In a sous vide bag, mix the shrimp with the tomatoes, spinach and the other ingredients, seal, submerge in the bath water and cook at 104 degrees F for 20 minutes. Divide into bowls and serve for lunch.

Nutrition: calories 152, fat 6, fiber 5, carbs 8, protein 5

Balsamic Calamari and Tomatoes
Preparation time: *10 minutes* | ***Cooking time:*** *30 minutes* | ***Servings:*** *2*

Ingredients:
- 1 cup calamari rings
- ½ cup tomato sauce
- 1 cup cherry tomatoes, halved
- 1 teaspoon chili powder
- 4 scallions, chopped
- ½ teaspoon balsamic vinegar
- A pinch of salt and black pepper

Directions:
In a sous vide bag, mix the calamari rings with the tomatoes and the other ingredients, toss, seal the bag, submerge in the water bath and cook at 170 degrees F for 30 minutes. Divide into bowls and serve for lunch.

Nutrition: calories 152, fat 6, fiber 2, carbs 6, protein 5

BBQ Cod Mix

***Preparation time:** 10 minutes | **Cooking time:** 30 minutes | **Servings:** 2*

Ingredients:
- 1 pound cod fillets, boneless
- 1 tablespoon chives, chopped
- ½ teaspoon coriander, ground
- 1 tablespoon olive oil
- 2 tablespoons BBQ sauce
- 1 tablespoon lime juice
- A pinch of salt and black pepper

Directions:
In a bowl, mix the cod with the bbq sauce and the other ingredients, toss gently and transfer to a sous vide bag. Seal the bag, introduce in the preheated water oven and cook at 140 degrees F for 30 minutes. Divide between plates and serve for lunch.

Nutrition: calories 200, fat 6, fiber 6, carbs 12, protein 6

Cod Salsa

***Preparation time:** 10 minutes | **Cooking time:** 30 minutes. | **Servings:** 2*

Ingredients:
- 1 pound cod fillets, boneless and skinless
- 1 cup mild salsa
- ½ teaspoon red pepper flakes, crushed
- ½ teaspoon sweet paprika
- 1 tablespoon rosemary, chopped
- ½ tablespoon olive oil
- Salt and black pepper to the taste

Directions:
In a sous vide bag, mix the fish with the salsa, pepper flakes and the other ingredients, seal the bag, submerge in the water oven and cook at 161 degrees F for 30 minutes. Divide between plates serve for lunch.

Nutrition: calories 172, fat 4, fiber 6, carbs 8, protein 8

Calamari, Salmon and Shrimp Bowls

***Preparation time:** 10 minutes | **Cooking time:** 50 minutes | **Servings:** 4*

Ingredients:
- 1 carrot, peeled and sliced
- 1 cup calamari rings
- 1 cup smoked salmon, skinless, boneless and cut into strips
- 1 cup shrimp, peeled and deveined
- 1 celery stalk, chopped
- 1 tablespoon black peppercorns
- 1 garlic clove, minced
- ¼ cup vinegar
- 1 shallot, chopped
- 1 teaspoon mustard
- Juice of 1 lime
- 1 teaspoon smoked paprika
- 1 tablespoon olive oil
- Salt and black pepper to the taste

Directions:
In a sous vide bag, combine the carrot with the calamari and the other ingredients, toss, seal, submerge in the water oven and cook at 185 degrees F for 50 minutes. Divide into bowls and serve.

Nutrition: calories 215, fat 4, fiber 8, carbs 12, protein 4

Mustard Salmon Mix

***Preparation time:** 10 minutes | **Cooking time:** 35 minutes | **Servings:** 4*

Ingredients:

- 1 pound salmon fillets, boneless and roughly cubed
- 2 tablespoons mustard
- 1 cup baby spinach
- 1 cup baby kale
- Salt and black pepper to the taste
- 1 tablespoon homemade mayonnaise
- Juice of 1 lemon
- Zest of 1 lemon, grated
- 2 scallions, chopped
- 2 tablespoons capers, chopped
- 2 tablespoons olive oil

Directions:

In a sous vide bag, combine the salmon with the spinach, mustard and the other ingredients, seal the bag, submerge in the water oven and cook at 170 degrees F for 35 minutes. Divide into bowls serve.

Nutrition: calories 201, fat 3, fiber 6, carbs 8, protein 6

Creamy Calamari

***Preparation time:** 10 minutes | **Cooking time:** 30 minutes | **Servings:** 2*

Ingredients:

- 2 cups calamari rings
- 1 cup heavy cream
- 1 cup baby spinach
- 1 cup cherry tomatoes, halved
- 1 cup corn
- 2 tablespoons olive oil
- Salt and black pepper to the taste
- 2 tablespoons chives, chopped

Directions:

In a sous vide bag, mix the calamari rings with the spinach, cream and the other ingredients, seal the bag, cook in the water bath at 180 degrees F for 30 minutes, divide into bowls and serve.

Nutrition: calories 199, fat 3, fiber 6, carbs 8, protein 7

Lime Lobster

***Preparation time:** 10 minutes | **Cooking time:** 30 minutes | **Servings:** 2*

Ingredients:

- 2 lobster tails
- 6 tablespoons butter, melted
- 1 teaspoon sweet paprika
- ½ teaspoon turmeric powder
- Juice of 1 lime
- Salt and black pepper to the taste

Directions:

In a sous vide bag, combine the lobster with the melted butter and the other ingredients, toss, seal the bag, introduce in the preheated water oven and cook at 140 degrees F for 30 minutes. Divide the lobster tails and lime sauce between plates and serve.

Nutrition: calories 166, fat 3, fiber 6, carbs 8, protein 5

Chicken, Shrimp and Rice

***Preparation time:** 10 minutes | **Cooking time:** 1 hour | **Servings:** 4*

Ingredients:

- 1 pound chicken breast, skinless, boneless and cubed
- 1 pound shrimp, peeled and deveined
- 1 cup wild rice
- 2 cups chicken stock
- 1 cup cherry tomatoes, halved
- ½ teaspoon chili powder
- 1 tablespoon Creole seasoning
- Salt and black pepper to the taste
- 1 green bell pepper, chopped
- 2 spring onions, chopped
- 3 garlic cloves, minced
- 1 tablespoon chives, chopped

Directions:

In a sous vide bag, mix the chicken with the shrimp, rice and the other ingredients, seal the bag, submerge in the water bath and cook at 180 degrees F for 1 hour. Divide into bowls and serve.

Nutrition: calories 243, fat 4, fiber 6, carbs 15, protein 5

Vanilla and Butter Shrimp

Preparation time: 10 minutes | *Cooking time:* 30 minutes | *Servings:* 2

Ingredients:
- ½ teaspoon vanilla extract
- 1 pound shrimp, peeled and deveined
- ¼ teaspoon sweet paprika
- A pinch of salt and black pepper
- 1 cup cherry tomatoes, halved
- 2 tablespoons butter, melted
- 1 tablespoon chives, chopped

Directions:
In a sous vide bag combine the shrimp with the vanilla, butter and the other ingredients, seal, introduce in the preheated sous vide machine and cook at 136 degrees F for 30 minutes. Divide into bowls and serve..

Nutrition: calories 188, fat 3, fiber 7, carbs 9, protein 5

Pork and Blueberries Mix

Preparation time: 10 minutes | *Cooking time:* 2 hours | *Servings:* 2

Ingredients:
- 2 pounds pork roast, sliced
- 1 tablespoon olive oil
- Salt and black pepper to the taste
- 1 tablespoon cinnamon powder
- A pinch of cayenne pepper
- 1 teaspoon cumin, ground
- 1 teaspoon fennel seeds, crushed
- 2 tablespoons soy sauce
- ½ cup blueberries
- 2 tablespoons stevia
- ½ teaspoon chili sauce
- 1 tablespoons chives, chopped

Directions:
In a sous vide bag, mix the roast with the oil, cinnamon and the other ingredients, seal the bag, cook in the water bath at 180 degrees F for 2 hours, divide between plates and serve.

Nutrition: calories 312, fat 5, fiber 7, carbs 16, protein 5

BBQ and Paprika Ribs

Preparation time: 10 minutes | *Cooking time:* 2 hours | *Servings:* 4

Ingredients:
- 2 pounds baby back pork ribs
- 2 tablespoons olive oil
- 1 cup bbq sauce
- Salt and black pepper to the taste
- 2 tablespoons sweet paprika
- 2 tablespoons cumin, ground
- 2 tablespoons garlic powder
- 1 tablespoon chives, chopped

Directions:
In a sous vide bag, mix the ribs with the oil, sauce and the other ingredients, toss, seal the bag, submerge in the water bath and cook at 180 degrees F for 2 hours. Divide between plates and serve them with a side salad.

Nutrition: calories 351, fat 6, fiber 7, carbs 9, protein 5

Herbed Pork and Sun dried Tomatoes

Preparation time: 10 minutes | *Cooking time:* 2 hours | *Servings:* 2

Ingredients:
- 2 pounds pork roast, sliced
- 1 cup sun-dried tomatoes, chopped
- 2 tablespoons olive oil
- Juice of 1 lime
- 1 tablespoon mustard
- Zest of 1 lime, grated
- ½ teaspoon cloves, crushed
- 1 teaspoon oregano, dried
- 1 teaspoon coriander, ground
- 1 teaspoon thyme, chopped
- 1 tablespoon chives, chopped

Directions:
In a large sous vide bag, combine the roast with the tomatoes, oil and the other ingredients, seal the bag, submerge in the sous vide machine and cook at 180 degrees F for 2 hours Divide between plates and serve right away.

Nutrition: calories 336, fat 6, fiber 6, carbs 16, protein 5

Buttery Pork Tenderloin

Preparation time: 10 minutes | Cooking time: 2 hours | Servings: 4

Ingredients:
- 2 pounds pork tenderloin, sliced
- ½ teaspoon turmeric powder
- 1 teaspoon chili powder
- Juice of 1 lime
- 1 and ½ tablespoons Italian seasoning
- Salt and black pepper to the taste
- 2 tablespoons butter, melted

Directions:
In a sous vide bag, combine the pork with the melted butter and the other ingredients, seal the bag, introduce it in the preheated water oven and cook at 135 degrees F for 2 hours. Divide between plates and serve with a side salad.

Nutrition: calories 321, fat 4, fiber 7, carbs 12, protein 5

Garlic and Nutmeg Pork

Preparation time: 10 minutes | Cooking time: 2 hours | Servings: 6

Ingredients:
- 2 pounds pork roast, sliced
- 4 garlic cloves, minced
- 1 teaspoon nutmeg, ground
- 2 tablespoons olive oil
- Juice of 1 lime
- Salt and black pepper to the taste
- 1 teaspoon rosemary, dried
- 2 bay leaves
- 1 tablespoon cilantro, chopped

Directions:
In a sous vide bag, combine the pork with the garlic, nutmeg and the other ingredients, seal, introduce them into your preheated water oven and cook at 180 degrees F for 2 hours. Divide between plates and serve.

Nutrition: calories 353, fat 7, fiber 8, carbs 15, protein 17

Thyme Pork and Carrots

Preparation time: 10 minutes | Cooking time: 3 hours | Servings: 4

Ingredients:
- 2 pounds pork roast, sliced
- ½ pound carrots, peeled and sliced
- 1 tablespoon thyme, chopped
- 1 cup red wine
- ½ teaspoon sweet paprika
- ½ teaspoon coriander, ground
- 2 garlic cloves, minced
- 2 tablespoons olive oil
- 2 tablespoons black peppercorns
- Salt and black pepper to the taste
- 2 bay leaves
- ½ teaspoon smoked paprika
- Salt and black pepper to the taste
- 1 tablespoon mustard powder

Directions:
In a large sous vide bag, combine the roast with the carrots, thyme and the other ingredients, seal, submerge in the water oven and cook at 190 degrees F for 3 hours Divide between plates and serve.

Nutrition: calories 400, fat 6, fiber 7, carbs 16, protein 22

Thyme Pork Chops

Preparation time: 10 minutes | Cooking time: 2 hours | Servings: 4

Ingredients:
- 4 pork chops, bone in
- 2 tablespoons thyme, chopped
- Juice of 1 lime
- ½ teaspoon chili powder
- Salt and black pepper to the taste
- A drizzle of olive oil

Directions:
In a sous vide bag, combine the pork chops with the thyme and the other ingredients, seal the bag, submerge in the preheated water oven and cook at 138 degrees F for 2 hours. Divide between plates and serve.

Nutrition: calories 312, fat 4, fiber 6, carbs 15, protein 17

Lamb Rack and Cherry Tomatoes Mix

Preparation time: 10 minutes | Cooking time: 2 hours | Servings: 4

Ingredients:
- 1 rack of lamb
- 1 cup cherry tomatoes, halved
- Salt and black pepper to the taste
- ½ teaspoon rosemary, dried
- ½ bunch mint, chopped
- ½ cup olive oil
- 2 garlic cloves, minced

Directions:
In a sous vide bag, combine the rack of lamb with the tomatoes and the other ingredients, seal the bag, submerge into your preheated water oven and cook at 150 degrees F for 2 hours. Divide the mix between plates and serve.

Nutrition: calories 276, fat 5, fiber 9, carbs 16, protein 20

Lamb and Pomegranate Mix

Preparation time: 10 minutes | Cooking time: 2 hours | Servings: 4

Ingredients:
- 1 cup pomegranate seeds
- 2 pounds lamb chops
- 2 cups pomegranate juice
- 2 tablespoons balsamic vinegar
- 2 rosemary springs, chopped
- Salt and black pepper to the taste
- 1 tablespoon butter, melted

Directions:
In sous vide bag, combine the lamb chops with the pomegranate seeds and the other ingredients, seal, introduce in the preheated water oven and cook at 160degrees F for 2 hours. Divide everything between plates and serve.

Nutrition: calories 300, fat 5, fiber 8, carbs 15, protein 20

Lamb, Leeks and Mushroom Mix

Preparation time: 10 minutes | Cooking time: 2 hours | Servings: 4

Ingredients:
- 2 pounds lamb chops
- 2 leeks, sliced
- 1 cup mushrooms, sliced
- 2 tablespoons balsamic vinegar
- 2 tablespoons olive oil
- Salt and black pepper to the taste
- 1 cup coconut cream
- 1 tablespoon chives, chopped

Directions:
In a sous vide bag, combine the lamb chops with the leeks and the other ingredients, seal the bag, submerge in the water bath, cook at 180 degrees F for 2 hours, divide between plates and serve.

Nutrition: calories 311, fat 4, fiber 7, carbs 18, protein 16

Coriander Leg Of Lamb

Preparation time: 10 minutes | *Cooking time:* 8 hours | *Servings:* 4

Ingredients:
- 2 pounds leg of lamb, boneless
- 3 garlic cloves, minced
- 2 tablespoons coriander, chopped
- Juice of 1 lime
- 2 tablespoons olive oil
- Salt and black pepper to the taste
- 2 teaspoons smoked paprika

Directions:

In a sous vide bag, combine the leg of lamb and the other ingredients, toss, seal, introduce in the preheated water oven and cook at 150 degrees F for 8 hours. Slice the meat, divide between plates, and serve.

Nutrition: calories 277, fat 6, fiber 8, carbs 16, protein 17

Lamb Fillets and Olives

Preparation time: 10 minutes | *Cooking time:* 3 hours | *Servings:* 4

Ingredients:
- 2 pounds lamb loin fillets
- Salt and black pepper to the taste
- 2 tablespoons olive oil
- 2 cups green olives, pitted and sliced
- Juice of 1 orange
- 1 tablespoon capers
- 2 tablespoons balsamic vinegar
- 1 cup cherry tomatoes, halved
- 1 cup parsley, chopped

Directions:

Divide the lamb fillets into 2 sous vide bags, add the oil, olives and the other ingredients, seal them, cook in the water oven at 160 degrees F for 3 hours, divide between plates and serve.

Nutrition: calories 300, fat 6, fiber 8, carbs 17, protein 5

Rack of Lamb and Baby Cauliflower Mix

Preparation time: 10 minutes | *Cooking time:* 2 hours | *Servings:* 4

Ingredients:
- 1 pound rack of lamb
- Salt and black pepper to the taste
- 1 tablespoon rosemary, chopped
- 2 shallots chopped
- 2 leeks, sliced
- 3 baby cauliflowers, florets separated
- 1 red onion, sliced
- 2 tablespoons balsamic vinegar
- Salt and black pepper to the taste

Directions:

In a sous vide bag, combine the rack of lamb with the rosemary and the other ingredients, seal the bag, submerge in the water bath, cook at 183 degrees F for 2 hours, divide between plates and serve.

Nutrition: calories 282, fat 5, fiber 8, carbs 18, protein 12

Garlic and Peppercorns Lamb Chops

Preparation time: 10 minutes | *Cooking time:* 2 hours | *Servings:* 2

Ingredients:
- 2 pounds lamb chops
- 2 garlic cloves, minced
- 2 tablespoons olive oil
- Juice of 1 lemon
- ½ teaspoon turmeric powder
- 1 teaspoon oregano, chopped
- 8 black peppercorns, crushed
- Salt and black pepper to the taste

Directions:

In a sous vide bag, combine the lamb chops with the garlic and the other ingredients, seal, submerge in the preheated water oven and cook at 132 degrees F for 2 hours. Divide between plates and serve.

Nutrition: calories 300, fat 8, fiber 9, carbs 17, protein 14

Sage Cajun Turkey

Preparation time: 10 minutes | *Cooking time:* 2 hours | *Servings:* 4

Ingredients:
- 2 pounds turkey breast, skinless, boneless and cut into strips
- 1 tablespoon Cajun seasoning
- 2 tablespoons balsamic vinegar
- A pinch of salt and black pepper
- 1 tablespoon black peppercorns
- 1 tablespoon sage, chopped
- ¼ cup chicken stock

Directions:
In a sous vide bag, combine the turkey with the seasoning and the other ingredients, seal the bag, introduce into your preheated water oven and cook at 176 degrees F for 2 hours. Divide between plates and serve with a side salad.

Nutrition: calories 342, fat 7, fiber 9, carbs 17, protein 6

Ginger and Shallot Duck

Preparation time: 10 minutes | *Cooking time:* 2 hours and 30 minutes | *Servings:* 2

Ingredients:
- 2 duck breasts, trimmed and some of the fat removed
- 1 teaspoon turmeric powder
- 1 tablespoon ginger paste
- 2 tablespoons olive oil
- 2 curry leaves
- 1 cup shallot, chopped
- ½ teaspoon chili powder
- 2 teaspoons coriander powder
- ½ teaspoon garam masala
- 1 cup coconut milk

Directions:
In a sous vide bag, combine the duck with the turmeric, ginger and the other ingredients, seal, submerge it in the preheated water oven and cook at 140 degrees F for 2 hours and 30 minutes. Divide duck breasts between plates, and serve.

Nutrition: calories 300, fat 5, fiber 8, carbs 17, protein 13

Curry Chicken Thighs

Preparation time: 10 minutes | *Cooking time:* 1 hour and 30 minutes | *Servings:* 4

Ingredients:
- 2 tablespoons avocado oil
- 2 pounds chicken thighs, boneless and skinless
- 1 tablespoon yellow curry paste
- Salt and black pepper to the taste
- 1 teaspoon garlic powder
- 6 tablespoons butter, melted

Directions:
In a sous vide bag, combine the chicken with the oil, butter and the other ingredients, seal the bag, introduce in the preheated water oven and cook at 150 degrees F for 1 hour and 30 minutes. Divide between plates and serve.

Nutrition: calories 241, fat 6, fiber 8, carbs 9, protein 12

Provence Chicken Breast

Preparation time: 10 minutes | *Cooking time:* 3 hours | *Servings:* 2

Ingredients:
- 2 pounds chicken breasts, skinless and boneless
- Salt and black pepper to the taste
- Juice of 1 lime
- ½ teaspoon garam masala
- 4 tablespoons butter, melted
- 1 tablespoon coriander, chopped
- 1 garlic clove, minced
- 1 teaspoon herbs de Provence

Directions:
In a sous vide bag, combine the chicken with the lime juice and the other ingredients, toss, seal the bag, introduce in the preheated water oven and cook at 140 degrees F for 3 hours. Divide between plates and serve with a side salad.

Nutrition: calories 226, fat 7, fiber 9, carbs 12, protein 17

Turkey Breast and Cranberries

Preparation time: 10 minutes | *Cooking time:* 3 hours | *Servings:* 4

Ingredients:
- 1 pound turkey breast, skinless, boneless and sliced
- 1 cup cranberries
- 1 tablespoon sage, chopped
- Salt and black pepper to the taste
- 2 tablespoons butter, melted
- ½ cup shallots, chopped
- ¼ cup red wine

Directions:

In a large sous vide bag, combine the turkey with the cranberries and the other ingredients, toss, seal the bag, submerge in the preheated water oven and cook at 156 degrees F for 3 hours. Divide the turkey between plates and serve with the cranberries mix on top.

Nutrition: calories 272, fat 8, fiber 6, carbs 18, protein 11

Chili Chicken

Preparation time: 10 minutes | *Cooking time:* 2 hours | *Servings:* 4

Ingredients:
- 2 pounds chicken breasts, skinless and boneless
- ½ tablespoon chili sauce
- 1 red chili, minced
- 1 yellow onion, quartered
- 2 tablespoons butter, melted
- 2 garlic cloves, minced
- Salt and black pepper to the taste

Directions:

In a sous vide bag, combine the chicken with the chili sauce and the other ingredients, seal the bag, submerge in the preheated water oven and cook the chicken at 146 degrees F for 2 hours. Serve the chicken with a side salad.

Nutrition: calories 221, fat 4, fiber 8, carbs 12, protein 6

Spring Onion and Soy Chicken

Preparation time: 10 minutes | *Cooking time:* 3 hours | *Servings:* 2

Ingredients:
- 1 bunch spring onions, roughly chopped
- 2 garlic cloves, minced
- 1 tablespoon avocado oil
- 2 pounds chicken breast, skinless, boneless and sliced
- 1 tablespoon soy sauce
- Salt and black pepper to the taste
- 1 tablespoon parsley, chopped

Directions:

In a sous vide bag, combine the chicken with the spring onions and the other ingredients, seal the bag, introduce in the preheated water oven and cook at 160 degrees F for 3 hours. Divide between plates and serve.

Nutrition: calories 201, fat 4, fiber 3, carbs 8, protein 6

Beet Cream Soup

Preparation time: 10 minutes | *Cooking time:* 1 hour | *Servings:* 8

Ingredients:
- 1 pound beets, peeled and cubed
- 1 red onion, sliced
- 4 carrots, chopped
- ½ tablespoon rosemary, chopped
- ½ red cabbage head, shredded
- 2 quarts veggie stock
- ½ cup chives, chopped
- 3 tablespoons red vinegar
- Salt and black pepper to the taste

Directions:

In a sous vide bag, mix the beets with the carrots, onion and the rest of the ingredients, toss, seal the bag, submerge in the water oven and cook at 182 degrees F for 1 hour. Transfer this to a blender, pulse well, divide into bowls and serve

Nutrition: calories 191, fat 3, fiber 7, carbs 8, protein 5

Chicken Soup

Preparation time: 10 minutes | Cooking time: 2 hours | Servings: 4

Ingredients:
- 1 red bell pepper, chopped
- 1 green bell pepper, chopped
- 2 cups rotisserie chicken, skinless, boneless and shredded
- ½ cup carrots, chopped
- 1 red onion, chopped
- ½ teaspoon garlic powder
- Salt and black pepper to the taste
- 1 tablespoon olive oil
- 1-quart chicken stock

Directions:

In a big sous vide bag, combine the chicken with the carrots and the other ingredients except the stock, toss well, seal the bag, introduce in the preheated water oven and cook at 182 degrees F for 1 hour and 30 minutes. Transfer the mix to a pot, add the stock, bring to a simmer, cook for 30 minutes over medium heat, divide into bowls and serve.

Nutrition: calories 200, fat 4, fiber 6, carbs 12, protein 6

Cauliflower Soup

Preparation time: 10 minutes | Cooking time: 1 hour | Servings: 4

Ingredients:
- 1 cauliflower head, florets separated
- 2 spring onions, chopped
- 4 cups chicken stock
- 4 garlic cloves, minced
- Salt and black pepper to the taste
- ½ teaspoon turmeric powder
- 1 tablespoon chives, chopped
- A drizzle of olive oil

Directions:

In a sous vide bag, combine the cauliflower with the spring onions, and the other ingredients except the stock, toss, seal the bag, submerge in the preheated water oven and cook at 190 degrees F for 1 hour. Transfer the veggies to a blender, add the stock, pulse well, divide into bowls and serve.

Nutrition: calories 211, fat 5, fiber 7, carbs 12, protein 4

Zucchini Cream

Preparation time: 10 minutes | Cooking time: 1 hour | Servings: 6

Ingredients:
- 1 pound zucchinis, roughly cubed
- A pinch of salt and black pepper
- 2 tablespoons butter, melted
- ½ teaspoon curry powder
- ½ teaspoon turmeric powder
- 1 yellow onion, chopped
- 1 garlic clove, minced
- 3 cups veggie stock
- 2 cups coconut cream

Directions:

In a sous vide bag, combine the zucchinis with the butter and the other ingredients except the stock and the cream, seal the bag, submerge in the water bath, cook at 170 degrees F for 1 hour, transfer to a blender, add the rest of the ingredients, pulse well, divide into bowls and serve.

Nutrition: calories 199, fat 3, fiber 6, carbs 8, protein 6

Roasted Pork and Apples

Preparation time: 10 minutes | Cooking time: 4 hours | Servings: 6

Ingredients:
- 1 cup red wine
- 1 tablespoon lemon zest, grated
- 1 tablespoon lemon juice
- 2 cups apples, cored and cut into wedges
- 2 pounds pork roast, sliced
- Salt and black pepper to the taste
- A drizzle of olive oil

Directions:
In a sous vide bag, combine the pork with the wine and the other ingredients, seal it, submerge in the preheated water oven in your sous vide machine and cook at 155 degrees F for 4 hours. Divide between plates and serve.

Nutrition: calories 356, fat 14, fiber 4, carbs 16, protein 25

Pork Chops and Mushrooms

Preparation time: 10 minutes | Cooking time: 3 hours | Servings: 4

Ingredients:
- 1 cup mushrooms, sliced
- 2 pounds pork chops
- 1 teaspoon garlic powder
- 1 teaspoon rosemary, chopped
- 1 teaspoon nutmeg
- 1 tablespoon balsamic vinegar
- ½ cup red wine

Directions:
in a sous vide bag, combine the pork chops with the mushrooms and the other ingredients, seal it, submerge in the preheated water oven and cook them at 1780 degrees F for 3 hours Divide pork chops between plates, and serve.

Nutrition: calories 370, fat 10, fiber 1, carbs 14, protein 30

Lemony and Parsley Beef

Preparation time: 10 minutes | Cooking time: 3 hours | Servings: 4

Ingredients:
- 1 tablespoons olive oil
- 2 pounds beef stew meat, cubed
- 1 cup beef stock
- Juice of ½ lemon
- Zest of 1 lemon, grated
- Salt and black pepper to the taste
- A pinch of lemon pepper
- 6 garlic cloves, minced
- 2 tablespoons parsley, chopped

Directions:
In a sous vide bag, mix the beef with the oil, stock and the other ingredients, seal the bag, submerge in the water oven and cook at 160 degrees F for 3 hours. Divide the mix between plates and serve with a side salad.

Nutrition: calories 366, fat 25, fiber 1, carbs 14, protein 40

Cranberry Beef

Preparation time: 10 minutes | Cooking time: 3 hours | Servings: 4

Ingredients:
- 1 tablespoon avocado oil
- 2 pounds beef steaks
- Salt and black pepper to the taste
- ½ teaspoon onion powder
- ½ teaspoon garlic powder
- ½ teaspoon ginger powder
- ½ cup cranberries
- 2 garlic cloves, minced
- Juice of 1 lime

Directions:
In a sous vide bag, combine the steaks with the oil, onion powder and the other ingredients, toss, seal the bag, submerge it in the preheated water oven and cook at 170 degrees F for 3 hours. Divide between plates and serve with a side salad.

Nutrition: calories 430, fat 23, fiber 2, carbs 15, protein 45

Maple Pork Chops

Preparation time: 10 minutes | *Cooking time:* 6 hours | *Servings:* 4

Ingredients:
- 3 scallions, chopped
- 2 tablespoons maple syrup
- 2 pounds pork chops
- Juice and zest of 1 lime
- Salt and black pepper to the taste
- ½ teaspoon rosemary, dried

Directions:
In 2 sous vide bags, combine the pork chops with the scallions, maple syrup and the other ingredients, seal the bag, submerge in the preheated water oven and cook them at 150 degrees F for 6 hours Divide everything between plates and serve.

Nutrition: calories 325, fat 18, fiber 1, carbs 16, protein 36

Pork Roast and Olives Salsa

Preparation time: 10 minutes | *Cooking time:* 6 hours | *Servings:* 4

Ingredients:
- 2 pounds pork roast, sliced
- 1 cup green olives, pitted and sliced
- 1 cup cherry tomatoes, halved
- 4 spring onions, chopped
- 2 tablespoons balsamic vinegar
- 2 tablespoons lime juice
- 2 tablespoons olive oil
- 1 tablespoon chives, chopped
- Salt and black pepper to the taste

Directions:
In a sous vide bag, combine the roast with the olives, tomatoes and the other ingredients, seal the bag, introduce in your preheated water oven and cook at 170 degrees F for 6 hours Divide everything between plates and serve right away.

Nutrition: calories 390, fat 16, fiber 2, carbs 22, protein 16

Lamb and Spinach Salad

Preparation time: 10 minutes | *Cooking time:* 5 hours | *Servings:* 4

Ingredients:
- 2 tablespoons olive oil
- 2 pounds lamb stew meat, cut into strips
- Salt and black pepper to the taste
- 1 teaspoon turmeric powder
- 2 garlic cloves, minced
- ½ cup pecans, toasted
- 1 cup cherry tomatoes, halved
- 2 cups spinach
- 1 tablespoon lime juice
- 1 cup mint, chopped

Directions:
In a sous vide bag, combine the lamb with the turmeric, garlic, half of the oil, salt and pepper, toss, seal the bag, submerge in the preheated water oven, cook at 180 degrees F for 5 hours, cool down and transfer to a salad bowl Add the rest of the ingredients, toss and serve.

Nutrition: calories 334, fat 33, fiber 3, carbs 14, protein 7

Harrisa Lamb Mix

Preparation time: 10 minutes | *Cooking time:* 3 hours | *Servings:* 4

Ingredients:
- 2 pounds lamb stew meat, roughly cubed
- 2 tablespoons olive oil
- 2 garlic cloves, minced
- 2 teaspoons oregano, dried
- 2 teaspoons rosemary, dried
- ¼ cup parsley, chopped
- 2 teaspoons harissa
- Salt and black pepper to the taste

Directions:
In a sous vide bag, mix the lamb with the oil, garlic and the other ingredients, toss, seal the bag, submerge in your preheated water oven and cook them at 160 degrees F for 3 hours Divide between plates and serve with a side salad.

Nutrition: calories 345, fat 32, fiber 6, carbs 14, protein 34

Lamb with Fennel and Tomatoes

Preparation time: 10 minutes | Cooking time: 3 hours | Servings: 4

Ingredients:
- 2 pounds lamb racks
- 2 fennel bulbs, sliced
- 1 cup cherry tomatoes, halved
- 2 tablespoons olive oil
- 2 tablespoons balsamic vinegar
- Salt and black pepper to the taste
- 1 tablespoon mint, chopped

Directions:

In a sous vide bag, combine the lamb with the fennel and the other ingredients, seal the bag, submerge in the preheated water oven, cook at 182 degrees F for 3 hours, divide between plates and serve.

Nutrition: calories 230, fat 3, fiber 3, carbs 14, protein 17

Beef and Yogurt Mix

Preparation time: 10 minutes | Cooking time: 4 hours | Servings: 4

Ingredients:
- 2 tablespoons olive oil
- 1 tablespoon lime juice
- 1 tablespoon lime zest, grated
- 2 pounds beef stew meat, cut into strips
- 1 cup Greek yogurt
- 1 teaspoon rosemary, dried
- 1 tablespoon chives, chopped
- 1 teaspoon thyme, dried
- Salt and black pepper to the taste
- 1 bay leaf
- 2 garlic cloves, minced

Directions:

In a sous vide bag, combine the beef with the oil, lime juice and the other ingredients, toss, seal the bag, submerge in the preheated water oven and cook at 170 degrees F for 4 hours Divide the mix between plates and serve with a side salad.

Nutrition: calories 435, fat 16, fiber 6, carbs 18, protein 45

Chili and Paprika Pork

Preparation time: 10 minutes | Cooking time: 6 hours | Servings: 4

Ingredients:
- 2 pound pork shoulder, sliced
- 1 tablespoon chili sauce
- ½ teaspoon sweet paprika
- 2 tablespoons olive oil
- 2 tablespoons lemon zest, grated
- Salt and black pepper to the taste
- ½ teaspoon celery salt
- A pinch of cayenne pepper
- 1 tablespoon garlic, minced

Directions:

In a big sous vide bag, combine the pork with the chili sauce, paprika and the other ingredients, toss, seal it, introduce in your preheated water oven and cook at 170 degrees F for 6 hours. Divide between plates and serve with a side salad.

Nutrition: calories 480, fat 5, fiber 6, carbs 16, protein 25

Greek Rosemary Lamb Chops

Preparation time: 10 minutes | Cooking time: 6 hours | Servings: 4

Ingredients:
- 2 pounds lamb chops
- 2 tablespoons olive oil
- 2 tablespoons rosemary, chopped
- ½ cup Greek yogurt
- 1 tablespoon mint, chopped
- Salt and black pepper to the taste
- 3 garlic cloves, minced

Directions:
In a large sous vide bag, combine the lamb with the oil, rosemary and the other ingredients, seal the bag, submerge in the water oven and cook at 140 degrees F for 6 hours. Divide the chops between plates and serve with a side salad.

Nutrition: calories 275, fat 2, fiber 1, carbs 12, protein 26

Curry and Coconut Pork Chops

Preparation time: 10 minutes | Cooking time: 6 hours | Servings: 4

Ingredients:
- ¼ cup lime juice
- 2 pounds pork chops
- 2 tablespoons avocado oil
- 2 tablespoons coconut butter, melted
- 2 tablespoons red curry paste
- 1 tablespoon rosemary, chopped
- 2 garlic cloves, minced
- ½ teaspoon chili powder
- 1 teaspoon cumin, ground
- Salt and black pepper to the taste

Directions:
In a large sous vide bag, combine the pork chops with the lime juice, oil and the other ingredients, seal the bag, submerge in your preheated water oven and cook at 145 degrees F for 6 hours. Divide the pork chops between plates and serve them with a side salad.

Nutrition: calories 360, fat 8, fiber 1, carbs 16, protein 26

Tomato and Eggplant Stew

Preparation time: 5 minutes | Cooking time: 30 minutes | Servings: 4

Ingredients:
- 1 pound tomatoes, cut into wedges
- 2 eggplants, cubed
- 1 red onion, chopped
- 1 tablespoon olive oil
- 2 garlic cloves, minced
- 1 teaspoon chili powder
- ½ cup tomato passata
- 1 tablespoon basil, chopped
- A pinch of salt and black pepper

Directions:
In a sous vide bag, mix the tomatoes with the eggplants, onion and the other ingredients, toss, seal the bag, submerge in the water oven and cook at 160 degrees F for 30 minutes. Divide the stew into bowls and serve.

Nutrition: calories 181, fat 7.3, fiber 1.4, carbs 4.6, protein 1.1

Lentils Stew

Preparation time: 10 minutes | Cooking time: 30 minutes | Servings: 4

Ingredients:
- 1 cup canned lentils, drained
- 2 spring onions, chopped
- ½ cup mild salsa
- 2 garlic cloves, minced
- 2 tablespoons olive oil
- A pinch of salt and black pepper
- 1 bunch cilantro, chopped
- ½ teaspoon chili powder
- ½ teaspoon sweet paprika
- 1 tablespoon cilantro, chopped

Directions:
In a sous vide bag, mix the lentils with the salsa and the other ingredients, toss, seal the bag, submerge in the water oven and cook at 165 degrees F for 30 minutes. Divide the stew into bowls and serve.

Nutrition: calories 671, fat 15.6, fiber 27.5, carbs 87.5, protein 27.1

Turmeric Veggies and Rice

Preparation time: 10 minutes | Cooking time: 30 minutes | Servings: 4

Ingredients:
- 1 red bell pepper, cubed
- 1 zucchini, cubed
- 1 eggplant, cubed
- ½ cup cherry tomatoes, halved
- 1 tablespoon olive oil
- 1 red onion, chopped
- 2 garlic cloves, minced
- 1 cup white rice
- 1 cup chicken stock
- ½ teaspoon turmeric powder
- Juice of ½ lemon
- 2 tablespoons parsley, chopped
- A pinch of salt and black pepper

Directions:
In a sous vide bag, mix the veggies with the rice, stock and the other ingredients, toss, seal the bag, submerge in the water oven and cook at 170 degrees F for 30 minutes. Divide into bowls and serve.

Nutrition: calories 342, fat 17.4, fiber 16.5, carbs 27.7, protein 26.4

Pork Bowls

Preparation time: 10 minutes | Cooking time: 30 minutes | Servings: 4

Ingredients:
- 1 pound pork stew meat, cubed
- 2 sweet potatoes, peeled and cubed
- 1 tablespoon olive oil
- 1 yellow onion, chopped
- ½ teaspoon chili powder
- A pinch of salt and black pepper
- 2 garlic cloves, minced
- ½ cup tomato passata
- 1/3 cup parsley, chopped

Directions:
In s sous vide bag, mix the pork with the sweet potatoes and the other ingredients, toss, seal the bag, submerge in the water oven and cook at 170 degrees F for 30 minutes. Divide into bowls and serve for lunch.

Nutrition: calories 435, fat 18.5, fiber 13.6, carbs 27.8, protein 25.6

Shrimp and Sweet Potato Bowls

Preparation time: 10 minutes | Cooking time: 20 minutes | Servings: 4

Ingredients:
- 1 cup sweet potatoes, peeled and cubed
- 1 tablespoon balsamic vinegar
- ½ pound shrimp, peeled and deveined
- 2 spring onions, chopped
- 1 tablespoon chives, chopped
- ½ teaspoon sweet paprika
- ½ teaspoon chili powder
- A pinch of salt and black pepper
- Juice of ½ lemon

Directions:
In a sous vide bag, mix the shrimp with the vinegar, potatoes and the other ingredients, toss, seal the bag, submerge in the water oven and cook at 140 degrees F fro 20 minutes. Divide everything into bowls and serve.

Nutrition: calories 253, fat 11.5, fiber 3.4, carbs 16.5, protein 23.2

Chicken and Eggplants

Preparation time: 10 minutes | *Cooking time:* 30 minutes | *Servings:* 4

Ingredients:
- 1 pound chicken breast, skinless, boneless and cubed
- 2 spring onions, chopped
- Juice of 1 lime
- ½ cup tomato passata
- 2 eggplants, cubed
- ½ teaspoon chili powder
- ½ teaspoon hot paprika
- 2 tablespoons balsamic vinegar
- ¼ cup parsley, chopped

Directions:
In a sous vide bag, mix the chicken with the eggplants and the other ingredients, toss, seal the bag, submerge in the water oven and cook at 170 degrees F for 30 minutes. Divide everything between plates and serve for lunch.

Nutrition: calories 266, fat 12.2, fiber 4.5, carbs 15.7, protein 3.7

Turkey Hash

Preparation time: 10 minutes | *Cooking time:* 30 minutes | *Servings:* 4

Ingredients:
- 1 red onion, chopped
- 1 cup hash browns
- 1 pound turkey breast, skinless, boneless and cubed
- 1 tablespoon olive oil
- ¼ cup chicken stock
- ¼ teaspoon red pepper flakes, crushed
- ¼ teaspoon garlic powder
- 2 tablespoons lemon juice
- ¼ cup parsley, chopped

Directions:
In a sous vide bag, mix the turkey with the onion, hash browns and the other ingredients, seal the bag and cook in the water oven at 170 degrees F for 30 minutes. Divide between plates and serve for lunch.

Nutrition: calories 364, fat 16.8, fiber 5.5, carbs 26.8, protein 23.4

Eggplant Stew

Preparation time: 10 minutes | *Cooking time:* 25 minutes | *Servings:* 4

Ingredients:
- 1 pound eggplant, cubed
- 2 tablespoons olive oil
- 1 red onion, chopped
- 2 garlic cloves, minced
- ½ teaspoon cumin, ground
- Zest and juice of 1 lemon
- A pinch of salt and black pepper
- 1 cup tomato passata
- 1 tablespoon parsley, chopped

Directions:
In a sous vide bag, mix the eggplants with the onion and the other ingredients, seal the bag and cook in the water oven at 170 degrees F for 25 minutes. Divide the stew into bowls and serve.

Nutrition: calories 512, fat 16.4, fiber 17.5, carbs 78, protein 17.2

Turmeric Shrimp Mix

Preparation time: 5 minutes | *Cooking time:* 20 minutes | *Servings:* 4

Ingredients:
- 1 pound shrimp, peeled and deveined
- 2 spring onions, chopped
- 1 tablespoon avocado oil
- ½ teaspoon turmeric powder
- 1 tablespoon lime juice
- A pinch of salt and black pepper
- ¼ cup chives, chopped

Directions:
In a sous vide bag, mix the shrimp with the spring onions and the other ingredients, seal the bag and cook in the water oven at 160 degrees F for 20 minutes. Divide everything into bowls and serve.

Nutrition: calories 281, fat 12.7, fiber 1.7, carbs 5.8, protein 36.5

Beef and Tomato Mix

Preparation time: 10 minutes | *Cooking time:* 1 hour | *Servings:* 4

Ingredients:
- 1 pound beef stew meat, ground
- 1 cup cherry tomatoes, halved
- ¼ tablespoon balsamic vinegar
- 1 red onion, chopped
- 1 tablespoon olive oil
- 1 teaspoon cumin, ground
- ½ teaspoon garam masala
- ½ teaspoon oregano, dried
- A pinch of salt and black pepper
- ¼ cup chives, chopped

Directions:
In a sous vide bag, mix the beef with the tomatoes, vinegar and the other ingredients, toss, seal the bag, submerge in the water oven and cook at 160 degrees F for 1 hours. Divide everything into bowls and serve.

Nutrition: calories 354, fat 19.2, fiber 4.5, carbs 24.7, protein 11.2

Lentils and Quinoa Stew

Preparation time: 10 minutes | *Cooking time:* 30 minutes | *Servings:* 4

Ingredients:
- 1 cup canned lentils, drained and rinsed
- 1 cup quinoa, cooked
- 1 zucchini, cubed
- 1 yellow onion, chopped
- ½ cup tomato passata
- 1 tablespoon olive oil
- ½ teaspoon sweet paprika
- ½ teaspoon red pepper flakes, crushed
- 1 tablespoon cilantro, chopped
- Salt and black pepper to the taste

Directions:
In a sous vide bag, mix the lentils with the quinoa, zucchini and the other ingredients, toss, seal the bag and cook in the water oven at 160 degrees F for 30 minutes. Divide into bowls and serve for lunch.

Nutrition: calories 263, fat 18.5, fiber 4.5, carbs 19.8, protein 14.5

Chickpeas Stew

Preparation time: 10 minutes | Cooking time: 30 minutes | Servings: 4

Ingredients:
- 2 cups canned chickpeas, drained
- ½ cup tomato passata
- 1 yellow onion, chopped
- 1 carrot, peeled and sliced
- Juice of 1 lime
- ¼ cup dill, chopped
- Salt and black pepper to the taste
- ½ teaspoon sweet paprika
- ½ teaspoon rosemary, dried

Directions:
In a sous vide bag, mix the chickpeas with the passata, onion and the other ingredients, toss, seal the bag and cook in the water oven at 160 degrees F for 30 minutes. Divide into bowls and serve.

Nutrition: calories 264, fat 17.5, fiber 4.8, carbs 28.7, protein 16.3

Peppers Stew

Preparation time: 10 minutes | Cooking time: 25 minutes | Servings: 2

Ingredients:
- ½ pound red bell peppers, cut into strips
- ½ cup cherry tomatoes, halved
- 1 red onion, chopped
- 1 tablespoon olive oil
- 2 garlic cloves, minced
- A pinch of salt and black pepper
- 2 tablespoons tomato paste
- ¼ cup parsley, chopped

Directions:
In a sous vide bag, mix the peppers with the tomatoes and the other ingredients, seal the bag, and cook in the water oven at 165 degrees F for 25 minutes. Divide the stew into bowls and serve.

Nutrition: calories 273, fat 11.2, fiber 3.4, carbs 15.7, protein 5.6

Potato Stew

Preparation time: 10 minutes | Cooking time: 30 minutes | Servings: 4

Ingredients:
- 1 red onion, chopped
- 1 tablespoon olive oil
- 1 pound gold potatoes, peeled and cut into wedges
- ½ cup tomato passata
- 1 carrot, sliced
- ½ cup cilantro, chopped
- 2 tablespoons ginger, grated
- 1 teaspoon turmeric powder
- 1 tablespoon chives, chopped
- A pinch of salt and black pepper

Directions:
In a sous vide bag, mix the potatoes with the onion, the oil and the other ingredients, seal the bag, submerge in the water oven and cook at 170 degrees F for 30 minutes. Divide into bowls and serve.

Nutrition: calories 238, fat 7.3, fiber 6.3, carbs 32, protein 14

Green Beans Salad

Preparation time: 10 minutes | Cooking time: 25 minutes | Servings: 4

Ingredients:
- 1 red onion, chopped
- 1 tablespoon olive oil
- 1 tablespoon lime juice
- 1 cup cherry tomatoes, halved
- 1 cup kalamata olives, pitted and halved
- 2 tablespoons balsamic vinegar
- 1 pound green beans, trimmed and halved
- ½ teaspoon turmeric powder
- ½ teaspoon chili powder
- A pinch of salt and black pepper

Directions:
In a sous vide bag, mix the green beans with the onion, oil and the other ingredients, seal the bag and cook in the water oven at 165 degrees F fro 25 minutes. Divide into bowls and serve for lunch.

Nutrition: calories 264, fat 17.5, fiber 4.5, carbs 23.7, protein 11.5

Sous Vide Side Dish Recipes

Cauliflower Salad

Preparation time: 10 minutes | Cooking time: 30 minutes | Servings: 2

Ingredients:
- 1 pound cauliflower florets
- ½ cup black olives, pitted and sliced
- Juice of 1 lime
- 2 tablespoons balsamic vinegar
- 6 tablespoons olive oil
- Salt and black pepper to the taste

Directions:

In a big sous vide bag mix the cauliflower with the olives and the other ingredients, toss, seal it, submerge it in the preheated water oven and cook at 183 degrees F for 30 minutes. Divide between plates and serve as a side salad.

Nutrition: calories 172, fat 4, fiber 5, carbs 8, protein 6

Spinach and Pear Salad

Preparation time: 10 minutes | Cooking time: 20 minutes | Servings: 4

Ingredients:
- 2 pears, peeled, cored and cubed
- 1 pound baby spinach
- 2 tablespoons olive oil
- A pinch of salt and black pepper
- 2 frisee heads, torn
- 1 cup walnuts, toasted
- 1 tablespoon lemon juice
- 1 tablespoon balsamic vinegar

Directions:

In a sous vide bag, mix the pears with half of the oil, salt, pepper, walnuts and lemon juice, seal the bag, submerge in the water oven and cook at 158 degrees F for 20 minutes. In a bowl, mix the pears with the spinach and the rest of the ingredients, toss, and serve as a side dish.

Nutrition: calories 183, fat 4, fiber 6, carbs 8, protein 5

Balsamic Beet Salad

Preparation time: 10 minutes | Cooking time: 1 hour | Servings: 4

Ingredients:
- 2 bunches red beets, trimmed, peeled and cut into wedges
- 2/3 cup walnuts, toasted
- 2 and ½ tablespoons balsamic vinegar
- Salt and black pepper to the taste
- 2 tablespoons olive oil
- ½ teaspoon sweet paprika

Directions:

In a sous vide bag, mix the beets with the walnuts and the other ingredients, seal the bag, put it your preheated water oven and cook at 180 degrees F for 1 hour. Divide between plates and serve as a side salad.

Nutrition: calories 188, fat 4, fiber 6, carbs 8, protein 5

Glazed Beets

Preparation time: 10 minutes | Cooking time: 1 hour | Servings: 4

Ingredients:
- 1 pound beets, peeled and cut into medium chunks
- Salt and black pepper to the taste
- 2 tablespoons butter, melted
- 1 tablespoon sugar
- 1 tablespoon parsley, chopped

Directions:

In a sous vide bag, combine the beets with the butter and the other ingredients, toss, seal the bag, submerge in the preheated water oven and cook at 183 degrees F for 1 hour. Divide them between plates and serve.

Nutrition: calories 177, fat 2, fiber 5, carbs 7, protein 5

Orange Green Beans

Preparation time: 10 minutes | Cooking time: 40 minutes | Servings: 4

Ingredients:
- 1 pound green beans, trimmed and halved
- A pinch of salt and black pepper
- ½ teaspoon chili powder
- ½ teaspoon coriander, ground
- 2 tablespoons butter, melted
- Zest of 2 oranges, grated
- Juice of 2 oranges

Directions:
In a sous vide bag, combine the green beans with the butter and the other ingredients, toss, seal the bag, submerge in the preheated water oven and cook at 185 degrees F for 40 minutes. Divide the mix between plates and serve.

Nutrition: calories 152, fat 2, fiber 5, carbs 5, protein 3

Lime Brussels Sprouts

Preparation time: 10 minutes | Cooking time: 30 minutes | Servings: 4

Ingredients:
- 1 pound Brussels sprouts, trimmed and halved
- 1 tablespoon lime juice
- Salt and black pepper to the taste
- A pinch of cayenne pepper
- 1 tablespoon avocado oil
- ½ teaspoon chili powder
- ½ teaspoon rosemary, dried
- 1 teaspoon sweet paprika

Directions:
In a sous vide bag, combine the sprouts with the lime juice, salt, pepper and the other ingredients, toss, seal the bag, introduce in your preheated water oven and cook at 183 degrees F for 30 minutes. Divide between plates and serve as a side dish.

Nutrition: calories 121, fat 3, fiber 2, carbs 5, protein 3

Buttery Squash Mix

Preparation time: 10 minutes | Cooking time: 1 hour | Servings: 4

Ingredients:
- 2 tablespoons butter, melted
- A pinch of salt and black pepper
- 3 scallions, chopped
- 1 teaspoon turmeric powder
- 2 pounds summer squash, quartered and sliced
- ½ cup coconut cream

Directions:
Divide the squash, butter and the other ingredients into sous vide bags, seal them, submerge them in the preheated water oven and cook at 176 degrees F for 1 hour. Divide this mix between plates and serve as a side dish.

Nutrition: calories 152, fat 3, fiber 6, carbs 12, protein 3

Parmesan Fennel

Preparation time: 10 minutes | Cooking time: 2 hours | Servings: 4

Ingredients:
- 2 fennel bulbs, trimmed and quartered
- 2 tablespoons butter, melted
- ½ teaspoon rosemary, dried
- ½ teaspoon coriander, ground
- ½ cup parmesan, grated
- Salt and black pepper to the taste

Directions:
Divide the fennel quarters into sous vide bags, add the butter and the other ingredients except the parmesan, toss, seal the bags, submerge them in the preheated water oven and cook at 183 degrees F for 2 hours. Divide fennel between plates, sprinkle parmesan on top and serve as a side dish.

Nutrition: calories 181, fat 2, fiber 6, carbs 9, protein 5

Soy Mushrooms

Preparation time: 10 minutes | Cooking time: 1 hour | Servings: 4

Ingredients:

- 2 tablespoons olive oil
- ½ teaspoon rosemary, dried
- 1 tablespoon soy sauce
- 1 pound white mushrooms, halved
- ½ teaspoon turmeric powder
- ½ teaspoon garam masala
- Salt and black pepper to the taste
- Juice of 1 lime
- 1 bay leaf

Directions:

In a sous vide bag, combine the mushrooms with the rosemary, oil and the other ingredients, toss, seal the bag, submerge in the preheated water oven and cook at 180 degrees F for 1 hour. Divide mushrooms between plates and serve as a side dish.

Nutrition: calories 161, fat 3, fiber 6, carbs 7, protein 5

Balsamic Carrots and Parsnips

Preparation time: 10 minutes | Cooking time: 2 hours | Servings: 4

Ingredients:

- 2 pounds baby carrots, peeled
- ½ pound parsnips, peeled and cut into matchsticks
- 2 tablespoons olive oil
- 1 tablespoon balsamic vinegar
- 2 tablespoons sugar
- ½ teaspoon rosemary, dried
- 1 tablespoon chives, chopped
- Salt and black pepper to the taste

Directions:

In a sous vide bag, combine the carrots with the parsnips, oil, vinegar and the other ingredients, seal the bag, submerge in your preheated water oven and cook at 185 degrees F for 2 hours. Divide between plates and serve as a side dish.

Nutrition: calories 121, fat 2, fiber 5, carbs 5, protein 4

Thai Eggplant Mix

Preparation time: 10 minutes | Cooking time: 2 hours | Servings: 4

Ingredients:

- 2 pounds eggplants, peeled and roughly cubed
- 3 garlic cloves, minced
- 2 Thai chilies, chopped
- 2 tablespoons balsamic vinegar
- 1 tablespoon olive oil
- Salt and black pepper to the taste
- 2 tablespoons lime juice
- 2 tablespoons soy sauce
- 2 tablespoons chives, chopped

Directions:

In a sous vide bag, combine the eggplants with the garlic, chilies and the other ingredients, toss, seal the bag, submerge in the preheated water oven and cook at 185 degrees F for 2 hours. Divide the mix between plates and serve as a side dish.

Nutrition: calories 212, fat 4, fiber 5, carbs 12, protein 4

Peppers and Eggplant Mix

Preparation time: 10 minutes | Cooking time: 2 hours | Servings: 4

Ingredients:

- 1 pound eggplant, roughly cubed
- 2 red bell peppers, cut into strips
- 2 tablespoons balsamic vinegar
- 2 tablespoons olive oil
- 4 garlic cloves, minced
- Salt and black pepper to the taste
- 1 red onion, sliced
- 1 tablespoon basil, chopped

Directions:

In a sous vide bag, combine the eggplants with the peppers, vinegar and the other ingredients, toss, seal the bag, submerge in the preheated water oven and cook at 180 degrees F for 2 hours. Divide between plates and serve as a side dish.

Nutrition: calories 189, fat 3, fiber 4, carbs 6, protein 4

Peppers and Seeds Mix

Preparation time: 10 minutes | Cooking time: 2 hours | Servings: 4

Ingredients:
- 1 pound red bell peppers, cut into strips
- 1 tablespoon sunflower seeds
- 1 tablespoon pine nuts, toasted
- 2 tablespoons olive oil
- Juice of 1 lime
- 2 garlic cloves, minced
- 1 tablespoon basil, chopped
- Salt and black pepper to the taste

Directions:
In a sous vide bag, combine the peppers with the seeds, nuts and the other ingredients, toss, introduce in your preheated water oven and cook at 180 degrees F for 2 hours. Divide between plates and serve.

Nutrition: calories 126, fat 1, fiber 3, carbs 6, protein 3

Parsley Asparagus

Preparation time: 10 minutes | Cooking time: 30 minutes | Servings: 2

Ingredients:
- 1 pound asparagus, trimmed
- 1 tablespoon balsamic vinegar
- 1 tablespoon parsley, chopped
- Juice of 1 lime
- ¼ cup olive oil
- 1 teaspoon mustard powder
- Salt and black pepper to the taste

Directions:
In a sous vide bag, combine the asparagus with the vinegar, parsley and the other ingredients, toss, seal the bag, submerge it in your preheated water oven and cook at 185 degrees F for 30 minutes. Divide this between plates and serve.

Nutrition: calories 144, fat 3, fiber 6, carbs 15, protein 4

Olives and Cauliflower

Preparation time: 10 minutes | Cooking time: 2 hours | Servings: 2

Ingredients:
- ¼ cup heavy cream
- 1 pound cauliflower florets
- 1 cup black olives, pitted and halved
- 1 cup kalamata olives, pitted and halved
- Salt and black pepper to the taste
- 2 tablespoons olive oil
- 2 tablespoons balsamic vinegar
- 2 tablespoons cilantro, chopped

Directions:
In a sous vide bag, combine the cauliflower with the olives, cream and the other ingredients, toss, seal the bag, submerge into preheated water oven and cook at 180 degrees F for 2 hours. Divide between plates and serve as a side dish.

Nutrition: calories 151, fat 4, fiber 2, carbs 12, protein 4

Tarragon Mushrooms

Preparation time: 10 minutes | Cooking time: 1 hour | Servings: 4

Ingredients:
- 1 pound brown mushrooms, halved
- Juice of 1 lime
- ½ teaspoon chili powder
- Salt and black pepper to the taste
- 2 tablespoons olive oil
- ½ teaspoon tarragon, dried
- 2 tablespoons balsamic vinegar

Directions:
In a sous vide bag, combine the mushrooms with the lime juice, chili powder and the other ingredients, seal the bag, introduce in the preheated water oven and cook at 182 degrees F for 1 hour. Divide between plates and serve as a side dish.

Nutrition: calories 100, fat 4, fiber 4, carbs 7, protein 4

Creamy Spinach

Preparation time: 10 minutes | Cooking time: 50 minutes | Servings: 2

Ingredients:
- 2 garlic cloves, minced
- 1 pound baby spinach
- ½ cup heavy cream
- 1 teaspoon turmeric powder
- ½ teaspoon curry powder
- Salt and black pepper to the taste
- 1 tablespoon butter, melted

Directions:

In a sous vide bag, mix the spinach with the garlic and the other ingredients, seal the bag, submerge in the preheated water oven and cook at 175 degrees F for 50 minutes. Divide between plates and serve as a side dish.

Nutrition: calories 133, fat 10, fiber 4, carbs 4, protein 2

Parsley Cauliflower

Preparation time: 10 minutes | Cooking time: 2 hours | Servings: 4

Ingredients:
- 2 pounds cauliflower florets
- 1 tablespoon lemon juice
- 1 tablespoon lemon zest, grated
- Salt and black pepper to the taste
- 1 tablespoon parsley, chopped
- 3 tablespoons olive oil
- 2 tablespoons soy sauce

Directions:

In a sous vide bag, combine the cauliflower with the lemon juice and the other ingredients, toss, seal, introduce in the preheated water oven and cook at 180 degrees F for 2 hours Divide between plates and serve.

Nutrition: calories 128, fat 2, fiber 3, carbs 7, protein 6

Mushroom and Broccoli Mix

Preparation time: 10 minutes | Cooking time: 1 hour | Servings: 4

Ingredients:
- 1 pound broccoli florets
- ½ pound white mushrooms, halved
- 2 tablespoons balsamic vinegar
- 2 tablespoons olive oil
- Salt and black pepper to the taste
- 2 garlic cloves, minced
- A handful parsley, chopped

Directions:

In a sous vide bag, combine the broccoli with the mushrooms, vinegar and the other ingredients, toss, seal the bag, introduce in your preheated water bag and cook at 175 degrees F for 1 hour. Divide between plates and serve.

Nutrition: calories 160, fat 4, fiber 6, carbs 2, protein 12

Cumin Okra

Preparation time: 10 minutes | Cooking time: 40 minutes | Servings: 4

Ingredients:
- 1 pound okra, sliced
- 2 tablespoons olive oil
- 1 red onion, sliced
- 1 tablespoon balsamic vinegar
- Salt and black pepper to the taste
- 1 tablespoon chives, chopped

Directions:

In a sous vide bag, combine the okra with the oil and the other ingredients, toss, seal the bag, submerge in the preheated water oven and cook at 180 degrees F for 40 minutes. Divide between plates and serve as a side dish.

Nutrition: calories 170, fat 2, fiber 3, carbs 12, protein 6

Eggplant and Okra Mix

Preparation time: 10 minutes | Cooking time: 1 hour | Servings: 4

Ingredients:
- 1 pound eggplant, sliced into thin rounds
- ½ pound okra, sliced
- 1 tablespoon olive oil
- 1 tablespoon lemon zest, grated
- 1 tablespoon red wine vinegar
- ½ teaspoon coriander, ground
- ½ teaspoon cumin, ground
- Salt and black pepper to the taste
- ¼ cup chives, chopped

Directions:
In a sous vide bag, combine the eggplant with the okra, oil and the other ingredients, toss, seal the bag, submerge in the preheated water oven and cook at 183 degrees F for 1 hour Divide between plates and serve.

Nutrition: calories 105, fat 1, fiber 1, carbs 6, protein 7

Lemony Okra

Preparation time: 10 minutes | Cooking time: 30 minutes | Servings: 4

Ingredients:
- 1 pound okra, sliced
- Juice of 1 lemon
- Zest of 1 lemon, grated
- Salt and black pepper to the taste
- ¼ cup almonds, blanched
- 2 tablespoons chives, chopped
- ½ teaspoon turmeric powder

Directions:
In a sous vide bag, combine the okra with the lemon juice, zest and the other ingredients, seal the bag, introduce it in the preheated water oven and cook at 180 degrees F for 30 minutes Divide the mix between plates and serve as a side dish.

Nutrition: calories 170, fat 15, fiber 4, carbs 7, protein 4

Cheesy Broccoli

Preparation time: 10 minutes | Cooking time: 1 hour | Servings: 4

Ingredients:
- 3 tablespoons olive oil
- 1 pound broccoli florets
- 1 garlic clove, minced
- 1 teaspoon chili powder
- 1 teaspoon cumin, ground
- 1 tablespoon goat cheese, crumbled
- Salt and black pepper to the taste

Directions:
In a sous vide bag, combine the broccoli with the garlic, chili and the other ingredients except the cheese, seal the bag, submerge in the preheated water oven and cook at 180 degrees F for 1 hour Divide broccoli between plates, sprinkle cheese all over and serve as a side dish.

Nutrition: calories 173, fat 14, fiber 3, carbs 6, protein 5

Tomato and Okra Mix

Preparation time: 10 minutes | Cooking time: 1 hour | Servings: 4

Ingredients:
- 1 pound cherry tomatoes, halved
- ½ pound okra, sliced
- 2 tablespoons olive oil
- 1 tablespoon soy sauce
- 1 tablespoon balsamic vinegar
- 1 teaspoon chili powder
- 1 tablespoon cilantro, chopped
- Salt and black pepper to the taste

Direction:
In a sous vide bag, combine the tomatoes with the okra, oil and the other ingredients, seal, submerge in the preheated water oven and cook at 185 degrees F for 1 hour Divide between plates and serve as a side dish.

Nutrition: calories 165, fat 11, fiber 4, carbs 6, protein 3

Italian Tomatoes

Preparation time: 10 minutes | *Cooking time:* 1 hour | *Servings:* 4

Ingredients:

- 1 red onion, sliced
- 1 pound tomatoes, cut into wedges
- 1 tablespoon olive oil
- ½ teaspoon sweet paprika
- Salt and black pepper to the taste
- 1 garlic clove, minced
- 1 teaspoon Italian seasoning
- 1 tablespoon dill, chopped

Directions:

In a sous vide bag, combine the tomatoes with the onion, oil and the other ingredients, seal the bag, submerge into the preheated water oven and cook at 180 degrees F for 1 hour Divide the mix between plates and serve as a side dish.

Nutrition: calories 120, fat 3, fiber 2, carbs 6, protein 4

Mushroom Salad

Preparation time: 10 minutes | *Cooking time:* 1 hour | *Servings:* 4

Ingredients:

- 2 tablespoons avocado oil
- 1 pound cremini mushrooms, cut into quarters
- 1 tablespoon balsamic vinegar
- 2 tablespoons red wine
- ½ teaspoon chili powder
- Salt and black pepper to the taste
- 1 cup cherry tomatoes, halved
- 1 cup kalamata olives, pitted and halved
- 1 cup baby spinach
- 1 tablespoon chives, chopped

Directions:

In a sous vide bag, combine the mushrooms with the oil, vinegar and the other ingredients, toss, seal the bag, submerge in the preheated water oven and cook at 180 degrees F for 1 hour. Divide between plates and serve as a side dish.

Nutrition: calories 160, fat 4, fiber 2, carbs 6, protein 6

Coriander Tomato and Spinach Mix

Preparation time: 10 minutes | *Cooking time:* 1 hour | *Servings:* 6

Ingredients:

- ½ pounds tomatoes, halved
- ½ pound baby spinach
- Juice of 1 lime
- 1 teaspoon coriander, ground
- ½ teaspoon chili powder
- 1 tablespoon extra virgin olive oil
- 3 garlic cloves, minced
- 1 tablespoon basil, chopped

Directions:

In a sous vide bag, combine the tomatoes with the spinach and the other ingredients, seal the bag, submerge in the preheated water oven and cook at 180 degrees F for 1 hour. Divide between plates and serve as a side dish.

Nutrition: calories 200, fat 2, fiber 2, carbs 7, protein 10

Tomato and Mango Salsa

Preparation time: 10 minutes | Cooking time: 1 hour | Servings: 4

Ingredients:
- 1 pound cherry tomatoes, halved
- 1 cup mango, peeled and cubed
- ½ cup black olives, pitted and halved
- 1 tablespoon olive oil
- 1 tablespoon balsamic vinegar
- Salt and black pepper to the taste
- 1/3 cup red onion, cut into wedges
- ¼ cup cilantro, finely chopped
- 3 tablespoons lemon juice

Directions:
In a sous vide bag, mix the tomatoes with the mango, olives and the other ingredients, seal the bag, submerge in the preheated water oven and cook at 140 degrees F for 1 hour. Divide the mix between plates and serve as a side dish.

Nutrition: calories 100, fat 1, fiber 2, carbs 7, protein 4

Balsamic Tomato and Pineapple Mix

Preparation time: 5 minutes | Cooking time: 1 hour | Servings: 4

Ingredients:
- 1 pound tomatoes, cut into wedges
- 1 cup pineapple, peeled and cubed
- 2 tablespoons extra virgin olive oil
- 2 tablespoons balsamic vinegar
- 1 tablespoon chives, chopped
- Salt and black pepper to the taste

Directions:
In a sous vide bag, combine the tomatoes with the pineapple and the other ingredients, seal the bag, submerge in the preheated water oven and cook at 140 degrees F for 1 hour. Divide between plates and serve as a side dish.

Nutrition: calories 100, fat 2, fiber 2, carbs 8, protein 9

Eggplant and Pearl Onion Mix

Preparation time: 10 minutes | Cooking time: 1 hour | Servings: 4

Ingredients:
- 1 pound eggplant, roughly cubed
- 1 cup pearl onions, peeled
- 2 tablespoons olive oil
- 1 tablespoon lemon juice
- 1 teaspoon mustard powder
- ½ teaspoon onion powder
- 1 tablespoon balsamic vinegar
- 1 tablespoon fresh oregano, chopped
- Salt and black pepper to the taste

Directions:
In a sous vide bag, combine the eggplants with the onions and the other ingredients, seal, submerge in the preheated water oven and cook at 180 degrees F for 1 hour. Divide the mix between plates serve as a side dish.

Nutrition: calories 160, fat 3, fiber 2, carbs 7, protein 8

Spicy Beets and Okra

Preparation time: 10 minutes | Cooking time: 1 hour | Servings: 4

Ingredients:
- 1 pound beets, peeled and cubed
- 1 cup okra, sliced
- 2 tablespoons olive oil
- 2 red chilies, chopped
- 1 teaspoon chili powder
- 2 tablespoons balsamic vinegar
- 1 teaspoon oregano, dried
- ¼ teaspoon basil, dried
- 1 tablespoon balsamic vinegar
- Salt and black pepper to the taste

Directions:
In a sous vide bag, combine the beets with the okra, oil and the other ingredients, toss, seal the bag, submerge in the water bath and cook at 180 degrees F for 1 hour. Divide the mix between plates and serve

Nutrition: calories 150, fat 1, fiber 2, carbs 7, protein 8

Coconut Endives and Radish

Preparation time: 10 minutes | **Cooking time:** 30 minutes | **Servings:** 4

Ingredients:

- 2 endives, roots and ends cut and thinly sliced crosswise
- 1 cup radishes, halved
- 2 tablespoons avocado oil
- 1 tablespoon lemon juice
- 1 shallot, chopped
- 1 tablespoon balsamic vinegar
- 6 tablespoons coconut cream
- Salt and black pepper to the taste
- 1 tablespoon parsley, chopped

Directions:

In a sous vide bag, combine the endives with the radishes and the other ingredients, seal it, submerge in the preheated water oven and cook at 180 degrees F for 30 minutes. Divide between plates and serve as a side dish.

Nutrition: calories 170, fat 3, fiber 5, carbs 7, protein 10

Cabbage and Carrots Mix

Preparation time: 10 minutes | **Cooking time:** 50 minutes | **Servings:** 4

Ingredients:

- 2 tablespoons olive oil
- 1 red cabbage, shredded
- 2 carrots, peeled and shredded
- 2 tablespoons balsamic vinegar
- 1 yellow onion, chopped
- 2 tablespoons capers, drained
- Juice of 1 lemon
- Salt and black pepper to the taste

Directions:

In a sous vide bag, combine the cabbage with the carrots and the other ingredients, seal the bag, submerge in the preheated water oven and cook at 185 degrees F for 50 minutes. Divide everything between plates and serve as a side dish.

Nutrition: calories 119, fat 7, fiber 3, carbs 7, protein 2

Kale and Spring Onions Mix

Preparation time: 10 minutes | **Cooking time:** 20 minutes | **Servings:** 4

Ingredients:

- 1 tablespoon olive oil
- 1 pound baby kale
- 1 cup spring onions, chopped
- 1/3 cup almonds, toasted
- 3 garlic cloves, minced
- 2 tablespoons lime juice
- ½ teaspoon chili powder
- ½ teaspoon rosemary, chopped
- 2 tablespoons chives, chopped

Directions:

In a sous vide bag, combine the kale with the spring onions, oil and the other ingredients, seal the bag, introduce in your preheated water oven and cook at 180 degrees F for 20 minutes Divide the mix between plates and serve as a side dish.

Nutrition: calories 170, fat 11, fiber 3, carbs 7, protein 4

Simple Cabbage and Avocado Mix

Preparation time: 10 minutes | Cooking time: 1 hour | Servings: 4

Ingredients:

- 1 pound green cabbage, roughly shredded
- 1 cup avocado, peeled, pitted and cubed
- ½ cup kalamata olives, pitted and halved
- 1 cup cherry tomatoes, halved
- 2 tablespoons olive oil
- Juice of 1 lime
- ½ teaspoon sweet paprika
- Salt and black pepper to the taste

Directions:

In a sous vide bag, combine the cabbage with the avocado, olives and the other ingredients, seal the bag, submerge in the preheated water oven and cook at 180 degrees F for 1 hou Divide the mix between plates and serve as a side dish.

Nutrition: calories 160, fat 4, fiber 2, carbs 7, protein 7

Green Beans and Walnuts Mix

Preparation time: 10 minutes | Cooking time: 1 hour | Servings: 4

Ingredients:

- 1 pound green beans, trimmed
- 1 cup walnuts, chopped
- 1 tablespoon soy sauce
- 1 tablespoon balsamic vinegar
- 2 tablespoons olive oil
- Salt and black pepper to the taste
- 5 scallions, chopped
- A handful cilantro, chopped

Directions:

In a sous vide bag, combine the green beans with the walnuts, soy sauce and the other ingredients, seal the bag, submerge in your preheated water oven and cook at 185 degrees F for 1 hour. Divide the mix between plates and serve as a side dish.

Nutrition: calories 170, fat 5, fiber 3, carbs 4, protein 6

Lemon Olives and Radish Mix

Preparation time: 10 minutes | Cooking time: 30 minutes | Servings: 4

Ingredients:

- 1 cup black olives, pitted
- 1 cup kalamata olives, pitted
- 1 cup radishes, halved
- 2 tablespoons olive oil
- 2 garlic cloves, minced
- 1 tablespoon lemon juice
- 1 teaspoon sweet paprika
- 1 teaspoon lemon zest, grated
- Salt and black pepper to the taste

Directions:

In a sous vide bag, combine the olives with the radishes, oil and the other ingredients, seal the bag, submerge into your preheated water oven and cook at 134 degrees F for 30 minutes Divide between plates and serve.

Nutrition: calories 130, fat 20, fiber 4, carbs 7, protein 1

Cauliflower and Chard Mix

Preparation time: 10 minutes | Cooking time: 1 hour | Servings: 6

Ingredients:
- 1 pound cauliflower florets
- 1 cup red chard, torn
- 1 tablespoon olive oil
- 1 tablespoon lemon juice
- 1 tablespoon balsamic vinegar
- 1 tablespoon lemon zest, grated
- ½ teaspoon garlic powder
- ½ teaspoon rosemary, dried
- Salt and black pepper to the taste
- 1 cup red onion, chopped
- 1 tablespoon chives, chopped

Directions:

In a sous vide bag, combine the cauliflower with the chard, oil and the other ingredients, toss, seal the bag, submerge in the preheated water oven and cook at 185 degrees F for 1 hour. Divide the mix between plates and serve as a side salad.

Nutrition: calories 171, fat 20, fiber 2, carbs 3, protein 4

Ginger Broccoli and Radish Mix

Preparation time: 10 minutes | Cooking time: 40 minutes | Servings: 4

Ingredients:
- 1 pound broccoli florets
- ½ pound radish, halved
- 2 tablespoons olive oil
- 1 tablespoon soy sauce
- 2 teaspoons coriander seeds, crushed
- 1 yellow onion, chopped
- Salt and black pepper to the taste
- A pinch of red pepper, crushed
- 1 tablespoon ginger, grated
- 1 garlic clove, minced
- 1 tablespoon chives, chopped

Directions:

In a sous vide bag, combine the broccoli with the radishes, oil and the other ingredients, seal the bag, submerge in the preheated water oven and cook at 183 degrees F for 40 minutes. Divide the mix between plates and serve as a side dish.

Nutrition: calories 150, fat 4, fiber 2, carbs 7, protein 12

Apple and Zucchini Mix

Preparation time: 10 minutes | Cooking time: 1 hour | Servings: 4

Ingredients:
- 2 apples, cored and cut into wedges
- 1 pound zucchinis, roughly cubed
- 1 tablespoon olive oil
- Juice of 1 lime
- 1 bunch green onion, chopped
- ½ teaspoon sweet paprika
- ½ teaspoon rosemary, dried
- Salt and black pepper to the taste
- 1 tablespoon parsley, chopped

Directions:

In a sous vide bag, mix the zucchinis with the apples, oil and the other ingredients, toss, seal the bag, submerge in the preheated water oven and cook at 180 degrees F for 1 hour. Divide between plates and serve as a side dish.

Nutrition: calories 170, fat 7, fiber 4, carbs 6, protein 10

Creamy Garlic Spinach and Corn

Preparation time: 10 minutes | Cooking time: 40 minutes | Servings: 4

Ingredients:
- 2 tablespoons butter, melted
- 1 pound baby spinach
- 1 cup corn
- 1 teaspoon turmeric powder
- ½ teaspoon coriander, ground
- 1 cup heavy cream
- 1 tablespoon chives, chopped
- 1 teaspoon garlic, minced
- Salt and black pepper to the taste
- ½ teaspoon nutmeg, ground

Directions:

In a sous vide bag, combine the spinach with the corn, turmeric and the other ingredients, toss, seal the bag, submerge in the preheated water bag and cook at 170 degrees F for 40 minutes. Divide everything between plates and serve as a side dish.

Nutrition: calories 245, fat 24, fiber 3, carbs 4, protein 6

Lemon Greens Mix

Preparation time: 10 minutes | Cooking time: 20 minutes | Servings: 4

Ingredients:
- 2 garlic cloves, minced
- 1 tablespoon olive oil
- 1 cup collard greens, chopped
- 1 cup red chard, torn
- 1 cup baby kale
- 1 cup baby spinach
- ½ teaspoon chili powder
- 1 teaspoon lemon juice
- 1 tablespoon butter, melted
- Salt and black pepper to the taste

Directions:

In a sous vide bag, combine the greens with the garlic, oil and the other ingredients, seal the bag, submerge in the preheated water oven and cook at 185 degrees F for 20 minutes. Divide the mix between plates and serve.

Nutrition: calories 151, fat 6, fiber 3, carbs 7, protein 8

Spicy Collards Greens

Preparation time: 10 minutes | Cooking time: 20 minutes | Servings: 4

Ingredients:
- 1 tablespoon olive oil
- 2 pounds collard greens, torn
- 2 red chilies, chopped
- 1 teaspoon hot paprika
- ½ teaspoon garam masala
- 1 tablespoon lemon juice
- 1 teaspoon red pepper flakes, crushed
- Salt and black pepper to the taste
- 1 yellow onion, chopped

Directions:

In a sous vide bag, mix the greens with the oil, chilies and the other ingredients, seal the bag, submerge in the preheated water oven and cook at 180 degrees F for 20 minutes. Divide between plates and serve as a side dish.

Nutrition: calories 150, fat 12, fiber 2, carbs 4, protein 8

Spinach, Mango and Tomatoes

Preparation time: 10 minutes | Cooking time: 20 minutes | Servings: 4

Ingredients:

- 1 pound baby spinach
- ½ pound cherry tomatoes, halved
- 1 cup mango, peeled and cubed
- 2 tablespoons olive oil
- Juice and zest of 1 lime
- ½ teaspoon rosemary, dried
- 1 tablespoon apple cider vinegar
- Salt and black pepper to the taste

Directions:

In a sous vide bag, combine the spinach with the tomatoes, mango and the other ingredients, seal the bag, submerge in the preheated water oven and cook at 180 degrees F for 20 minutes. Divide the whole mix between plates and serve.

Nutrition: calories 150, fat 8, fiber 1, carbs 3, protein 7

Mustard Greens, Olives and Kale Salad

Preparation time: 5 minutes | Cooking time: 20 minutes | Servings: 4

Ingredients:

- 2 garlic cloves, minced
- 1 pound baby kale
- 2 tomatoes, cubed
- 1 cup kalamata olives, pitted and halved
- 1 cup black olives, pitted and halved
- 1 pound mustard greens, torn
- 1 tablespoon olive oil
- ½ cup scallions, chopped
- Juice of 1 lime
- Salt and black pepper to the taste
- 3 tablespoons veggie stock
- 1 tablespoon chives, chopped

Directions:

In a sous vide bag, combine the kale with the olives, greens and the other ingredients, toss seal the bag, submerge in the preheated water oven and cook at 180 degrees F for 20 minutes. Divide between plates, and serve as a side dish.

Nutrition: calories 120, fat 3, fiber 1, carbs 7, protein 6

Greens and Shallots Mix

Preparation time: 10 minutes | Cooking time: 20 minutes | Servings: 4

Ingredients:

- 2 cups mustard greens, torn
- 1 cup shallots, chopped
- ½ cup black olives, pitted and halved
- 1 cup cherry tomatoes halved
- 1 tablespoon olive oil
- Salt and black pepper to the taste
- 2 tablespoons soy sauce
- 2 teaspoons ginger, grated

Directions:

In a sous vide bag, combine the greens with the shallots and the other ingredients, toss, seal the bag, submerge into preheated water oven and cook at 180 degrees F for 20 minutes. Divide between plates and serve as a side dish.

Nutrition: calories 140, fat 2, fiber 1, carbs 6, protein 7

Jalapeno Greens Mix

Preparation time: 10 minutes | Cooking time: 20 minutes | Servings: 4

Ingredients:
- 1 pound mustard greens, torn
- 1 cup red chard, torn
- 1 cup baby kale
- 2 jalapeno peppers, chopped
- 1 tablespoon balsamic vinegar
- 1 tablespoon avocado oil
- 1 teaspoon coriander seeds
- 1 cup shallots, chopped
- 1 tablespoon garlic, minced
- 1 tablespoon ginger, grated
- Salt and black pepper to the taste
- ½ teaspoon paprika

Directions:
In a sous vide bag, combine the greens with the jalapenos and the other ingredients, seal the bag, submerge in the preheated water oven and cook at 185 degrees F for 20 minutes. Divide the mix between plates and serve as a side dish.

Nutrition: calories 143, fat 6, fiber 3, carbs 7, protein 7

Sprouts Salad

Preparation time: 10 minutes | Cooking time: 40 minutes | Servings: 4

Ingredients:
- 1 green apple, cored and cubed
- 1 cup cherry tomatoes, halved
- 1 cup shallots, chopped
- 1 pound Brussels sprouts, trimmed and halved
- 2 tablespoons olive oil
- Juice of ½ lemon
- ½ teaspoon chili powder
- 1 tablespoon balsamic vinegar
- Salt and black pepper to the taste

Directions:
In a sous vide bag, mix the sprouts with the shallots, tomatoes and the other ingredients, seal the bag, submerge in the preheated water oven and cook at 183 degrees F for 40 minutes. Divide between plates and serve as a side dish.

Nutrition: calories 160, fat 3, fiber 1, carbs 6, protein 6

Mango and Radishes Mix

Preparation time: 10 minutes | Cooking time: 40 minutes | Servings: 4

Ingredients:
- 1 pound radishes, halved
- 1 cup mango, peeled and cubed
- 1 tablespoon olive oil
- 1 tablespoon balsamic vinegar
- ½ teaspoon chili powder
- 2 scallions, chopped
- Salt and black pepper to the taste
- 1 tablespoon chives, chopped

Directions:
In a sous vide bag, mix the radishes with the mango and the other ingredients, seal the bag, submerge in the preheated water oven and cook at 185 degrees F for 40 minutes. Divide between plates and serve.

Nutrition: calories 30, fat 1, fiber 0.4, carbs 1, protein 1

Creamy Radish and Corn Mix

Preparation time: 10 minutes | Cooking time: 30 minutes | Servings: 4

Ingredients:
- ½ pound radishes, halved
- 1 cup corn
- ½ cup heavy cream
- 1 tablespoon butter, melted
- 1 tablespoon green onion, chopped
- 1 tablespoon chives, chopped
- Salt and black pepper to the taste

Directions:
In a sous vide bag, combine the radishes with the corn and the other ingredients, toss, seal the bag, submerge in the preheated water oven and cook at 185 degrees F for 30 minutes. Divide everything between plates and serve as a side dish.

Nutrition: calories 140, fat 23, fiber 3, carbs 6, protein 5

Balsamic Carrots

Preparation time: 10 minutes | Cooking time: 30 minutes | Servings: 4

Ingredients:
- 1 pound baby carrots, peeled
- 2 tablespoons olive oil
- 2 tablespoons balsamic vinegar
- 1 teaspoon rosemary, dried
- A pinch of salt and black pepper
- 1 teaspoon chili powder

Directions:
In a sous vide bag, mix the carrots with the vinegar and the other ingredients, seal and cook in the water oven at 170 degrees F for 30 minutes. Divide between plates and serve.

Nutrition: calories 149, fat 5, fiber 3, carbs 33, protein 4

Creamy Corn

Preparation time: 10 minutes | Cooking time: 20 minutes | Servings: 2

Ingredients:
- 2 cups fresh corn
- 2 spring onions, chopped
- ½ cup heavy cream
- ½ teaspoon turmeric powder
- A pinch of salt and black pepper
- 1 tablespoon cilantro, chopped

Directions:
In a sous vide bag, mix the corn with the cream and the other ingredients, seal the bag, submerge in the water oven and cook at 165 degrees F for 20 minutes. Divide the mix between plates and serve as a side dish.

Nutrition: calories 293, fat 19, fiber 2, carbs 28, protein 6

Rosemary Broccoli Mix

Preparation time: 10 minutes | Cooking time: 30 minutes | Servings: 4

Ingredients:
- 1 pound broccoli florets
- 1 tablespoon avocado oil
- 2 scallions, chopped
- Juice of 1 lime
- 1 tablespoon rosemary, chopped
- 1 tablespoon coriander powder
- 1 tablespoon chives, chopped
- A pinch of salt and black pepper

Directions:
In a sous vide bag, mix the broccoli with the oil, scallions and the other ingredients, seal the bag and cook in the water oven and cook at 160 degrees F for 30 minutes. Divide the mix between plates and serve as a side dish.

Nutrition: calories 168, fat 12, fiber 6, carbs 14, protein 5

Creamy Tomatoes

Preparation time: 10 minutes | Cooking time: 20 minutes | Servings: 2

Ingredients:
- 4 scallions, chopped
- 1 tablespoon avocado oil
- 1 pound cherry tomatoes, halved
- ½ teaspoon chili powder
- ¼ cup heavy cream
- A pinch of salt and black pepper
- 1 tablespoon dill, chopped

Directions:
In a sous vide bag, mix the tomatoes with the scallions and the other ingredients, seal the bag and cook in the water oven at 165 degrees F for 20 minutes. Divide the mix between plates and serve.

Nutrition: calories 122, fat 7, fiber 3, carbs 10, protein 4

Hot Cauliflower

Preparation time: 10 minutes | Cooking time: 20 minutes | Servings: 4

Ingredients:
- 1 tablespoon avocado oil
- 1 teaspoon chili powder
- Juice of 1 lime
- 1 red chili pepper, chopped
- 1 pound cauliflower florets
- 2 garlic cloves, minced
- A pinch of salt and black pepper
- ½ teaspoon turmeric powder
- ½ teaspoon red pepper flakes, crushed

Directions:

In a sous vide bag, mix the cauliflower with the oil, chili and the other ingredients, toss, seal the bag and cook in the water oven at 170 degrees F for 20 minutes. Divide between plates and serve as a side dish.

Nutrition: calories 166, fat 13, fiber 3, carbs 9.6, protein 5

Ginger Green Beans

Preparation time: 10 minutes | Cooking time: 25 minutes | Servings: 4

Ingredients:
- 2 cups green beans, trimmed and halved
- 1 tablespoon lemon zest, grated
- 1 tablespoon balsamic vinegar
- 1 tablespoon avocado oil
- 1 red chili pepper, minced
- 1 tablespoon ginger, grated
- 2 garlic cloves, minced
- Salt and black pepper to the taste
- 1 tablespoon cilantro, chopped

Directions:

In a sous vide bag, mix the green beans with the vinegar, lemon zest and the other ingredients, seal the bag, submerge in the water oven and cook at 160 degrees F for 25 minutes. Divide the mix between plates and serve as a side dish.

Nutrition: calories 256, fat 14, fiber 5, carbs 15, protein 5

Dill Eggplant

Preparation time: 5 minutes | Cooking time: 30 minutes | Servings: 4

Ingredients:
- 1 pound eggplant, roughly cubed
- 1 tablespoon dill, chopped
- 1 tablespoon olive oil
- 1 red onion, chopped
- Juice of 1 lime
- ½ teaspoon coriander, ground
- ½ teaspoon rosemary, dried
- A pinch of salt and black pepper

Directions:

In a sous vide bag, mix the eggplant with the dill, oil and the other ingredients, seal the bag and cook in the water oven at 170 degrees F for 30 minutes. Divide the mix between plates and serve.

Nutrition: calories 230, fat 12, fiber 4, carbs 8, protein 5

Chives Potatoes

***Preparation time:** 10 minutes | **Cooking time:** 30 minutes | **Servings:** 2*

Ingredients:
- 2 tablespoons butter, melted
- 1 pound gold potatoes, peeled and cut into wedges
- 2 tablespoons balsamic vinegar
- A pinch of salt and black pepper
- 1 tablespoon chives, chopped

Directions:

In a sous vide bag, mix the potatoes with the melted butter and the other ingredients, seal the bag and cook in the water oven and cook at 180 degrees F for 30 minutes. Divide between plates and serve as a side dish.

Nutrition: calories 152, fat 4, fiber 4, carbs 12, protein 5.3

Black Beans Mix

***Preparation time:** 5 minutes | **Cooking time:** 20 minutes | **Servings:** 4*

Ingredients:
- 2 cups canned black beans, drained and rinsed
- 1 tablespoon coriander, chopped
- 2 tablespoons butter, soft
- 1 tablespoon balsamic vinegar
- 1 tablespoon chives, chopped
- A pinch of salt and white pepper

Directions:

In a sous vide bag, mix the beans with the coriander and the other ingredients, toss, seal the bag and cook in the water oven at 170 degrees F for 20 minutes. Divide between plates and serve as a side dish.

Nutrition: calories 170, fat 6, fiber 3, carbs 22, protein 5

Dill Peas

***Preparation time:** 10 minutes | **Cooking time:** 25 minutes | **Servings:** 2*

Ingredients:
- 1 tablespoon olive oil
- 2 cups green peas
- Juice of 1 lime
- ½ teaspoon rosemary, dried
- 1 teaspoon turmeric powder
- A pinch of salt and black pepper
- 1 tablespoon dill, chopped

Directions:

In a sous vide bag, mix the peas with the oil, lime juice and the other ingredients, toss, seal the bag and cook in the water oven at 150 degrees F for 25 minutes. Divide the mix between plates and serve as a side dish,

Nutrition: calories 220, fat 15, fiber 4, carbs 18, protein 4

Sous Vide Snack and Appetizer Recipes

Turkey Meatballs

Preparation time: 10 minutes | Cooking time: 3 hours | Servings: 8

Ingredients:
- 1 pound turkey breast, skinless, boneless and ground
- Salt and black pepper to the taste
- 1 egg, whisked
- 1 tablespoon coconut flour
- 1 red onion, chopped
- 1 tablespoon chives, chopped
- 2 tablespoons parsley, chopped
- 3 tablespoons parmesan, grated

Directions:
In a bowl, mix the meat with the egg, flour and the other ingredients, stir well and shape medium meatballs out of this mix. Put the meatballs in a sous vide bag, seal, put it in the water oven and cook them at 135 degrees F for 3 hours. Arrange the meatballs on a platter and serve them as an appetizer.

Nutrition: calories 200, fat 6, fiber 6, carbs 8, protein 5

Pearl Onions Bowls

Preparation time: 10 minutes | Cooking time: 1 hour | Servings: 8

Ingredients:
- 2 cups pearl onions, peeled
- 2 tablespoons olive oil
- 1 tablespoon balsamic vinegar
- 1 tablespoon goat cheese, crumbled

Directions:
In a sous vide bag, mix the pearl onions with the oil and the other ingredients, toss, seal the bag, submerge them in the preheated water oven and cook at 185 degrees F for 1 hour. Divide into bowls and serve as a snack.

Nutrition: calories 162, fat 5, fiber 6, carbs 9, protein 5

Thyme Shrimp Platter

Preparation time: 10 minutes | Cooking time: 20 minutes | Servings: 4

Ingredients:
- 1 pound shrimp, peeled and deveined
- Juice of 1 lime
- 2 spring onions, chopped
- Salt and black pepper to the taste
- 2 tablespoons thyme, chopped

Directions:
In a sous vide bag, mix the shrimp with the lime juice and the other ingredients, toss, seal, put the bag in the water oven and cook at 150 degrees F for 20 minutes. Arrange the shrimp on a platter, and serve.

Nutrition: calories 181, fat 3, fiber 5, carbs 7, protein 6

Cauliflower Spread

Preparation time: 10 minutes | Cooking time: 1 hour | Servings: 12

Ingredients:
- ¼ cup chicken stock
- 1 pound cauliflower florets
- ¼ cup mayonnaise
- 1 yellow onion, cut into wedges
- ¾ cup heavy cream
- ½ teaspoon chili powder
- Salt and black pepper to the taste

Directions:
In a sous vide bag, mix the cauliflower with the chicken stock, onion, salt and pepper, seal the bag, submerge in the water oven and cook at 183 degrees F for 1 hour. Transfer this to a blender, add the rest of the ingredients, pulse well, divide into bowls and serve as a party spread.

Nutrition: calories 100, fat 4, fiber 1, carbs 7, protein 1

Coconut Cheese Dip

Preparation time: 10 minutes | Cooking time: 30 minutes | Servings: 4

Ingredients:
- 2 cups mozzarella cheese, shredded
- ¼ cup coconut cream
- 2 tablespoons garlic, chopped
- 1 red chili, chopped
- 1 tablespoon chives, chopped
- 2 teaspoons cumin, ground
- A pinch of salt and white pepper

Directions:
In a sous vide bag, mix the cheese with the cream, garlic and the other ingredients, seal the bag, submerge in the preheated water oven and cook at 175 degrees F for 30 minutes. Transfer the cheese dip to a bowl and serve.

Nutrition: calories 150, fat 14, fiber 2, carbs 4, protein 2

Shrimp and Pineapple Bowls

Preparation time: 10 minutes | Cooking time: 30 minutes | Servings: 2

Ingredients:
- 2 tablespoons olive oil
- 2 pounds shrimp, peeled and deveined
- 1 cup black olives, pitted and halved
- 1 cup pineapple, peeled and cubed
- 1 tablespoon lime juice
- 1 tablespoons mint, chopped

Directions:
In a sous vide bag, mix the shrimp with the pineapple and the other ingredients, seal, submerge in the preheated water oven and cook at 140 degrees F for 30 minutes. Divide into bowls and serve.

Nutrition: calories 205, fat 12, fiber 2, carbs 6, protein 14

Peppers Salsa

Preparation time: 10 minutes | Cooking time: 1 hour | Servings: 6

Ingredients:
- 1 pound red bell peppers, roughly cubed
- 1 cup cherry tomatoes, halved
- 1 cup spring onions, chopped
- 1 cup kalamata olives, pitted and halved
- 1 tablespoon olive oil
- Juice of 1 lime
- ½ teaspoon chili powder
- Salt and black pepper to the taste
- 1 teaspoon garlic powder
- 1 teaspoon sweet paprika
- ½ teaspoon oregano, dried
- ¼ teaspoon red pepper flakes
- 1 tablespoon chives, chopped

Directions:
In a sous vide bag, combine the bell peppers with the tomatoes, spring onions and the other ingredients, toss, seal, submerge in the preheated water oven and cook at 185 degrees F for 1 hour. Divide into small bowls and serve.

Nutrition: calories 250, fat 22, fiber 3, carbs 6, protein 15

Radish Chips

Preparation time: 10 minutes | Cooking time: 30 minutes | Servings: 4

Ingredients:
- Juice of 1 lime
- ½ pound radishes, thinly sliced
- ½ teaspoon chili powder
- Salt and black pepper to the taste
- ½ teaspoon rosemary, dried
- Cooking spray

Directions:
Spray the radish chips with cooking spray, add the chili powder and the other ingredients, transfer the mix to a sous vide bag, seal, submerge in the preheated water oven and cook at 183 degrees F for 30 minutes. Divide into bowls and serve as a snack.

Nutrition: calories 150, fat 4, fiber 2, carbs 6, protein 4

Zucchini Salsa

Preparation time: 10 minutes | Cooking time: 30 minutes | Servings: 4

Ingredients:
- 1 pound zucchinis, cubed
- 1 cup cherry tomatoes, halved
- 1 cup avocado, peeled, pitted and cubed
- 4 spring onions, chopped
- ½ teaspoon rosemary, dried
- Salt and black pepper to the taste
- 2 tablespoons olive oil
- 2 tablespoons balsamic vinegar

Directions:
In a sous vide bag, combine the zucchinis with the cherry tomatoes and the other ingredients, seal, submerge in the preheated water oven and cook at 183 degrees F for 30 minutes. Divide into bowls and serve.

Nutrition: calories 100, fat 3, fiber 7, carbs 3, protein 7

Crab Dip

Preparation time: 10 minutes | Cooking time: 30 minutes | Servings: 8

Ingredients:
- 2 cups crab meat
- ½ cup mayonnaise
- ½ cup heavy cream
- 8 ounces cream cheese
- ½ teaspoon turmeric powder
- 2 spring onions, chopped
- 2 tablespoons lemon juice
- Salt and black pepper to the taste
- 4 garlic cloves, minced
- 1 tablespoon chives, chopped
- Salt and black pepper to the taste

Directions:
In a sous vide bag, mix the crab with the mayo, cream and the other ingredients, seal the bag, submerge in the preheated water oven and cook at 154 degrees F for 30 minutes. Divide into bowls and serve as a snack.

Nutrition: calories 180, fat 7, fiber 2, carbs 4, protein 6

Olives Balls

Preparation time: 10 minutes | Cooking time: 10 minutes | Servings: 12

Ingredients:
- 4 tablespoons butter, melted
- 2 cups black olives, pitted and chopped
- 1 cup kalamata olives, pitted and chopped
- 2 eggs
- 1 cup almond flour
- ¼ teaspoon sweet paprika
- 1/3 cup parmesan, grated
- Salt and black pepper to the taste
- 1 tablespoon garlic, minced
- 3 tablespoons whipping cream

Directions:

In a bowl, combine the olives with the eggs, butter and the other ingredients, stir well and shape medium balls out of this mix Divide the balls in sous vide bags, seal them, submerge them in the water oven and cook at 180 degrees F for 10 minutes. Serve as a party appetizer.

Nutrition: calories 60, fat 5, fiber 1, carbs 0.7, protein 2

Spinach Dip

Preparation time: 10 minutes | Cooking time: 10 minutes | Servings: 6

Ingredients:
- ½ pound baby spinach
- ½ cup coconut cream
- 8 ounces cream cheese, soft
- 1 tablespoon parsley, chopped
- 1 tablespoon lemon juice
- Salt and black pepper to the taste
- 1 tablespoon chives, chopped

Directions:

In a sous vide bag, combine the spinach with the cream and the other ingredients, seal the bag, submerge it in the preheated water oven and cook at 180 degrees F for 10 minutes. Transfer to a blender, pulse well, divide into small bowls and serve as a party dip.

Nutrition: calories 245, fat 12, fiber 3, carbs 6, protein 8

Stuffed Mushrooms

Preparation time: 10 minutes | Cooking time: 1 hour | Servings: 4

Ingredients:
- 1 teaspoon garlic powder
- 1 red onion, chopped
- 2 spring onions, chopped
- 1 cup black olives, pitted and chopped
- 1 pound white mushroom caps
- Salt and black pepper to the taste
- 1 teaspoon curry powder
- 4 ounces cream cheese, soft
- Salt and black pepper to the taste

Directions:

In a bowl, combine the spring onions with the garlic powder and the other ingredients except the mushroom caps, stir well and stuff the mushrooms with this mix. Divide them into sous vide bags, seal them, submerge them in your preheated water oven and cook at 180 degrees F for 1 hour. Arrange on a platter and serve.

Nutrition: calories 204, fat 12, fiber 3, carbs 7, protein 14

Spicy Meatballs

Preparation time: 10 minutes | Cooking time: 1 hour | Servings: 12

Ingredients:
- 2 eggs, whisked
- 1 pound beef stew meat, ground
- 1 tablespoon garlic, minced
- ½ teaspoon chili powder
- ½ teaspoon hot paprika
- 4 spring onions, chopped
- Salt and black pepper to the taste
- ¼ cup almond flour
- ½ teaspoon garlic powder
- 2 tablespoon basil, chopped

Directions:
In a bowl, combine the meat with the eggs and the other ingredients, stir well and shape medium meatballs out of this mix. Divide them into sous vide bags and keep them in the freezer for 10 minutes. Submerge sous vide bags in the preheated water oven and cook at 145 degrees F for 1 hour. Arrange the meatballs on a platter and serve.

Nutrition: calories 130, fat 6, fiber 3, carbs 5, protein 7

Parmesan Chicken Wings

Preparation time: 10 minutes | Cooking time: 4 hours | Servings: 6

Ingredients:
- 2 pounds chicken wings, halved
- 2 tablespoons olive oil
- 1 tablespoon soy sauce
- 1 tablespoon sugar
- Salt and black pepper to the taste
- ½ teaspoon Italian seasoning
- ½ cup parmesan cheese, grated

Directions:
In a sous vide bag, combine the chicken wings with the oil and the other ingredients except the parmesan, toss, seal the bag, submerge them in the preheated water oven and cook at 170 degrees F for 4 hours. Arrange the chicken wings on a platter, sprinkle the parmesan on top and serve as an appetizer.

Nutrition: calories 154, fat 8, fiber 1, carbs 6, protein 14

Cauliflower Bowls

Preparation time: 10 minutes | Cooking time: 50 minutes | Servings: 8

Ingredients:
- 2 eggs, whisked
- 2 cups cauliflower florets
- 1/3 cup parmesan, grated
- 1/3 cup breadcrumbs
- 2 tablespoons chives, chopped
- Cooking spray
- Salt and black pepper to the taste

Directions:
In a sous vide bag, combine the cauliflower with salt and pepper, grease with cooking spray, toss, seal the bag, submerge it in your preheated water oven and cook at 183 degrees F for 40 minutes. In a bowl, mix the cauliflower with the rest of the ingredients, toss well, transfer the bites to another sous vide bag, seal, submerge them in the water oven and cook them at 180 degrees F for 10 minutes. Divide into bowls and serve as a snack.

Nutrition: calories 140, fat 4, fiber 2, carbs 7, protein 7

Artichoke Dip

Preparation time: 10 minutes | Cooking time: 1 hour | Servings: 8

Ingredients:

- 1 cup heavy cream
- 4 spring onions, chopped
- 2 cups canned artichoke hearts, drained and chopped
- 1 tablespoon olive oil
- 2 garlic cloves, minced
- ½ cup cream cheese
- 1 cup mozzarella cheese, shredded
- 1 teaspoon turmeric powder
- Salt and black pepper to the taste
- 1 tablespoon chives, chopped

Directions:

In a sous vide bag, combine the artichokes with the cream and the other ingredients, whisk, seal the bag, submerge them in the preheated water oven and cook at 183 degrees F for 1 hour. Divide into bowls and serve as a dip.

Nutrition: calories 144, fat 12, fiber 2, carbs 5, protein 5

Shrimp Bites

Preparation time: 10 minutes | Cooking time: 30 minutes | Servings: 6

Ingredients:

- 2 pounds shrimp, peeled and deveined
- Salt and black pepper to the taste
- A drizzle of olive oil
- 1 tablespoon chives, chopped
- 3 tablespoons lemon juice
- 4 garlic cloves, minced
- ½ teaspoon chili powder

Directions:

In a sous vide bag, combine the shrimp with the oil, chives and the other ingredients, toss, seal the bag, submerge in the preheated water oven and cook them at 160 degrees F for 30 minutes. Divide into bowls and serve.

Nutrition: calories 182, fat 12, fiber 1, carbs 6, protein 14

Lemon Oysters

Preparation time: 10 minutes | Cooking time: 30 minutes | Servings: 4

Ingredients:

- 8 oysters, shucked
- Juice of 1 lemon
- Zest of 1 lemon, grated
- ½ teaspoon chili powder
- 1 tablespoon parsley, chopped
- A pinch of sweet paprika
- 2 tablespoons chives, chopped

Directions:

Top each oyster with lemon juice, zest and the other ingredients, put them in separate sous vide bags, seal them, submerge them in the preheated water oven and cook them at 140 degrees F for 30 minutes. Arrange on a platter and serve them as an appetizer.

Nutrition: calories 100, fat 1, fiber 1, carbs 4, protein 1

Parsley Calamari Bites

Preparation time: 10 minutes | Cooking time: 40 minutes | Servings: 4

Ingredients:
- 2 garlic cloves, minced
- 2 cups calamari rings
- 1 tablespoon lime juice
- ½ teaspoon sweet paprika
- 1 tablespoon olive oil
- Salt and black pepper to the taste
- ¼ cup parsley, chopped

Directions:
In a sous vide bag, combine the calamari with the garlic and the other ingredients, seal the bag, submerge it in the preheated water oven and cook them at 130 degrees F for 40 minutes. Divide into bowls and serve as an appetizer.

Nutrition: calories 240, fat 12, fiber 1, carbs 5, protein 25

Salmon Salsa

Preparation time: 10 minutes | Cooking time: 40 minutes | Servings: 4

Ingredients:
- 1 pound salmon fillets, skinless, boneless and cubed
- 1 tablespoon olive oil
- Salt and black pepper to the taste
- 1 teaspoon turmeric powder
- 2 red chilies, minced
- 1 teaspoon sweet paprika
- 2 red onions, chopped
- 1 cup cherry tomatoes, halved
- 2 tablespoons cilantro, chopped
- Juice of 2 limes
- Salt and black pepper to the taste

Directions:
In a sous vide bag, combine the salmon with the oil, turmeric and the other ingredients, toss, seal the bag, submerge in the preheated water oven and cook them at 140 degrees F for 40 minutes. Divide into bowls and serve as an appetizer.

Nutrition: calories 250, fat 14, fiber 4, carbs 5, protein 15

Tuna Bites

Preparation time: 15 minutes | Cooking time: 30 minutes | Servings: 6

Ingredients:
- 1 pound tuna fillets, boneless and roughly cubed
- 1 tablespoon olive oil
- 1 tablespoon soy sauce
- 1 teaspoon chili powder
- ½ teaspoon dill, dried
- 1 tablespoon parsley, chopped
- Salt and black pepper to the taste

Directions:
In a sous vide bag, combine the tuna with the oil, soy sauce and the other ingredients, toss, seal, submerge in the preheated water oven and cook at 130 degrees F for 30 minutes. Arrange the tuna bites on a platter and serve them as an appetizer.

Nutrition: calories 170, fat 2, fiber 1, carbs 6, protein 6

Shrimp and Cucumber Salad
Preparation time: *10 minutes* | ***Cooking time:*** *30 minutes* | ***Servings:*** *4*

Ingredients:
- 3 cucumbers, cut with a spiralizer
- ½ cup mint, chopped
- 2 pounds shrimp, peeled and deveined
- 1 cup black olives, pitted and halved
- 1 tablespoon olive oil
- Salt and black pepper to the taste
- 2 tablespoons lime juice
- 2 teaspoons chili garlic sauce
- 1 tablespoon chives, chopped

Directions:
In a sous vide bag, combine the shrimp with the cucumbers, mint and the other ingredients, toss, seal the bag, submerge it in your preheated water oven and cook at 140 degrees F for 30 minutes. Divide into bowls and serve.

Nutrition: calories 150, fat 2, fiber 3, carbs 6, protein 6

Lemon Mussels
Preparation time: *5 minutes* | ***Cooking time:*** *20 minutes* | ***Servings:*** *4*

Ingredients:
- 2 pounds mussels, debearded and scrubbed
- ½ teaspoon rosemary, dried
- ½ teaspoon sweet paprika
- 1 tablespoon butter, melted
- 1 tablespoon lemon juice

Directions:
Put the mussels in a sous vide bag, add the rosemary and the other ingredients, seal the bag, submerge in the preheated water oven and cook at 194 degrees F for 20 minutes. Arrange mussels on a platter, and serve.

Nutrition: calories 100, fat 1, fiber 1, carbs 6, protein 2

Squid Salad
Preparation time: *10 minutes* | ***Cooking time:*** *2 hours* | ***Servings:*** *2*

Ingredients:
- 1 pound squid, cut into medium rings
- 1 cup cherry tomatoes, halved
- 1 cup kalamata olives, pitted and halved
- 1 cup zucchinis, cubed
- 2 tablespoons olive oil
- 1 tablespoon balsamic vinegar
- A pinch of cayenne pepper
- Salt and black pepper to the taste
- 1 tablespoons lemon juice
- 1 tablespoon chives, chopped
- 1 teaspoon sriracha sauce

Directions:
In a sous vide bag, combine the squid rings with the tomatoes, olives and the other ingredients, toss, seal, submerge in the preheated water oven and cook at 136 degrees F for 2 hours. Divide the salad into bowls and serve.

Nutrition: calories 245, fat 32, fiber 3, carbs 12, protein 17

Calamari and Radish Salad

Preparation time: 10 minutes | Cooking time: 2 hours | Servings: 4

Ingredients:
- 2 cups calamari rings
- 1 cup radishes, sliced
- 1 cup kalamata olives, pitted and halved
- 1 tablespoon olive oil
- Juice of 1 lime
- A splash of Worcestershire sauce
- Salt and black pepper to the taste
- ½ teaspoon turmeric powder
- 1 tablespoon chives, chopped

Directions:
In a sous vide bag, combine the calamari with the radishes and the other ingredients, seal the bag, submerge in the preheated water oven and cook at 145 degrees F for 2 hours. Divide into bowls and serve as an appetizer.

Nutrition: calories 368, fat 23, fiber 3, carbs 10, protein 34

Octopus and Mango Salad

Preparation time: 10 minutes | Cooking time: 5 hours | Servings: 2

Ingredients:
- 2 pounds octopus, rinsed
- 1 cup mango, peeled and cubed
- 1 cup cherry tomatoes, halved
- 1 cup black olives, pitted and halved
- 1 cup cucumber, cubed
- 1 tablespoon balsamic vinegar
- 4 tablespoons olive oil
- 1 tablespoon chives, chopped
- Juice of 1 lemon
- Salt and black pepper to the taste
- 2 tablespoons parsley, chopped

Directions:
Put the octopus in a sous vide bag, drizzle half of the oil over it, season with salt and pepper, seal the bag, submerge it in the preheated water oven and cook at 170 degrees F for 5 hours. Chop octopus, transfer to a bowl, add the rest of the ingredients, toss, divide into bowls and serve.

Nutrition: calories 200, fat 10, fiber 3, carbs 6, protein 23

Clam Bowls

Preparation time: 10 minutes | Cooking time: 20 minutes | Servings: 4

Ingredients:
- 1 cup shallots, chopped
- 1 cup corn
- 1 cup kalamata olives, pitted and halved
- Juice of 1 lime
- ½ teaspoon chili powder
- Salt and black pepper to the taste
- 1 cup chicken stock
- 14 ounces baby clams
- 1 cup heavy cream
- 1 cup onion, chopped
- 1 tablespoon chives, chopped

Directions:
Put the clams in a sous vide bag, add salt, pepper and the stock, seal the bag, submerge it in the preheated water oven and cook at 190 degrees F for 20 minutes. Open the clams, transfer the meat to a bowl, add the rest of the ingredients, toss, divide between plates and serve.

Nutrition: calories 220, fat 12, fiber 7, carbs 8, protein 13

Italian Shrimp Salad

Preparation time: 10 minutes | Cooking time: 30 minutes | Servings: 4

Ingredients:
- 2 tablespoons avocado oil
- 1 cup pineapple, peeled and cubed
- 1 cup avocado, peeled, pitted and cubed
- 1 cup radishes, cubed
- 1 pound shrimp, peeled and deveined
- Salt and black pepper to the taste
- 2 tablespoons lime juice
- 2 teaspoons mint, chopped
- 1 tablespoon tarragon, chopped
- 1 tablespoon lemon juice
- 1 teaspoon lime zest, grated
- ½ cup heavy cream

Directions:
In a sous vide bag, combine the shrimp with the oil, pineapple and the other ingredients, seal the bag, submerge it in the preheated water oven and cook at 140 degrees F for 30 minutes. Divide small bowls and serve as an appetizer.

Nutrition: calories 180, fat 11, fiber 2, carbs 8, protein 13

Cod Salsa

Preparation time: 10 minutes | Cooking time: 40 minutes | Servings: 4

Ingredients:
- ½ cup spring onions, chopped
- 2 pounds cod fillets, boneless and cubed
- 1 cup radishes, cubed
- 1 cup mango, peeled and cubed
- 1 cup green olives, pitted and halved
- Juice of 1 lime
- 1 tablespoon avocado oil
- 1 teaspoon red pepper flakes, crushed
- 1 tablespoon parsley, chopped
- 5 garlic cloves, minced

Directions:
In a sous vide bag, combine the cod with the spring onions and the other ingredients, seal the bag, submerge in the preheated water oven and cook them at 180 degrees F for 40 minutes. Divide the mix into bowls and serve as an appetizer.

Nutrition: calories 204, fat 15, fiber 2, carbs 3, protein 4

Apple and Shrimp Salsa

Preparation time: 10 minutes | Cooking time: 30 minutes | Servings: 4

Ingredients:
- 2 pounds shrimp, peeled and deveined
- 1 cup green apple, cored and cubed
- 1 cup cherry tomatoes, halved
- 2 tablespoons balsamic vinegar
- 1 tablespoon olive oil
- Juice of ½ lemon
- 2 garlic cloves, minced
- Salt and black pepper to the taste
- Juice of ½ lemon
- 1 tablespoon chives, chopped
- 2 thyme springs, chopped

Directions:
In a sous vide bag, combine the shrimp with the apple, tomatoes and the other ingredients, seal, submerge in the preheated water oven and cook them at 180 degrees F for 30 minutes. Divide the mix appetizer bowls and serve.

Nutrition: calories 140, fat 2, fiber 1, carbs 8, protein 10

Shrimp and Pico De Gallo

Preparation time: 10 minutes | Cooking time: 30 minutes | Servings: 4

Ingredients:
- 1 pound shrimp, peeled and deveined
- 1 tablespoon olive oil
- ½ teaspoon sweet paprika
- A handful cilantro, chopped
- 2 tomatoes, cubed
- 1 jalapeno pepper, chopped
- ¼ cup red onion, chopped
- Salt and black pepper to the taste
- Zest of 1 lime, grated
- 1 tablespoon chives, chopped
- Juice of 1 lime

Directions:
In a sous vide bag, combine the shrimp with the oil, paprika and the other ingredients, toss, seal the bag, submerge in the preheated water oven and cook them at 185 degrees F for 30 minutes. Divide into bowls and serve.

Nutrition: calories 100, fat 2, fiber 6, carbs 8, protein 1

Scallops and Radish Salad

Preparation time: 10 minutes | Cooking time: 1 hour | Servings: 2

Ingredients:
- 6 scallops
- 1 cup radishes, halved
- 1 cup cherry tomatoes, halved
- 1 cup kalamata olives, pitted and halved
- 1 tablespoon chives, chopped
- 1 tablespoon parsley, chopped
- Juice of 1 lime
- Zest of 1 lime, grated
- 2 tablespoons olive oil
- Salt and black pepper to the taste

Directions:
Season scallops with salt and pepper, put them in a sous vide bag, seal, submerge in the preheated water oven and cook them at 140 degrees F for 1 hour. In a bowl, combine the scallops with the radishes, tomatoes and the other ingredients, toss and serve as an appetizer.

Nutrition: calories 240, fat 14, fiber 4, carbs 12, protein 15

Tuna Salad

Preparation time: 10 minutes | Cooking time: 40 minutes | Servings: 4

Ingredients:
- 1 pound tuna fillets, boneless and cubed
- 2 beets, peeled and cubed
- 1 cup kalamata olives, pitted and halved
- 1 tablespoon olive oil
- 1 cup broccoli florets
- 2 tablespoons green onions, chopped
- A pinch of salt and black pepper
- Some cloves sprouts
- 2 tablespoons soy sauce
- 1 tablespoon apple cider vinegar
- A pinch of salt and black pepper
- 1 tablespoon cilantro, chopped

Directions:
In a sous vide bag, combine the tuna with the beets, olives and the other ingredients, toss gently, seal it, submerge it in the preheated water oven, cook at 130 degrees F for 40 minutes, transfer small bowls and serve as an appetizer.

Nutrition: calories 281, fat 12, fiber 6, carbs 6, protein 15

Tuna Bites and Mint Sauce

Preparation time: 10 minutes | Cooking time: 40 minutes | Servings: 4

Ingredients:
- 2 pounds tuna fillets, boneless and cubed
- 1 tablespoon turmeric powder
- 1 tablespoon ginger, grated
- ½ teaspoon sweet paprika
- Salt and black pepper to the taste
- 2 tablespoons olive oil
- Juice of ½ lemon
- 1 cup mint leaves
- 2 tablespoons chives, chopped
- 1 tablespoon pine nuts, toasted and chopped
- 1 tablespoon water
- Salt and black pepper to the taste

Directions:
In a blender, combine the mint with the oil, lemon juice, pine nuts, water, salt and pepper and pulse well. In a sous vide bag, combine the tuna with the turmeric, the other ingredients and the mint sauce, toss, seal the bag, submerge in the water oven and cook at 175 degrees F for 40 minutes. Arrange the tuna and sauce on a platter and serve as an appetizer.

Nutrition: calories 140, fat 5, fiber 1, carbs 7, protein 9

Bbq Chicken Meatballs

Preparation time: 10 minutes | Cooking time: 2 hours | Servings: 4

Ingredients:
- 1 pound chicken meat, ground
- 1 cup bbq sauce
- 2 eggs, whisked
- 4 scallions, chopped
- Salt and black pepper to the taste
- 2 tablespoons lime juice
- Cooking spray
- ½ cup almond flour
- ¼ cup cheddar cheese, grated
- 1 tablespoon cilantro, chopped

Directions:
In a bowl, mix the chicken with the eggs, scallions and the other ingredients except the cooking spray and the bbq sauce, stir and shape medium meatballs out of this mix Divide the meatballs into sous vide bags, grease them with cooking spray, cover with the bbq sauce, seal the bags, submerge in the preheated water oven and cook them at 150 degrees F for 2 hours Arrange the meatballs on a platter and serve them as an appetizer.

Nutrition: calories 156, fat 11, fiber 1, carbs 2, protein 12

Creamy Corn Dip

Preparation time: 10 minutes | Cooking time: 30 minutes | Servings: 4

Ingredients:
- 2 cups corn
- 1 cup heavy cream
- 1 cup cream cheese
- 4 spring onions, chopped
- ½ teaspoon turmeric powder
- Juice of 1 lime
- 1 handful cilantro, chopped
- 2 garlic cloves, minced
- 1 jalapeno pepper, chopped
- Salt and black pepper to the taste

Directions:
In a vide bag, combine the corn with the cream, cream cheese and the other ingredients, toss, seal, submerge in the preheated water oven and cook at 160 degrees F for 30 minutes. Divide the mix into bowls and serve as a party dip.

Nutrition: calories 172, fat 5, fiber 1, carbs 5, protein 12

Chicken Salad

Preparation time: 10 minutes | Cooking time: 1 hour | Servings: 4

Ingredients:
- 2 pounds chicken breasts, skinless, boneless and cut into strips
- 1 cup baby kale
- 1 teaspoon chili powder
- 2 tablespoons olive oil
- 1 tablespoon balsamic vinegar
- 1 cup kalamata olives, pitted and cubed
- 1 cup mango, peeled and cubed
- 2 tablespoons lime juice
- Salt and black pepper to the taste
- 1 teaspoon sweet paprika
- 1 green bell pepper, cubed
- 1 red onion, chopped
- 1 tablespoon cilantro, chopped
- 1 tablespoon chives, chopped

Directions:
In a sous vide bag, mix the chicken with the kale, chili powder and the other ingredients, toss, seal the bag, submerge in the preheated water oven and cook them at 170 degrees F for 1 hour.ь Divide the mix into bowls and serve.

Nutrition: calories 240, fat 10, fiber 2, carbs 5, protein 20

Duck and Spinach Salad

Preparation time: 10 minutes | Cooking time: 1 hour and 30 minutes | Servings: 4

Ingredients:
- 2 pounds duck breast, boneless and skin scored
- 1 red onion, chopped
- 2 tablespoons red vinegar
- 2 tablespoons olive oil
- ¾ cup raspberries
- 1 tablespoon lime juice
- Salt and black pepper to the taste
- 2 cups baby spinach
- Salt and black pepper to the taste
- ½ cup walnuts, chopped
- 1 tablespoon chives, chopped

Directions:
Season the duck with salt and pepper, drizzle half of the oil, divide into 2 sous vide bags, seal the bags, submerge them in the preheated water oven and cook at 140 degrees F for 1 hour and 30 minutes. In a bowl, combine the spinach with the other ingredients and toss. Slice duck breasts, add them to the salad, toss and serve as an appetizer.

Nutrition: calories 355, fat 40, fiber 4, carbs 6, protein 18

Stuffed Peppers

Preparation time: 10 minutes | Cooking time: 1 hour | Servings: 4

Ingredients:
- Salt and black pepper to the taste
- 1 small yellow onion, chopped
- 2 tablespoons spring onions, chopped
- 1 pound beef stew meat, ground
- 2 tomatoes, chopped
- 1 tablespoon olive oil
- 8 bell peppers, tops cut off and seeds removed
- 2/3 cup tomato sauce

Directions:
In a bowl mix the beef with the onion, spring onions, tomatoes, salt and pepper, stir and stuff the peppers with this mix. Divide the stuffed peppers into individual sous vide bags, also divide the tomato sauce, seal them, submerge in the water oven and cook at 185 degrees F for 1 hour. Arrange the peppers on a platter and serve.

Nutrition: calories 200, fat 6, fiber 3, carbs 6, protein 14

Chicken Dip

Preparation time: 10 minutes | Cooking time: 1 hour and 10 minutes | Servings: 4

Ingredients:
- 1 tablespoon chives, chopped
- 1 pound chicken breast, skinless, boneless and ground
- 1 tablespoon olive oil
- 1 yellow onion, chopped
- 1 cup baby spinach
- 1 cup heavy cream
- Juice of 1 lime
- 1 teaspoon turmeric powder
- 1 cup cream cheese
- Salt and black pepper to the taste

Directions:
Heat up a pan with the oil over medium heat, add the onion and the meat and brown for 10 minutes. In a bowl, mix browned meat with the other ingredients, stir well and divide into 4 ramekins. Put the ramekins in the water oven, fill it with water halfway and cook the dip at 160 degrees F for 1 hour. Serve as a party dip.

Nutrition: calories 260, fat 45, fiber 4, carbs 5, protein 16

Chinese Beef Bites

Preparation time: 10 minutes | Cooking time: 3 hours | Servings: 4

Ingredients:
- 2 pounds beef stew meat, cubed
- 2 tablespoons olive oil
- Salt and black pepper to the taste
- 3 tablespoons balsamic vinegar
- 1 teaspoon five spice
- ½ teaspoon allspice, ground
- 3 tablespoons balsamic vinegar
- ¼ cup scallions, chopped

Directions:
In a bowl, mix beef bites with the oil, vinegar and the other ingredients, toss, transfer to a sous vide bag, submerge in the preheated water oven and cook at 160 degrees F for 3 hours. Arrange on a platter and serve.

Nutrition: calories 415, fat 23, fiber 3, carbs 8, protein 27

Mushroom Dip

Preparation time: 10 minutes | Cooking time: 1 hour | Servings: 6

Ingredients:
- 1 pound mushrooms, sliced
- 1 tablespoon olive oil
- 4 ounces cream cheese
- ½ teaspoon rosemary, dried
- 1 teaspoon Italian seasoning
- 4 tablespoons hot sauce
- ½ cup mozzarella, shredded
- 1 cup heavy cream
- 4 spring onions, chopped
- Salt and black pepper to the taste

Directions:
Heat up a pan with the oil over medium heat, add the mushrooms, cook for 10 minutes and transfer to a bowl Add the rest of the ingredients, toss well and divide into 6 ramekins Arrange the ramekins in the water oven, cover them with tin foil, fill the water oven with water halfway and cook at 170 degrees F for 1 hour. Serve the mix as a party dip.

Nutrition: calories 200, fat 4, fiber 1, carbs 7, protein 7

Shrimp Meatballs

Preparation time: 10 minutes | Cooking time: 1 hour | Servings: 6

Ingredients:

- ½ cup coconut flour
- 2 pounds shrimp, peeled, deveined and chopped
- 2 eggs, whisked
- 4 scallions, chopped
- Salt and black pepper to the taste
- 3 teaspoons soy sauce
- 1 tablespoon chives, chopped
- Cooking spray
- ½ teaspoon mustard powder
- ¼ teaspoon sweet paprika

Directions:

In a bowl, mix the shrimp with the scallions, flour and the other ingredients except the cooking spray, stir well and shape medium meatballs out of this mix Divide the shrimp meatballs into sous vide bags, grease them with the cooking spray, seal the bags, submerge in the water oven and cook at 140 degrees F for 1 hour Arrange them on a platter and serve as an appetizer

Nutrition: calories 332, fat 18, fiber 1, carbs 7, protein 15

Sausage Bites

Preparation time: 10 minutes | Cooking time: 1 hour and 30 minutes | Servings: 4

Ingredients:

- 1 pound beef sausages, sliced
- 1 tablespoon olive oil
- 1 tablespoon balsamic vinegar
- Salt and black pepper to taste
- 1 teaspoon sweet paprika
- 3 tablespoons tomato sauce
- ¼ teaspoon red pepper flakes
- ¼ teaspoon onion powder
- ½ teaspoon garlic powder

Directions:

In large sous vide bag, mix the sausage bites with the oil, vinegar and the other ingredients, toss, seal, submerge in the preheated water oven and cook them at 140 degrees F for 1 hour and 30 minutes Divide the sausage bites into bowls and serve as a snack.

Nutrition: calories 316, fat 35, fiber 3, carbs 4, protein 16

Radish Dip

Preparation time: 10 minutes | Cooking time: 1 hour | Servings: 6

Ingredients:

- 1 pound radishes, chopped
- 1 cup scallions, chopped
- 1 cup heavy cream
- 1 cup cream cheese
- 1 tablespoon chives, chopped
- Juice of 1 lime
- Salt and black pepper to the taste
- ½ teaspoon garlic powder
- 1 tablespoon parsley, chopped

Directions:

In a bowl, mix the radishes with the scallions, cream and the other ingredients, stir well and divide into 6 ramekins Cover the ramekins with tin foil, put them in the water oven, add water halfway into the oven, and cook at 140 degrees F for 1 hour Serve as a party dip.

Nutrition: calories 325, fat 23, fiber 4, carbs 6, protein 22

Sriracha Turkey Bites

Preparation time: 10 minutes | Cooking time: 2 hours | Servings: 4

Ingredients:

- 2 pounds turkey breast, skinless, boneless and cubed
- 1 tablespoon olive oil
- 1 tablespoon soy sauce
- 2 tablespoons tomato sauce
- 2 teaspoons sriracha sauce
- ¼ cup chives, chopped
- ½ teaspoon chili powder
- Salt and black pepper to the taste

Directions:

In a sous vide bag, combine the turkey with the oil, sriracha sauce and the other ingredients, toss, seal the bag, submerge in the preheated water oven, cook at 146 degrees F for 2 hours, arrange on a platter and serve as an appetizer.

Nutrition: calories 320, fat 23, fiber 0, carbs 12, protein 37

Beet Salsa

Preparation time: 10 minutes | Cooking time: 1 hour | Servings: 4

Ingredients:

- 1 pound red beets, peeled and cubed
- 1 cup green olives, pitted and halved
- 1 cup cherry tomatoes, halved
- Juice of 1 lime
- 2 tablespoons olive oil
- Salt and black pepper to the taste
- ½ teaspoon herbs de Provence
- 2 red onions, chopped
- 1 tablespoon chives, chopped

Directions:

In a large sous vide bag, combine the beets with the olives and the other ingredients, toss, seal the bag, introduce in the preheated water oven and cook at 185 degrees F for 1 hour Serve as a snack.

Nutrition: calories 320, fat 8, fiber 4, carbs 12, protein 10

Fennel and Shrimp Salad

Preparation time: 10 minutes | Cooking time: 50 minutes | Servings: 4

Ingredients:

- 1 pound shrimp, peeled and deveined
- 2 fennel bulbs, sliced
- 1 cup mango, peeled and cubed
- 1 cup kalamata olives, pitted and cubed
- 1 tablespoon lime juice
- 2 tablespoons olive oil
- ¼ cup walnuts, toasted and chopped
- 2 tablespoons cilantro, chopped
- 1 tablespoon chives, chopped
- Salt and black pepper to the taste
- A pinch of cayenne pepper

Directions:

In a large sous vide bag, combine the shrimp with the mango, fennel and the other ingredients, toss, seal, submerge in the preheated water oven, cook them at 146 degrees F for 50 minutes, divide between appetizer plates and serve.

Nutrition: calories 200, fat 10, fiber 1, carbs 6, protein 7

Pesto Radish and Corn Dip

Preparation time: 10 minutes | *Cooking time: 1 hour* | *Servings: 4*

Ingredients:
- 1 pound radishes, cubed
- 2 cups corn
- 3 tablespoons basil pesto
- 1 cup heavy cream
- 1 cup cream cheese
- 1 tablespoon chives, chopped
- Salt and black pepper to the taste

Directions:
In a bowl, mix the radishes with the corn, pesto and the other ingredients, whisk and divide into 4 ramekins. Cover the ramekins with tin foil, put them in the water oven, fill it halfway with water and cook the dip at 180 degrees F for 1 hour. Serve the mix as a party dip warm.

Nutrition: calories 357, fat 23, fiber 5, carbs 8, protein 26

Balsamic Salmon Bites

Preparation time: 10 minutes | *Cooking time: 20 minutes* | *Servings: 6*

Ingredients:
- 1 pound salmon fillets, boneless and cubed
- 2 tablespoons olive oil
- ½ tablespoon honey
- 2 tablespoons balsamic vinegar
- 1 tablespoon parsley, chopped

Directions:
In a sous vide bag, mix the salmon with the oil and the other ingredients, toss, seal the bag and cook in the water oven at 170 degrees F for 20 minutes. Arrange the bites on a platter and serve as an appetizer.

Nutrition: calories 222, fat 11.2, fiber 4.5, carbs 3.4, protein 12.6

Spicy Lentils Bowls

Preparation time: 10 minutes | *Cooking time: 20 minutes* | *Servings: 4*

Ingredients:
- 2 cups canned lentils, drained and rinsed
- 1 tablespoon olive oil
- 1 teaspoon hot paprika
- Juice of 1 lime
- 1 red chili pepper, chopped
- ½ tablespoon red pepper, crushed
- A pinch of salt and black pepper
- 1 tablespoon chives, chopped

Directions:
In a sous vide bag, mix the lentils with the paprika and the other ingredients, toss, seal the bag, submerge in the water oven and cook at 160 degrees F for 20 minutes. Divide the mix into bowls and serve as a snack.

Nutrition: calories 200, fat 11.2, fiber 2.4, carbs 5.3, protein 2.3

Eggplant Dip

Preparation time: 10 minutes | *Cooking time: 25 minutes* | *Servings: 4*

Ingredients:
- 1 cup heavy cream
- 1 cup eggplant, chopped
- ½ teaspoon rosemary, dried
- A pinch of salt and black pepper
- 2 scallions, chopped
- 1 tablespoon parsley, chopped
- 1 red onion, chopped

Directions:
In a sous vide bag, mix the eggplants with the cream and the other ingredients, seal the bag and cook in the water oven at 170 degrees F for 25 minutes. Transfer to a blender, pulse well divide into bowls, and serve the dip right away.

Nutrition: calories 232, fat 9.8, fiber 2.3, carbs 5.7, protein 4.3

Chickpeas Spread

Preparation time: 10 minutes | *Cooking time:* 25 minutes | *Servings:* 6

Ingredients:
- 1 cup canned chickpeas, drained and rinsed
- 2 tablespoons chives, chopped
- A pinch of salt and black pepper
- 2 tablespoons olive oil
- 2 tablespoons tahini paste
- 2 tablespoons lime juice
- 2 scallions, chopped

Directions:

In a sous vide bag, mix the chickpeas with the oil, lime juice and the other ingredients, seal the bag and cook in the water oven at 170 degrees F for 25 minutes. Transfer the mix to a blender, pulse well, divide into bowls and serve.

Nutrition: calories 300, fat 12, fiber 4, carbs 12, protein 5

Garlic Chicken Bites

Preparation time: 10 minutes | *Cooking time:* 40 minutes | *Servings:* 6

Ingredients:
- 2 pounds chicken breast, skinless, boneless and cubed
- 4 garlic cloves, minced
- 2 tablespoons olive oil
- 1 tablespoon balsamic vinegar
- ½ cup honey
- A pinch of salt and black pepper
- ½ teaspoon hot paprika

Directions:

In a sous vide bag, mix the chicken with the garlic and the other ingredients, toss, seal, and cook in the water oven at 180 degrees F for 40 minutes. Arrange on a platter and serve as an appetizer.

Nutrition: calories 234, fat 11, fiber 3, carbs 20, protein 12

Coconut Dip

Preparation time: 5 minutes | *Cooking time:* 20 minutes | *Servings:* 4

Ingredients:
- 1 cup coconut cream
- ½ cup coconut flakes
- ½ teaspoon turmeric powder
- 1 tablespoon olive oil
- 1 cup almonds, chopped
- A pinch of salt and black pepper

Directions:

In a blender, mix the cream with the almonds and the other ingredients, pulse well and divide into 4 ramekins. Put the ramekins in the water bath, fill it with water halfway, and cook at 180 degrees F for 20 minutes. Serve right away as a party dip.

Nutrition: calories 132, fat 1, fiber 2, carbs 6, protein 5

Pesto Dip

Preparation time: 5 minutes | *Cooking time:* 20 minutes | *Servings:* 4

Ingredients:
- 2 tablespoons basil pesto
- 1 cup Greek yogurt
- 4 scallions, chopped
- 1 tablespoon lime zest, grated
- 1 tablespoon lime juice
- 1 tablespoon olive oil
- ½ teaspoon garam masala
- A pinch of salt and black pepper

Directions:

In a blender, mix the yogurt with the pesto and the other ingredients, pulse well and transfer to 4 ramekins Put the ramekins in the water oven and cook at 180 degrees F for 20 minutes. Serve as a dip.

Nutrition: calories 140, fat 4, fiber 3, carbs 6, protein 6

Shrimp and Olives Bowls

Preparation time: 5 minutes | *Cooking time:* 20 minutes | *Servings:* 4

Ingredients:

- 2 pounds shrimp, peeled and deveined
- 1 tablespoon avocado oil
- 1 cup kalamata olives, pitted and halved
- 1 tablespoon chives, chopped
- Juice of 1 lime
- 1 tablespoon balsamic vinegar
- 1 tablespoon capers, drained
- 2 spring onions, chopped

Directions:

In a sous vide bag, mix the shrimp with the oil, olives and the other ingredients, seal the bag and cook in the water oven at 180 degrees F for 20 minutes. Divide the mix into bowls and serve as an appetizer.

Nutrition: calories 170, fat 9, fiber 4, carbs 7, protein 6

Mussels Bowls

Preparation time: 5 minutes | *Cooking time:* 20 minutes | *Servings:* 4

Ingredients:

- 1 pound mussels, scrubbed
- 2 scallions, chopped
- 1 cup kalamata olives, pitted and halved
- ½ cup cherry tomatoes, halved
- Juice of 1 lime
- ½ cup white wine
- ½ teaspoon Italian seasoning
- 1 tablespoon olive oil
- 1 tablespoon chives, chopped

Directions:

In a sous vide bag, mix the mussels with the scallions and the other ingredients, seal the bag, submerge in the water oven and cook at 170 degrees F for 20 minutes. Divide into bowls and serve as an appetizer.

Nutrition: calories 180, fat 3, fiber 3, carbs 7, protein 9

Walnuts Bowls

Preparation time: 5 minutes | *Cooking time:* 20 minutes | *Servings:* 4

Ingredients:

- 2 cups walnuts
- ½ teaspoon hot paprika
- 1 tablespoon olive oil
- 1 teaspoon red pepper flakes, crushed
- 1 tablespoon lime juice
- 1 tablespoon capers, drained
- 1 tablespoon chives, chopped

Directions:

In a sous vide bag, mix the walnuts with the paprika and the other ingredients, toss, seal, submerge in the water oven and cook at 180 degrees F for 20 minutes. Divide the mix into bowls and serve as a snack.

Nutrition: calories 150, fat 9, fiber 2, carbs 6, protein 6

Sous Vide Fish and Seafood Recipes

Lemon Salmon

Preparation time: 10 minutes | Cooking time: 30 minutes | Servings: 4

Ingredients:
- 1 pound salmon fillets, boneless and cubed
- ½ teaspoon turmeric powder
- 1 tablespoon lemon juice
- 1 tablespoon rosemary, chopped
- A pinch of salt and black pepper
- 1 tablespoon chives, chopped

Directions:

In a sous vide bag, mix the salmon with the turmeric and the other ingredients, seal the bag, and cook at 180 degrees F for 30 minutes. Divide between plates and serve.

Nutrition: calories 198, fat 7, fiber 2, carbs 6, protein 7

Chili Tuna

Preparation time: 10 minutes | Cooking time: 30 minutes | Servings: 4

Ingredients:
- 2 tablespoons avocado oil
- 1 pound tuna fillets, boneless and cubed
- 2 red chilies, chopped
- ½ teaspoon chili powder
- 1 tablespoon chives, chopped
- A pinch of salt and black pepper

Directions:

In a sous vide bag, mix the tuna with the oil and the other ingredients, seal, and cook in the water oven at 200 degrees F for 30 minutes. Divide the mix into bowls and serve.

Nutrition: calories 221, fat 8, fiber 3, carbs 6, protein 7

Shrimp and Tomatoes Mix

Preparation time: 5 minutes | Cooking time: 20 minutes | Servings: 4

Ingredients:
- 1 pound shrimp, peeled and deveined
- 1 tablespoon olive oil
- 1 cup cherry tomatoes, halved
- 1 tablespoon lemon juice
- 3 garlic cloves, crushed
- A pinch of salt and black pepper

Directions:

In a sous vide bag, mix the shrimp with the tomatoes and the other ingredients, seal and cook in the water oven at 180 degrees F for 20 minutes. Divide the mix into bowls and serve.

Nutrition: calories 235, fat 8, fiber 4, carbs 7, protein 9

Paprika Cod

Preparation time: 10 minutes | Cooking time: 25 minutes | Servings: 4

Ingredients:
1. 1 tablespoon avocado oil
2. 2 pounds cod fillets, boneless
3. ½ cup white wine
4. 1 teaspoon sweet paprika
5. A pinch of salt and black pepper

Directions:

In a sous vide bag, mix the cod with the wine and the other ingredients, seal and cook in the water oven at 170 degrees F for 25 minutes. Divide everything into bowls and serve.

Nutrition: calories 211, fat 8, fiber 4, carbs 8, protein 8

Shrimp and Spinach

Preparation time: 10 minutes | Cooking time: 20 minutes | Servings: 4

Ingredients:
- 1 pound shrimp, peeled and deveined
- Juice of 1 lemon
- 1 cup baby spinach
- ½ teaspoon chili powder
- ½ teaspoon red pepper flakes, crushed
- 2 tablespoons avocado oil
- A pinch of salt and black pepper
- 1 tablespoon chives, chopped

Directions:
In a sous vide bag, mix the shrimp with the lemon juice and the other ingredients, seal and cook n the water oven at 170 degrees F for 20 minutes. Transfer the mix to bowls and serve.

Nutrition: calories 193, fat 7, fiber 3, carbs 6, protein 6

Cod and Green Beans

Preparation time: 5 minutes | Cooking time: 25 minutes | Servings: 4

Ingredients:
- 1 pound cod fillets, boneless and roughly cubed
- 1 cup green beans, trimmed and halved
- 1 tablespoon olive oil
- ½ teaspoon ginger, ground
- Juice of 1 lime
- 1 tablespoon chives, chopped
- A pinch of salt and black pepper

Directions:
In a sous vide bag, mix the cod with the green beans and the other ingredients, seal the bag, submerge in the water oven and cook at 180 degrees F for 25 minutes. Divide the mix into bowls and serve.

Nutrition: calories 200, fat 11, fiber 4, carbs 5, protein 12

Turmeric Tuna

Preparation time: 10 minutes | Cooking time: 25 minutes | Servings: 4

Ingredients:
- 1 pound tuna fillets, boneless and roughly cubed
- 1 teaspoon turmeric powder
- 1 tablespoon avocado oil
- ½ teaspoon sweet paprika
- 2 spring onions, chopped
- Juice of ½ lemon
- 1 tablespoon chives, chopped

Directions:
In a sous vide bag, mix the tuna with the turmeric, oil and the other ingredients, seal the bag and cook in the water oven at 180 degrees F for 25 minutes. Divide the mix between plates and serve.

Nutrition: calories 200, fat 12, fiber 3, carbs 7, protein 9

Salmon and Avocado Mix

Preparation time: 5 minutes | Cooking time: 25 minutes | Servings: 4

Ingredients:
- 1 pound salmon fillets, boneless and roughly cubed
- 1 cup avocado, peeled, pitted and cubed
- 2 scallions, chopped
- Juice of 1 lime
- 1 tablespoon olive oil
- A pinch of salt and black pepper
- 1 teaspoon ginger powder
- ½ teaspoon basil, dried
- 1 tablespoon cilantro, chopped

Directions:
In a sous vide bag, mix the salmon with the avocado, scallions and the other ingredients, seal and cook in the water oven at 176 degrees F for 25 minutes. Divide the mix into bowls and serve.

Nutrition: calories 232, fat 10, fiber 4, carbs 6, protein 9

Shrimp and Corn

Preparation time: 10 minutes | Cooking time: 20 minutes | Servings: 4

Ingredients:
- 1 pound shrimp, peeled and deveined
- 1 cup corn
- 3 scallions, minced
- ½ teaspoon garam masala
- 1 tablespoon olive oil
- 1 tablespoon lemon juice
- 1 tablespoon chives, chopped
- Salt and black pepper to the taste

Directions:
In a sous vide bag, mix the shrimp with the corn and the other ingredients, seal and cook in the water oven at 165 degrees F for 20 minutes. Divide the mix into between plates and serve.

Nutrition: calories 182, fat 7, fiber 3, carbs 6, protein 9

Lemon Cod and Peas

Preparation time: 5 minutes | Cooking time: 30 minutes | Servings: 4

Ingredients:
- 1 pound cod fillets, boneless
- 1 cup peas
- 1 tablespoon avocado oil
- 2 spring onions, chopped
- ½ teaspoon red pepper flakes, crushed
- ½ tablespoon lemon juice
- 1 tablespoon lemon zest, grated
- 1 tablespoon chives, chopped
- A pinch of salt and black pepper

Directions:
In a sous vide bag, mix the cod with the peas and the other ingredients, seal the bag and cook in the water oven at 180 degrees F for 30 minutes. Divide between plates and serve.

Nutrition: calories 210, fat 8, fiber 3, carbs 6, protein 14

Ginger Cod

Preparation time: 5 minutes | Cooking time: 30 minutes | Servings: 4

Ingredients:
- 1 pound cod fillets, boneless
- Juice of 1 lime
- 1 tablespoon ginger, grated
- 1 red onion, chopped
- ½ teaspoon turmeric powder
- 2 tablespoons avocado oil
- Salt and black pepper to the taste
- 1 tablespoon chives, chopped

Directions:
In a sous vide bag, mix the cod with the lime juice and the other ingredients, seal the bag and cook in the water oven at 180 degrees F for 30 minutes. Divide between plates and serve.

Nutrition: calories 200, fat 12, fiber 3, carbs 6, protein 11

Salmon and Olives

Preparation time: 5 minutes | Cooking time: 30 minutes | Servings: 4

Ingredients:
- 1 pound salmon fillets, boneless
- 1 cup kalamata olives, pitted and halved
- ½ teaspoon rosemary, dried
- ¼ cup tomato passata
- 2 garlic cloves, minced
- 1 tablespoon olive oil
- Salt and black pepper to the taste

Directions:
In a sous vide bag, mix the salmon with the olives, rosemary and the other ingredients, seal the bag and cook in the water oven at 170 degrees F for 30 minutes. Divide everything between plates and serve.

Nutrition: calories 132, fat 9, fiber 2, carbs 5, protein 11

Curry Shrimp

Preparation time: 10 minutes | Cooking time: 25 minutes | Servings: 4

Ingredients:
- 1 pound shrimp, peeled and deveined
- 2 scallions, chopped
- 2 tablespoons avocado oil
- ½ cup coconut cream
- 1 tablespoon yellow curry paste
- A pinch of salt and black pepper
- 2 tablespoons cilantro, chopped

Directions:
In a sous vide bag, mix the shrimp with the scallions and the other ingredients, seal and cook in the water oven at 165 degrees F for 25 minutes. Divide the mix into bowls and serve.

Nutrition: calories 200, fat 12, fiber 2, carbs 6, protein 11

Chives Shrimp Mix

Preparation time: 5 minutes | Cooking time: 20 minutes | Servings: 4

Ingredients:
- 2 pounds shrimp, peeled and deveined
- 2 tablespoons chives, chopped
- 1 cup white wine
- 2 tablespoons olive oil
- Juice of 1 lime
- 1 teaspoon sweet paprika
- Salt and black pepper to the taste

Directions:
In a sous vide bag, mix the shrimp with the wine and the other ingredients, seal the bag and cook in the water oven at 170 degrees F for 20 minutes. Divide the mix into bowls and serve.

Nutrition: calories 200, fat 12, fiber 2, carbs 6, protein 9

Pesto Sea Bass

Preparation time: 10 minutes | Cooking time: 35 minutes | Servings: 4

Ingredients:
- 1 pound sea bass fillets, boneless and roughly cubed
- 2 tablespoons basil pesto
- 1 tablespoon olive oil
- Juice of 1 lime
- ½ teaspoon turmeric powder
- ½ teaspoon chili powder
- 1 tablespoon chives, chopped
- A pinch of salt and black pepper

Directions:
In a sous vide bag, mix the fish with the pesto and the other ingredients, seal the bag and cook in the water oven at 180 degrees F for 35 minutes. Divide the mix between plates and serve.

Nutrition: calories 211, fat 13, fiber 2, carbs 7, protein 11

Shrimp and Pineapple Bowls

Preparation time: 5 minutes | Cooking time: 20 minutes | Servings: 4

Ingredients:
- 1 pound shrimp, peeled and deveined
- 1 tablespoon olive oil
- Juice of ½ lemon
- 1 cup pineapple, peeled and cubed
- 1 red chili pepper, chopped
- 2 scallions, chopped
- 2 tablespoons chives, chopped
- A pinch of salt and black pepper

Directions:
In a sous vide bag, mix the shrimp with the oil, lemon juice and the other ingredients, seal the bag, submerge in the water oven and cook at 170 degrees F for 20 minutes. Divide the mix into bowls and serve.

Nutrition: calories 200, fat 12, fiber 4, carbs 6, protein 8

Garlic Sea Bass

***Preparation time:** 5 minutes | **Cooking time:** 35 minutes | **Servings:** 4*

Ingredients:

- 1 pound sea bass fillets, boneless
- 4 garlic cloves, minced
- 1 tablespoon lime zest, grated
- 1 tablespoon lime juice
- 2 tablespoons olive oil
- ½ teaspoon sweet paprika
- ½ teaspoon rosemary, dried
- A pinch of salt and black pepper
- 1 tablespoon cilantro, chopped

Directions:

In 4 sous vide bags, mix the sea bass fillets with the garlic, lime juice and the other ingredients, seal them, submerge in the water oven and cook at 180 degrees F for 30 minutes. Divide the mix between plates and serve with a side salad.

Nutrition: calories 232, fat 7, fiber 3, carbs 7, protein 9

Shrimp and Broccoli

***Preparation time:** 5 minutes | **Cooking time:** 25 minutes | **Servings:** 4*

Ingredients:

- 2 pounds shrimp, peeled and deveined
- 1 cup broccoli florets
- Juice of ½ lemon
- 2 tablespoons balsamic vinegar
- 1 red onion, chopped
- 2 tablespoons avocado oil
- A pinch of salt and black pepper
- 1 tablespoon cilantro, chopped

Directions:

In a large sous vide bag, mix the shrimp with the broccoli, lemon juice and the other ingredients, toss, seal the bag and cook in the water oven at 170 degrees F for 25 minutes. Divide the mix between plates and serve.

Nutrition: calories 232, fat 9, fiber 2, carbs 6, protein 8

Tuna and Brussels Sprouts

***Preparation time:** 10 minutes | **Cooking time:** 30 minutes | **Servings:** 4*

Ingredients:

- 1 pound tuna fillets, boneless and roughly cubed
- 1 cup Brussels sprouts, trimmed and halved
- 1 tablespoon lime juice
- 1 tablespoon soy sauce
- 1 tablespoon balsamic vinegar
- 3 scallions, chopped
- 1 tablespoon olive oil
- ½ teaspoon sweet paprika
- ½ teaspoon chili powder
- A pinch of salt and black pepper
- 1 tablespoon chives, chopped

Directions:

In a large sous vide bag, mix the tuna with the sprouts, lime juice and the other ingredients, seal the bag and cook in the water oven at 180 degrees F for 30 minutes. Divide the mix between plates and serve.

Nutrition: calories 200, fat 13, fiber 3, carbs 6, protein 11

Mackerel and Avocado Mix

Preparation time: 5 minutes | Cooking time: 30 minutes | Servings: 4

Ingredients:

- 1 pound mackerel fillets, boneless
- 1 cup avocado, peeled, pitted and cubed
- 3 scallions, minced
- Juice of 1 lime
- 1 tablespoon avocado oil
- 1 tablespoon balsamic vinegar
- ½ teaspoon turmeric powder
- A pinch of salt and black pepper
- 1 tablespoon chives, chopped

Directions:

In a sous vide bag, mix the mackerel with the avocado, scallions and the other ingredients, seal the bag and cook in the water oven at 180 degrees F for 30 minutes. Divide the mix between plates and serve.

Nutrition: calories 200, fat 12, fiber 2, carbs 6, protein 9

Tuna and Asparagus

Preparation time: 10 minutes | Cooking time: 25 minutes | Servings: 4

Ingredients:

- 1 pound tuna fillets, boneless
- ¼ pound asparagus spears, trimmed
- ½ cup white wine
- 1 tablespoon avocado oil
- 1 tablespoon lime juice
- A pinch of salt and black pepper
- 2 tablespoons chives, chopped

Directions:

Divide the tuna, asparagus and the other ingredients in 4 sous vide bags, seal and submerge them in the water oven. Cook at 180 degrees F for 25 minutes, divide the whole mix between plates and serve.

Nutrition: calories 200, fat 12, fiber 2, carbs 5, protein 6

Cod and Carrots

Preparation time: 10 minutes | Cooking time: 35 minutes | Servings: 4

Ingredients:

- 1 tablespoon olive oil
- 1 pound cod fillets, boneless and cubed
- 2 cups baby carrots, peeled
- 1 teaspoon lemon juice
- 1 tablespoon cilantro, chopped
- ½ teaspoon sweet paprika
- ½ teaspoon chili powder
- A pinch of salt and black pepper

Directions:

In a large sous vide bag, mix the cod with the oil, carrots and the other ingredients, seal and submerge it in the water oven. Cook at 180 degrees F for 35 minutes, divide the mix between plates and serve.

Nutrition: calories 192, fat 9, fiber 2, carbs 8, protein 7

Chili Cod

Preparation time: 10 minutes | Cooking time: 35 minutes | Servings: 4

Ingredients:

- 1 pound cod fillets, skinless, boneless and cubed
- 1 red chili pepper, chopped
- 1 teaspoon chili powder
- 1 red onion, chopped
- 1 tablespoon lime juice
- ½ teaspoon rosemary, dried
- 1 tablespoon olive oil
- ½ cup chicken stock
- A pinch of salt and black pepper
- 1 tablespoon chives, chopped

Directions:

In a large sous vide bag, mix the cod with the chili pepper, chili powder and the other ingredients, seal the bag and cook in the water oven at 180 degrees F for 35 minutes Divide the mix between plates and serve.

Nutrition: calories 210, fat 9, fiber 2, carbs 6, protein 7

Balsamic Salmon and Beans

Preparation time: 5 minutes | Cooking time: 35 minutes | Servings: 4

Ingredients:

- 4 salmon fillets, boneless and cubed
- 1 cup canned black beans, drained and rinsed
- 3 garlic cloves, minced
- 1 tablespoon avocado oil
- Juice of 1 lime
- 2 tablespoons balsamic vinegar
- 2 tablespoons parsley, chopped
- A pinch of salt and black pepper

Directions:

In a sous vide bag, mix the salmon with the black beans, garlic and the other ingredients, seal the bag, submerge in the water oven and cook at 180 degrees F for 35 minutes. Divide the mix between plates and serve.

Nutrition: calories 200, fat 10, fiber 2, carbs 5, protein 9

Lemon Trout and Cabbage

Preparation time: 10 minutes | Cooking time: 35 minutes | Servings: 4

Ingredients:

- 1 pound trout fillets, boneless
- 1 cup red cabbage, shredded
- 1 tablespoon soy sauce
- 3 scallions, minced
- 2 tablespoons avocado oil
- 2 tablespoons lemon juice
- 1 teaspoon lemon zest, grated
- 1 tablespoon chives, chopped
- A pinch of salt and black pepper

Directions:

In a large sous vide bag, mix the trout with the cabbage, soy sauce and the other ingredients, seal, submerge the bag and cook in the water oven at 180 degrees F for 35 minutes. Divide everything between plates and serve.

Nutrition: calories 200, fat 13, fiber 3, carbs 6, protein 11

Lime and Chili Mussels

Preparation time: 10 minutes | *Cooking time:* 40 minutes | *Servings:* 4

Ingredients:
- 1 pound mussels, scrubbed
- 1 tablespoon olive oil
- Juice of 1 lime
- 2 red chilies, minced
- 1 teaspoon turmeric powder
- ½ cup white wine
- A pinch of salt and black pepper

Directions:
In a sous vide bag, combine the mussels with the oil, lime juice and the other ingredients, seal the bag, submerge in preheated water bath and cook at 170 degrees F for 40 minutes. Divide the mussels into bowls and serve.

Nutrition: calories 198, fat 7, fiber 2, carbs 6, protein 7

Chives Cod

Preparation time: 10 minutes | *Cooking time:* 40 minutes | *Servings:* 4

Ingredients:
- 1 tablespoon avocado oil
- 1 pound cod fillets, boneless
- 2 tablespoons chives, chopped
- 2 garlic cloves, minced
- ¼ cup white wine
- A pinch of salt and black pepper

Directions:
In a sous vide bag, mix the cod with the oil and the other ingredients, seal the bag, submerge in the water bath and cook at 180 degrees F for 40 minutes. Divide between plates and serve with a side salad.

Nutrition: calories 221, fat 8, fiber 3, carbs 6, protein 7

Tuna Bites with Pineapple

Preparation time: 5 minutes | *Cooking time:* 40 minutes | *Servings:* 4

Ingredients:
- 1 pounds tuna fillets, boneless, skinless and cubed
- 1 cup pineapple, peeled and cubed
- 1 tablespoon avocado oil
- Juice of 1 lime
- 3 garlic cloves, crushed
- 1 tablespoon chives, chopped
- A pinch of salt and black pepper

Directions:
In a sous vide bag, mix the tuna bites with the pineapple, oil and the other ingredients, seal the bag, submerge in the water bath and cook at 180 degrees F for 40 minutes Divide between plates and serve.

Nutrition: calories 235, fat 8, fiber 4, carbs 7, protein 9

Sea Bass and Avocado

Preparation time: 10 minutes | *Cooking time:* 40 minutes | *Servings:* 4

Ingredients:
- 1 tablespoon olive oil
- 1 pound sea bass fillets, boneless
- 1 cup avocado, peeled, pitted and cubed
- Juice of 1 lime
- ½ teaspoon rosemary, dried
- ½ teaspoon turmeric powder
- 1 teaspoon sweet paprika
- A pinch of salt and black pepper

Directions:
In a sous vide bag, mix the sea bass with the oil, avocado and the other ingredients, seal the bag and cook in the water bath for 40 minutes at 180 degrees F Divide everything between plates and serve.

Nutrition: calories 211, fat 8, fiber 4, carbs 8, protein 8

Smoked Salmon and Chives

Preparation time: 10 minutes | Cooking time: 20 minutes | Servings: 4

Ingredients:
- 1 pound smoked salmon fillets, boneless
- 1 tablespoon olive oil
- 1 cup baby spinach
- 1 tablespoon chives, chopped
- ¼ cup lime juice
- 2 scallions, chopped
- 1 tablespoon smoked paprika
- A pinch of salt and black pepper

Directions:

In a sous vide bag, mix the smoked salmon with the oil, spinach and the other ingredients, seal the bag, submerge in the water bath and cook at 180 degrees F for 20 minutes. Transfer the mix to bowls and serve.

Nutrition: calories 193, fat 7, fiber 3, carbs 6, protein 6

Shrimp and Eggplant

Preparation time: 5 minutes | Cooking time: 20 minutes | Servings: 4

Ingredients:
- 1 pound shrimp, peeled and deveined
- 1 tablespoon avocado oil
- 2 eggplants, cubed
- 1 red onion, chopped
- 4 garlic cloves, minced
- 1 tablespoon chives, chopped
- A pinch of salt and black pepper

Directions:

In a sous vide bag, mix the shrimp with the eggplant, oil and the other ingredients, seal the bag, submerge in preheated water bath and cook at 170 degrees F for 20 minutes. Divide the mix into bowls and serve.

Nutrition: calories 200, fat 11, fiber 4, carbs 5, protein 12

Garlic Mackerel

Preparation time: 10 minutes | Cooking time: 30 minutes | Servings: 4

Ingredients:
- 1 pound mackerel fillets, boneless
- 4 garlic cloves, minced
- 1 tablespoon avocado oil
- ½ teaspoon turmeric powder
- ½ teaspoon garam masala
- Juice of ½ lemon
- 1 tablespoon chives, chopped

Directions:

In a sous vide bag, mix the mackerel with the garlic, oil and the other ingredients, seal the bag, submerge in the water bath and cook at 180 degrees F for 30 minutes. Divide between plates and serve with a side salad.

Nutrition: calories 200, fat 12, fiber 3, carbs 7, protein 9

Coconut Cod

Preparation time: 5 minutes | Cooking time: 40 minutes | Servings: 4

Ingredients:
- 1 pound cod fillets, boneless, skinless and cubed
- 1 tablespoon olive oil
- 1 cup coconut cream
- ½ teaspoon turmeric powder
- ½ teaspoon cumin, ground
- A pinch of salt and black pepper
- 1 tablespoon chives, chopped

Directions:

Divide the cod, oil, cream and the other ingredients in 2 sous vide bags, seal, submerge them in the water bath and cook at 180 degrees F for 40 minutes. Divide into bowls and serve.

Nutrition: calories 232, fat 10, fiber 4, carbs 6, protein 9

Shrimp and Peas

Preparation time: 10 minutes | Cooking time: 20 minutes | Servings: 4

Ingredients:
- 1 pound shrimp, peeled and deveined
- 1 tablespoon olive oil
- 1 cup fresh peas
- ¼ cup lemon juice
- 1 tablespoon lemon zest, grated
- ½ teaspoon oregano, dried
- 1 teaspoon chili powder
- Salt and black pepper to the taste

Directions:
In a sous vide bag, mix the shrimp with the oil, peas and the other ingredients, seal and cook at 180 degrees F for 20 minutes. Divide the mix into bowls and serve.

Nutrition: calories 182, fat 7, fiber 3, carbs 6, protein 9

Italian Mackerel

Preparation time: 10 minutes | Cooking time: 35 minutes | Servings: 4

Ingredients:
- 1 pound mackerel fillets, boneless
- 4 spring onions, chopped
- 1 tablespoon Italian seasoning
- Juice of 1 lime
- 2 green chilies, chopped
- A pinch of salt and black pepper
- 1 tablespoon rosemary, chopped

Directions:
In a sous vide bag, mix the mackerel with the spring onions, seasoning and the other ingredients, seal the bag and cook in the water bath at 180 degrees F for 35 minutes. Divide the mix between plates and serve.

Nutrition: calories 210, fat 8, fiber 3, carbs 6, protein 14

Honey Cod

Preparation time: 5 minutes | Cooking time: 30 minutes | Servings: 4

Ingredients:
- 1 pound cod fillets, boneless
- 2 tablespoons olive oil
- ½ teaspoon coriander, ground
- 1 tablespoon balsamic vinegar
- 2 tablespoons honey
- Salt and black pepper to the taste
- Juice of 1 lime
- 1 tablespoon chives, chopped

Directions:
In a sous vide bag, mix the cod with the oil, honey, coriander and the other ingredients, seal the bag, submerge in the water bath and cook at 175 degrees F for 30 minutes. Divide the mix into bowls and serve.

Nutrition: calories 200, fat 12, fiber 3, carbs 6, protein 11

Basil Shrimp

Preparation time: 5 minutes | Cooking time: 20 minutes | Servings: 4

Ingredients:
- 1 pound shrimp, peeled and deveined
- Juice of 1 lemon
- 1 tablespoon basil, chopped
- 1 tablespoon olive oil
- ½ teaspoon rosemary, dried
- ½ teaspoon cumin, ground
- 2 garlic cloves, minced
- Salt and black pepper to the taste

Directions:
In a sous vide bag, mix the shrimp with the lemon juice and the other ingredients, seal the bag, submerge in the water bath and cook at 180 degrees F for 20 minutes. Divide everything between plates and serve.

Nutrition: calories 132, fat 9, fiber 2, carbs 5, protein 11

Curry Sea Bass

Preparation time: 10 minutes | Cooking time: 40 minutes | Servings: 4

Ingredients:

- 1 pound sea bass fillets, boneless
- 1 tablespoon olive oil
- ½ teaspoon rosemary, dried
- Juice of 1 lime
- ½ teaspoon curry powder
- 1 red onion, chopped
- A pinch of salt and black pepper
- 2 tablespoons cilantro, chopped

Directions:

In a sous vide bag, mix the sea bass with the oil and the other ingredients, seal the bag, submerge in the water bath and cook at 180 degrees F for 40 minutes. Divide the mix between plates and serve with a side salad.

Nutrition: calories 200, fat 12, fiber 2, carbs 6, protein 11

Calamari and Mushrooms

Preparation time: 10 minutes | Cooking time: 35 minutes | Servings: 4

Ingredients:

- 1 pound calamari rings
- 1 cup brown mushrooms, halved
- 4 scallions, minced
- ½ cup white wine
- 2 tablespoons avocado oil
- Juice of 1 lime
- 1 tablespoon rosemary, dried
- Salt and black pepper to the taste
- 1 tablespoon parsley, chopped

Directions:

In a sous vide bag, mix the calamari with the mushrooms, scallions and the other ingredients, seal the bag, submerge in the water bath and cook at 180 degrees F for 35 minutes. Divide the mix between plates and serve.

Nutrition: calories 200, fat 12, fiber 2, carbs 6, protein 9

Curry Trout and Green Beans

Preparation time: 10 minutes | Cooking time: 35 minutes | Servings: 4

Ingredients:

- 4 trout fillets, boneless
- ½ pound green beans, trimmed and halved
- 1 tablespoon green curry paste
- 1 cup coconut cream
- 1 tablespoon avocado oil
- ½ teaspoon basil, dried
- ½ teaspoon curry powder
- A pinch of salt and black pepper

Directions:

In a sous vide bag, mix the trout with the green beans, curry paste and the other ingredients, seal the bag, submerge in the water bath and cook at 180 degrees F for 35 minutes. Divide the whole mix between plates and serve.

Nutrition: calories 211, fat 13, fiber 2, carbs 7, protein 11

Coriander Shrimp Mix

Preparation time: 5 minutes | Cooking time: 20 minutes | Servings: 4

Ingredients:

- 1 pound shrimp, peeled and deveined
- Juice of 1 lime
- 1 tablespoon olive oil
- ½ cup white wine
- ½ teaspoon turmeric powder
- 2 tablespoons coriander, chopped
- A pinch of salt and black pepper

Directions:

In a sous vide bag, mix the shrimp with the oil, lime juice and the other ingredients, seal the bag, submerge in the water bath and cook at 180 degrees F for 20 minutes. Divide the mix into bowls and serve.

Nutrition: calories 200, fat 12, fiber 4, carbs 6, protein 8

Shrimp and Mustard Sauce

Preparation time: 5 minutes | Cooking time: 20 minutes | Servings: 4

Ingredients:
- 1 pound shrimp, peeled and deveined
- 1 tablespoon mustard
- 1 cup heavy cream
- ½ teaspoon garam masala
- 1 tablespoon lime zest, grated
- ½ teaspoon rosemary, dried
- A pinch of salt and black pepper
- 1 tablespoon cilantro, chopped

Directions:
In a sous vide bag, mix the shrimp with the mustard, heavy cream and the other ingredients, seal the bag and cook in the water bath and cook at 175 degrees F for 25 minutes. Divide the mix into bowls and serve.

Nutrition: calories 232, fat 7, fiber 3, carbs 7, protein 9

Shrimp and Quinoa

Preparation time: 5 minutes | Cooking time: 20 minutes | Servings: 4

Ingredients:
- 1 pound shrimp, peeled and deveined
- 1 cup quinoa, cooked
- ½ cup lemon juice
- ½ teaspoon turmeric powder
- 1 tablespoon capers, drained
- ½ cup tomatoes, cubed
- 1 tablespoon olive oil
- 1 red onion, chopped
- ½ teaspoon sweet paprika
- A pinch of salt and black pepper
- 1 tablespoon cilantro, chopped

Directions:
In a sous vide bag, mix the shrimp with the quinoa, lemon juice and the other ingredients, seal the bag, submerge in the water bath and cook at 180 degrees F for 20 minutes. Divide into bowls and serve.

Nutrition: calories 232, fat 9, fiber 2, carbs 6, protein 8

Shrimp and Rice

Preparation time: 5 minutes | Cooking time: 30 minutes | Servings: 4

Ingredients:
- 1 pound shrimp, peeled and deveined
- 1 cup wild rice
- 1 cup chicken stock
- 1 tablespoon lime zest, grated
- 1 cup baby spinach
- 1 red onion, sliced
- 1 tablespoon olive oil
- ½ teaspoon sweet paprika
- A pinch of salt and black pepper
- 1 tablespoon chives, chopped

Directions:
In a sous vide bag, mix the shrimp with the rice, stock and the other ingredients, seal the bag, submerge in the water bath and cook at 180 degrees F for 30 minutes. Divide the mix into bowls and serve.

Nutrition: calories 200, fat 13, fiber 3, carbs 6, protein 11

Parsley Cod

Preparation time: 5 minutes | Cooking time: 30 minutes | Servings: 4

Ingredients:
- 1 pound cod fillets, boneless
- 1 tablespoon capers, drained
- 1 tablespoon parsley, chopped
- 1 cup heavy cream
- ½ teaspoon turmeric powder
- Juice of 1 lime
- 1 tablespoon olive oil
- ½ teaspoon garam masala
- A pinch of salt and black pepper

Directions:
In a sous vide bag, mix the cod with the capers, parsley and the other ingredients, toss gently, seal the bag, and cook in the water bath at 180 degrees F for 30 minutes. Divide between plates and serve.

Nutrition: calories 200, fat 12, fiber 2, carbs 6, protein 9

Cod, Olives and Zucchinis

Preparation time: 10 minutes | Cooking time: 30 minutes | Servings: 4

Ingredients:
- 1 pound cod fillets, boneless and roughly cubed
- 1 cup black olives, pitted and halved
- 2 zucchinis, cubed
- 2 tablespoons olive oil
- 3 spring onions, chopped
- ¼ cup chicken stock
- 1 tablespoon lime juice
- ½ teaspoon sweet paprika
- A pinch of salt and black pepper
- 2 tablespoons chives, chopped

Directions:
Divide the cod, olives, zucchinis and the other ingredients between 2 sous vide bags, seal them and cook in the water bath at 180 degrees F for 30 minutes. Divide between plates and serve.

Nutrition: calories 200, fat 12, fiber 2, carbs 5, protein 6

Creamy Salmon Mix

Preparation time: 5 minutes | Cooking time: 30 minutes | Servings: 4

Ingredients:
- 1 pound salmon fillets, boneless and roughly cubed
- 1 cup heavy cream
- 1 tablespoon lime juice
- 1 tablespoon lime zest, grated
- 1 yellow onion, chopped
- ½ teaspoon turmeric powder
- ½ teaspoon chili powder
- A pinch of salt and black pepper
- 1 tablespoon chives, chopped

Directions:
In a big sous vide bag, mix the salmon with the cream, lime juice and the other ingredients, seal the bag and cook in the water bath at 175 degrees F for 30 minutes Divide the mix into bowls and serve.

Nutrition: calories 210, fat 9, fiber 2, carbs 6, protein 7

Trout and Capers Mix

Preparation time: 10 minutes | Cooking time: 30 minutes | Servings: 4

Ingredients:
- 1 pound trout fillets, boneless
- 2 tablespoons capers, drained
- 1 red onion, sliced
- 1 tablespoon olive oil
- ½ cup white wine
- Juice of 1 lime
- 2 tablespoons chives, chopped
- ½ teaspoon chili powder
- A pinch of salt and black pepper

Directions:
In a large sous vide bag, mix the trout fillets with the capers, onion and the other ingredients, seal the bag and cook in the water bath at 175 degrees F for 30 minutes Divide the mix between plates and serve.

Nutrition: calories 200, fat 10, fiber 2, carbs 5, protein 9

Balsamic Sea Bass

Preparation time: 5 minutes | Cooking time: 30 minutes | Servings: 4

Ingredients:
- 1 pound sea bass fillets, boneless
- 2 tablespoons balsamic vinegar
- 1 cup kalamata olives, pitted and halved
- 2 tablespoons olive oil
- 2 tablespoons garlic, minced
- A pinch of salt and black pepper

Directions:
In a sous vide bag, mix the sea bass with the vinegar, olives and the other ingredients, seal the bag, submerge in the water bath and cook at 180 degrees F for 30 minutes. Divide everything between plates and serve.

Nutrition: calories 200, fat 13, fiber 3, carbs 6, protein 11

Creole Calamari

Preparation time: 5 minutes | Cooking time: 35 minutes | Servings: 4

Ingredients:
- 1 pound calamari rings
- ½ cup white wine
- 2 tablespoons avocado oil
- 1 tablespoon lime juice
- 1 tablespoon Creole seasoning
- ½ teaspoon chili powder
- 1 tablespoon chives, chopped

Directions:
In a sous vide bag, mix the calamari rings with the wine, oil and the other ingredients, seal the bag, submerge in the water bath and cook at 190 degrees F for 35 minutes. Divide the mix into bowls and serve.

Nutrition: calories 211, fat 12, fiber 3, carbs 6, protein 7

Clams and Wine Sauce

Preparation time: 10 minutes | Cooking time: 25 minutes | Servings: 4

Ingredients:
- 1 pound clams, scrubbed
- ½ cup white wine
- Juice of ½ lemon
- Zest of 1 lemon, grated
- A pinch of salt and black pepper
- 1 tablespoon chives, chopped

Directions:
In a sous vide bag, mix the clams with the wine, lemon juice and the other ingredients, seal the bag and cook in the water bath at 175 degrees F for 25 minutes. Divide the mix into bowls and serve.

Nutrition: calories 198, fat 7, fiber 2, carbs 6, protein 7

Tarragon Trout

***Preparation time:** 10 minutes | **Cooking time:** 30 minutes | **Servings:** 4*

Ingredients:
- 1 tablespoon avocado oil
- 1 pound trout fillets, boneless
- ½ teaspoon chili powder
- 1 tablespoon tarragon, chopped
- ½ cup chicken stock
- A pinch of salt and black pepper
- Juice of ½ lemon

Directions:
In a large sous vide bag, mix the trout with the oil, chili powder and the other ingredients, seal the bag and cook in the water bath at 180 degrees F for 30 minutes Divide the mix between plates and serve.

Nutrition: calories 221, fat 8, fiber 3, carbs 6, protein 7

Shrimp, Corn and Tomato Bowls

***Preparation time:** 5 minutes | **Cooking time:** 20 minutes | **Servings:** 4*

Ingredients:
- 1 pounds shrimp, peeled and deveined
- 1 cup corn
- 1 cup cherry tomatoes, halved
- Juice of 1 lime
- 1 tablespoon olive oil
- ½ teaspoon rosemary, dried
- 3 garlic cloves, crushed
- 2 tablespoons chives, chopped
- ½ cup chicken stock
- A pinch of salt and black pepper

Directions:
In a large sous vide bag, mix the shrimp with the corn, tomatoes and the other ingredients, seal the bag and cook in the water bath at 175 degrees F for 20 minutes Divide into bowls and serve.

Nutrition: calories 235, fat 8, fiber 4, carbs 7, protein 9

Shrimp, Crab and Avocado Bowls

***Preparation time:** 10 minutes | **Cooking time:** 20 minutes | **Servings:** 4*

Ingredients:
- 1 tablespoon olive oil
- 1 cup crab meat
- 1 pound shrimp, peeled and deveined
- 1 cup avocado, peeled, pitted and cubed
- Juice of 1 lime
- 1 tablespoon lime zest, grated
- ½ teaspoon chili powder
- 1 cup chicken stock
- 1 teaspoon sweet paprika
- A pinch of salt and black pepper

Directions:
In a sous vide bag, mix the crab with the shrimp and the other ingredients, seal the bag and cook in the water bath at 180 degrees F for 20 minutes. Divide everything into bowls and serve.

Nutrition: calories 211, fat 8, fiber 4, carbs 8, protein 8

Salmon and Kale

Preparation time: 10 minutes | *Cooking time:* 30 minutes | *Servings:* 4

Ingredients:
- 1 pound salmon fillets, boneless and cubed
- 1 cup baby kale
- Juice of 1 lime
- 2 tablespoons avocado oil
- 1 tablespoon smoked paprika
- A pinch of salt and black pepper
- 2 garlic cloves, minced
- 1 tablespoon cilantro, chopped

Directions:
In a sous vide bag, mix the salmon with the kale and the other ingredients, seal the bag and cook in the water bath at 180 degrees F for 30 minutes. Transfer the mix to bowls and serve.

Nutrition: calories 193, fat 7, fiber 3, carbs 6, protein 6

Rosemary Calamari

Preparation time: 5 minutes | *Cooking time:* 30 minutes | *Servings:* 4

Ingredients:
- 1 pound calamari rings
- Juice of 1 lime
- ½ teaspoon chili powder
- 1 tablespoon rosemary, chopped
- ½ cup red wine
- 1 red onion, chopped
- 4 garlic cloves, minced
- A pinch of salt and black pepper

Directions:
In a sous vide bag, mix the calamari with the lime juice and the other ingredients, seal the bag and cook in the water bath at 180 degrees F for 30 minutes. Divide into bowls and serve.

Nutrition: calories 200, fat 11, fiber 4, carbs 5, protein 12

Salmon and Sweet Potatoes

Preparation time: 10 minutes | *Cooking time:* 30 minutes | *Servings:* 4

Ingredients:
- 1 pound salmon fillets, boneless
- 1 cup chicken stock
- ½ teaspoon garam masala
- ½ teaspoon sweet paprika
- 2 sweet potatoes, peeled and cubed
- 2 spring onions, chopped
- 2 tablespoons olive oil
- 1 tablespoon chives, chopped

Directions:
In a large sous vide bag, mix the salmon with the stock, garam masala and the other ingredients, seal the bag and cook in the water bath at 180 degrees F for 30 minutes. Divide the mix into bowls and serve.

Nutrition: calories 200, fat 12, fiber 3, carbs 7, protein 9

Creamy Cod and Zucchinis

Preparation time: 5 minutes | *Cooking time:* 30 minutes | *Servings:* 4

Ingredients:
- 1 pound cod fillets, boneless, skinless and cubed
- 2 zucchinis, cubed
- 1 tablespoon olive oil
- 1 cup heavy cream
- A pinch of salt and black pepper
- ½ teaspoon turmeric powder
- 1 tablespoon cilantro, chopped

Directions:
In a sous vide bag, mix the cod with the zucchinis and the other ingredients, seal the bag and cook in the water bath at 180 degrees F for 30 minutes. Divide the mix into bowls and serve.

Nutrition: calories 232, fat 10, fiber 4, carbs 6, protein 9

Salmon with Quinoa and Rice

***Preparation time:** 6 minutes | **Cooking time:** 30 minutes | **Servings:** 4*

Ingredients:

- 1 pound smoked salmon, skinless and flaked
- 1 cup quinoa, cooked
- 1 cup corn
- 1 cup chicken stock
- 1 tablespoon olive oil
- 2 spring onions, chopped
- 1 tablespoon olive oil
- ½ teaspoon rosemary, dried
- 1 teaspoon sweet paprika
- Salt and black pepper to the taste

Directions:

In a large sous vide bag, mix the salmon with the corn, quinoa and the other ingredients, seal the bag and cook in the water bath at 176 degrees F for 30 minutes. Divide the mix into bowls and serve right away.

Nutrition: calories 182, fat 7, fiber 3, carbs 6, protein 9

Lemon Sea Bass and Olives

***Preparation time:** 10 minutes | **Cooking time:** 30 minutes | **Servings:** 4*

Ingredients:

- 1 pound sea bass fillets, skinless, boneless and cubed
- 2 spring onions, chopped
- 1 cup kalamata olives, pitted and halved
- 1 cup green olives, pitted and halved
- 2 tablespoons olive oil
- ¼ cup white wine
- 2 green chilies, chopped
- ½ tablespoon lemon juice
- 1 tablespoon coriander, chopped
- A pinch of salt and black pepper

Directions:

In a large sous vide bag, mix the sea bass with the spring onions, olives and the other ingredients, seal the bag, submerge in the water bath and cook at 180 degrees F for 30 minutes. Divide everything between plates and serve.

Nutrition: calories 210, fat 8, fiber 3, carbs 6, protein 14

Sous Vide Poultry Recipes

Lime Duck and Eggplant Mix

Preparation time: 10 minutes | Cooking time: 1 hour | Servings: 4

Ingredients:
- 2 pounds duck breast, skinless, boneless and cubed
- 2 tablespoons olive oil
- 2 eggplants, cubed
- Juice of 1 lime
- Zest of 1 lime, grated
- 1 red onion, chopped
- 4 garlic cloves, minced
- 1 tablespoon chives, chopped
- A pinch of salt and black pepper

Directions:
In a large sous vide bag, mix the duck with the oil, eggplants and the other ingredients, seal the bag and cook in the water bath at 180 degrees F for 1 hour. Divide everything between plates and serve.

Nutrition: calories 263, fat 12, fiber 3, carbs 6, protein 14

Pesto Turkey

Preparation time: 10 minutes | Cooking time: 50 minutes | Servings: 4

Ingredients:
- 1 pound turkey breasts, skinless, boneless and cubed
- ½ cup chicken stock
- 1 tablespoon basil pesto
- 1 tablespoon lime juice
- 2 tablespoons olive oil
- 1 teaspoon chili powder
- A pinch of salt and black pepper
- 1 tablespoon chives, chopped

Directions:
In a large sous vide bag, mix the turkey with the stock, pesto and the other ingredients, seal the bag and cook in the water bath at 180 degrees F for 50 minutes. Divide everything between plates and serve.

Nutrition: calories 162, fat 8, fiber 2, carbs 5, protein 9

Mustard Chicken and Capers

Preparation time: 10 minutes | Cooking time: 50 minutes | Servings: 4

Ingredients:
1. 2 tablespoons avocado oil
2. 2 pounds chicken breasts, skinless, boneless and cut into strips
3. 1 tablespoon capers, drained
4. 3 scallions minced
5. 1 tablespoon mustard
6. 1 tablespoon lime zest, grated
7. Juice 1 lime
8. ¾ cup chicken stock
9. A pinch of salt and black pepper
10. 1 tablespoon parsley, chopped

Directions:
In a large sous vide bag, mix the chicken with the oil, capers and the other ingredients, seal the bag and cook in the water bath at 180 degrees F for 50 minutes Divide the mix between plates and serve.

Nutrition: calories 200, fat 9, fiber 2, carbs 5, protein 10

Orange Chicken Mix

Preparation time: 10 minutes | *Cooking time:* 2 hours | *Servings:* 4

Ingredients:
- 1 pound chicken breast, skinless, boneless and roughly cubed
- 1 cup orange, peeled and cut into segments
- 1 tablespoon avocado oil
- 1 cup orange juice
- 1 tablespoon chives, chopped
- A pinch of salt and black pepper

Directions:
In a large sous vide bag, mix the chicken with the orange, oil and the other ingredients, toss, seal the bag, submerge in the water bath and cook at 175 degrees F for 2 hours. Divide the mix into bowls and serve.

Nutrition: calories 200, fat 7, fiber 2, carbs 6, protein 11

Turkey with Sauce

Preparation time: 10 minutes | *Cooking time:* 1 hour | *Servings:* 4

Ingredients:
- 1 pound turkey breasts, skinless, boneless and cubed
- 1 tablespoon mustard
- 1 tablespoon lime zest, grated
- 1 cup heavy cream
- 1 tablespoon olive oil
- 1 red onion, sliced
- ½ teaspoon garam masala
- 1 red chili, minced
- 1 teaspoon sweet paprika
- ½ cup chives, chopped

Directions:
In a large sous vide bag, combine the turkey with the mustard, cream and the other ingredients, toss, seal the bag, submerge in the water bath, cook at 170 degrees F for 1 hour, divide the mix between plates and serve.

Nutrition: calories 210, fat 8, fiber 2, carbs 6, protein 11

Italian Turkey and Carrots

Preparation time: 10 minutes | *Cooking time:* 1 hour | *Servings:* 4

Ingredients:
- 1 pound turkey breast, skinless, boneless and roughly cubed
- ½ pound baby carrots, peeled
- 1 cup chicken stock
- 1 tablespoon avocado oil
- 1 teaspoon Italian seasoning
- ½ teaspoon rosemary, dried
- ½ teaspoon turmeric powder
- A pinch of salt and black pepper
- 1 tablespoon cilantro, chopped

Directions:
Divide the turkey, carrots, stock and the other ingredients into 4 sous vide bags and seal them. Submerge in the water bath, cook at 170 degrees F for 1 hour, divide between plates and serve.

Nutrition: calories 220, fat 8, fiber 2, carbs 5, protein 11

Chicken and Green Beans

Preparation time: 10 minutes | Cooking time: 1 hour | Servings: 4

Ingredients:

- 1 pound chicken breasts, skinless, boneless and cut into strips
- 2 cups green beans, trimmed and halved
- 1 teaspoon curry powder
- ½ teaspoon chili powder
- ½ teaspoon rosemary, dried
- 1 red onion, chopped
- 1 cup tomato passata
- 2 tablespoons olive oil
- Salt and black pepper to the taste
- 1 tablespoon cilantro, chopped

Directions:

Divide the chicken, green beans, curry powder and the other ingredients into 2 sous vide bags, seal them, submerge in the water bath, cook at 170 degrees F for 1 hour, divide the mix between plates and serve.

Nutrition: calories 192, fat 12, fiber 3, carbs 5, protein 12

Duck and Tomatoes

Preparation time: 10 minutes | Cooking time: 1 hour and 10 minutes | Servings: 4

Ingredients:

- 1 pound duck breasts, skinless, boneless and cubed
- 1 cup cherry tomatoes, halved
- ½ cup chicken stock
- Juice of 1 lime
- ½ teaspoon chili powder
- ½ teaspoon cumin, ground
- 2 tablespoons olive oil
- ½ teaspoon coriander, ground
- ½ teaspoon turmeric powder
- 1 tablespoon chives, chopped

Directions:

In a sous vide bag, mix the duck with the tomatoes, stock and the other ingredients, seal the bag and cook in the water bath at 170 degrees F for 1 hour and 10 minutes. Divide the mix between plates and serve.

Nutrition: calories 200, fat 7, fiber 1, carbs 5, protein 12

Garlic Chicken Mix

Preparation time: 10 minutes | Cooking time: 1 hour | Servings: 4

Ingredients:

- 1 pound chicken breast, skinless, boneless and cubed
- 1 tablespoon olive oil
- 4 garlic cloves, minced
- Juice of 1 lime
- ½ teaspoon coriander, ground
- 3 scallions, chopped
- A pinch of salt and black pepper
- 1 tablespoon parsley, chopped

Directions:

In a sous vide bag, mix the chicken with the oil, garlic and the other ingredients, seal the bag and cook in the water bath at 170 degrees F for 1 hour. Divide the mix between plates and serve.

Nutrition: calories 231, fat 7, fiber 2, carbs 6, protein 12

Chicken and Avocado

Preparation time: 10 minutes | Cooking time: 45 minutes | Servings: 4

Ingredients:
- 1 pound chicken breast, skinless, boneless and cubed
- 1 cup avocado, peeled, pitted and cubed
- 1 tablespoon olive oil
- Juice of 1 lime
- 2 scallions, chopped
- ½ teaspoon sweet paprika
- ½ teaspoon chili powder
- A pinch of salt and black pepper
- 1 tablespoon chives, chopped

Directions:
In a sous vide bag, mix the chicken with the avocado, oil and the other ingredients, seal the bag, submerge in the water bath and cook at 180 degrees F for 45 minutes. Divide everything between plates and serve.

Nutrition: calories 252, fat 12, fiber 4, carbs 7, protein 13

Turkey and Tomato Sauce

Preparation time: 10 minutes | Cooking time: 1 hour | Servings: 4

Ingredients:
- 1 pound turkey breasts, skinless, boneless and cubed
- 1 carrot, sliced
- 1 parsnip, sliced
- Juice of 1 lime
- 1 red onion, chopped
- 2 tablespoons olive oil
- A pinch of salt and black pepper
- 1 cup tomato passata
- 1 tablespoon chives, chopped

Directions:
In a sous vide bag, combine the turkey with the carrot, parsnip and the other ingredients, seal the bag, submerge into preheated water bath and cook at 175 degrees F for 1 hour. Divide everything between plates and serve.

Nutrition: calories 221, fat 14, fiber 3, carbs 7, protein 14

Turkey Medley

Preparation time: 10 minutes | Cooking time: 1 hour | Servings: 4

Ingredients:
- 1 pound turkey breast, skinless, boneless and cut into strips
- 1 tablespoon olive oil
- ½ cup white wine
- 2 scallions, chopped
- 1 cup black olives, pitted and halved
- 1 eggplant, cubed
- 1 cup green beans, trimmed and halved
- 2 tablespoons balsamic vinegar
- A handful cilantro, chopped
- A pinch of salt and black pepper

Directions:
In a large sous vide bag, combine the turkey with the oil, wine, scallions and the other ingredients, seal, submerge in the water oven and cook at 176 degrees F for 1 hour. Divide the mix between plates and serve.

Nutrition: calories 263, fat 14, fiber 1, carbs 8, protein 12

Chili Chicken

Preparation time: 10 minutes | Cooking time: 1 hour | Servings: 4

Ingredients:

- 1 pound chicken breast, skinless, boneless and cubed
- 2 green chilies, chopped
- Juice of 1 lime
- ½ teaspoon sweet paprika
- 2 tablespoons olive oil
- ½ cup chicken stock
- A pinch of salt and black pepper
- 1 tablespoon cilantro, chopped

Directions:

In a large sous vide bag, mix the chicken with the chilies, lime juice and the other ingredients, seal the bag and cook in the water oven at 175 degrees F for 1 hour. Divide everything between plates and serve.

Nutrition: calories 263, fat 12, fiber 3, carbs 6, protein 14

Chicken and Mango Mi

Preparation time: 10 minutes | Cooking time: 1 hour | Servings: 4

Ingredients:

- 1 pound chicken breast, skinless, boneless and sliced
- 1 cup mango, peeled and cubed
- 1 tablespoon olive oil
- Juice of 1 lime
- 1 teaspoon garam masala
- ½ teaspoon turmeric powder
- 1 tablespoon chives, chopped
- A pinch of salt and black pepper

Directions:

In a sous vide bag, mix the chicken with the mango, oil and the other ingredients, seal the bag, submerge in the water oven and cook at 190 degrees F for 1 hour. Divide the mix between plates and serve.

Nutrition: calories 253, fat 13, fiber 2, carbs 7, protein 16

Ginger Turkey

Preparation time: 10 minutes | Cooking time: 50 minutes | Servings: 4

Ingredients:

- 1 pound turkey breast, skinless, boneless and cubed
- 1 tablespoon ginger, grated
- 1 tablespoon balsamic vinegar
- Juice of ½ lime
- 3 scallions, chopped
- ¼ cup chives, chopped
- A pinch of salt and black pepper
- 1 tablespoon chives, chopped

Directions:

In a sous vide bag, mix the turkey with the ginger, vinegar and the other ingredients, seal the bag and cook in the water oven at 185 degrees F for 50 minutes. Divide everything between plates and serve.

Nutrition: calories 234, fat 14, fiber 4, carbs 7, protein 15

Turkey and Potatoes

Preparation time: 10 minutes | Cooking time: 1 hour | Servings: 4

Ingredients:
- 1 pound turkey breast, skinless, boneless and sliced
- ½ pound gold potatoes, peeled and cut into wedges
- 1 red onion, sliced
- 2 tablespoons avocado oil
- Juice of ½ lemon
- ½ teaspoon chili powder
- 3 garlic cloves, minced
- A pinch of salt and black pepper
- 1 tablespoon cilantro, chopped

Directions:
In a sous vide bag, mix the turkey with the potatoes, onion and the other ingredients, seal the bag and cook in the water oven at 185 degrees F for 1 hour. Divide the mix between plates and serve.

Nutrition: calories 263, fat 13, fiber 2, carbs 7, protein 15

Chicken and Asparagus

Preparation time: 5 minutes | Cooking time: 1 hour | Servings: 4

Ingredients:
- 1 pound chicken breasts, skinless, boneless and cubed
- 2 tablespoons avocado oil
- ½ pound asparagus, trimmed and halved
- 2 garlic cloves, minced
- ½ teaspoon sweet paprika
- 1 cup chicken stock
- 1 tablespoon cilantro, chopped
- A pinch of salt and black pepper

Directions:
In a large sous vide bag, mix the chicken with the oil, and the other ingredients except the asparagus and cook in the water bath at 180 degrees F for 50 minutes. Open the bag, add the asparagus, seal the bag again, cook for another 10 minutes, divide everything between plates and serve.

Nutrition: calories 200, fat 13, fiber 2, carbs 5, protein 16

Sage Turkey and Olives

Preparation time: 5 minutes | Cooking time: 1 hour | Servings: 4

Ingredients:
- 1 pound turkey breast, skinless, boneless and cubed
- 2 tablespoons sage, chopped
- Juice of ½ lemon
- 1 tablespoon garlic, minced
- 1 tablespoon lemon zest, grated
- 2 tablespoons olive oil
- ½ teaspoon mustard seeds, crushed
- A pinch of salt and black pepper
- 1 tablespoon chives, chopped

Directions:
In a large sous vide bag, mix the turkey with the sage, lemon juice and the other ingredients, seal the bag, submerge in the water oven and cook at 175 degrees F for 1 hour. Divide the mix between plates and serve.

Nutrition: calories 200, fat 12, fiber 2, carbs 6, protein 15

Chicken with Brussels Sprouts Mix

Preparation time: 10 minutes | Cooking time: 50 minutes | Servings: 4

Ingredients:

- 1 pound chicken breast, skinless, boneless and cubed
- 2 tablespoons olive oil
- 2 cups Brussels sprouts, trimmed and halved
- 2 tablespoons lime juice
- 2 tablespoons lime zest, grated
- ½ teaspoon chili powder
- 3 garlic cloves, minced
- A pinch of salt and black pepper
- 1 tablespoon parsley, chopped

Directions:

In a large sous vide bag, mix the chicken with the oil, sprouts and the other ingredients, toss, seal the bag, submerge in the water oven, cook at 175 degrees F for 50 minutes, divide the mix between plates and serve.

Nutrition: calories 253, fat 14, fiber 2, carbs 7, protein 16

Turkey and Fennel

Preparation time: 10 minutes | Cooking time: 1 hour | Servings: 4

Ingredients:

- 2 pounds turkey breast, skinless, boneless and roughly cubed
- 1 tablespoon olive oil
- 2 fennel bulbs, sliced
- Juice of 1 lime
- 1 teaspoon sweet paprika
- 1 tablespoon rosemary, chopped
- A pinch of salt and black pepper
- 1 tablespoon dill, chopped

Directions:

In a sous vide bag, mix the turkey with the oil, fennel and the other ingredients, seal the bag, cook in the water oven at 175 degrees F for 1 hour, divide the mix between plates and serve.

Nutrition: calories 273, fat 13, fiber 3, carbs 7, protein 17

Chicken with Endives

Preparation time: 10 minutes | Cooking time: 1 hour | Servings: 4

Ingredients:

- 1 pound chicken breast, skinless, boneless and sliced
- 2 endives, shredded
- 1 red onion, sliced
- ½ cup white wine
- Zest of 1 lime, grated
- ½ teaspoon coriander, ground
- ½ teaspoon cumin, ground
- ½ teaspoon basil, dried
- ½ tablespoon olive oil
- 1 tablespoon chives, chopped

Directions:

In a large sous vide bag, mix the chicken with the endives, onion and the other ingredients, toss, seal the bag, submerge in the water oven and cook at 180 degrees F for 1 hour. Divide the mix between plates and serve.

Nutrition: calories 276, fat 15, fiber 3, carbs 7, protein 16

Balsamic Turkey

Preparation time: 10 minutes | Cooking time: 1 hour | Servings: 4

Ingredients:
- 1 pound turkey breast, skinless, boneless and sliced
- 2 tablespoons olive oil
- 2 tablespoons balsamic vinegar
- 2 garlic cloves, minced
- A pinch of salt and black pepper
- 1 tablespoon chives, chopped

Directions:
In a sous vide bag, mix the turkey with the oil, vinegar and the other ingredients, seal the bag and cook in the water bath at 174 degrees F for 1 hour. Divide the mix between plates and serve with a side salad.

Nutrition: calories 252, fat 15, fiber 2, carbs 6, protein 15

Chicken and Squash Mix

Preparation time: 10 minutes | Cooking time: 1 hour | Servings: 4

Ingredients:
- 1 pound chicken breast, skinless, boneless and cubed
- 1 cup butternut squash, peeled and roughly cubed
- 2 tablespoons lime juice
- 2 tablespoons olive oil
- 2 spring onions, chopped
- 1 tablespoon oregano, chopped
- ½ teaspoon chili powder
- A pinch of salt and black pepper
- 1 tablespoon chives, chopped

Directions:
In a large sous vide bag, mix the chicken with the squash, lime juice and the other ingredients, seal the bag, submerge in the water bath and cook at 180 degrees F for 1 hour. Divide everything between plates and serve.

Nutrition: calories 234, fat 12, fiber 3, carbs 5, protein 7

Paprika Turkey Mix

Preparation time: 10 minutes | Cooking time: 50 minutes | Servings: 4

Ingredients:
- 2 pounds turkey breast, skinless, boneless and sliced
- Juice of 1 lime
- 1 tablespoon sweet paprika
- 1 tablespoon avocado oil
- 4 scallions, minced
- A pinch of salt and black pepper
- 1 tablespoon chives, chopped

Directions:
In a large sous vide bag, mix the turkey with the lime juice, paprika and the other ingredients, seal the bag, submerge in the water bath and cook at 175 degrees F for 50 minutes. Divide everything between plates and serve.

Nutrition: calories 263, fat 14, fiber 3, carbs 7, protein 16

BBQ Chicken Wings

Preparation time: 10 minutes | Cooking time: 1 hour | Servings: 4

Ingredients:

- 2 pounds chicken wings
- ½ cup bbq sauce
- 2 tablespoons avocado oil
- 2 tablespoons chives, chopped
- ½ teaspoon chili powder
- ½ teaspoon cumin, ground
- A pinch of salt and black pepper

Directions:

In a large sous vide bag, mix the chicken wings with the bbq sauce and the other ingredients, toss, seal the bag and cook in the water bath at 175 degrees F for 1 hour. Divide the chicken wings between plates and serve.

Nutrition: calories 263, fat 12, fiber 2, carbs 7, protein 18

Chicken and Salsa

Preparation time: 10 minutes | Cooking time: 1 hour | Servings: 4

Ingredients:

- 1 pound chicken breasts, skinless, boneless and cubed
- A pinch of salt and black pepper
- 1 cup cherry tomatoes, cubed
- 1 cup avocado, peeled, pitted and cubed
- 1 tablespoon basil, chopped
- Juice of 1 lime
- 2 tablespoons avocado oil
- ½ cup black olives, pitted and halved
- 3 spring onions, chopped
- 1 tablespoon balsamic vinegar

Directions:

In a large sous vide bag, mix the chicken with the tomatoes, avocado and the other ingredients, seal the bag and cook in the water bath at 180 degrees F for 1 hour. Divide the mix between plates and serve.

Nutrition: calories 201, fat 7, fiber 3, carbs 6, protein 8

Coconut Turkey

Preparation time: 10 minutes | Cooking time: 50 minutes | Servings: 4

Ingredients:

- 2 pounds turkey breast, skinless, boneless and cubed
- 1 cup coconut cream
- 1 tablespoon lime zest, grated
- 1 tablespoon lime juice
- 2 tablespoons avocado oil
- 3 scallions, chopped
- 1 tablespoon garam masala
- A pinch of salt and black pepper
- 1 tablespoon chives, chopped

Directions:

In a large sous vide bag, mix the turkey with the cream, lime juice and the other ingredients, seal the bag and cook in the water bath at 180 degrees F for 50 minutes Divide the mix between plates and serve.

Nutrition: calories 263, fat 12, fiber 3, carbs 7, protein 15

Cumin Turkey

Preparation time: 10 minutes | Cooking time: 50 minutes | Servings: 4

Ingredients:

- 1 red onion, sliced
- 2 pounds turkey breast, skinless, boneless and sliced
- Juice of ½ lemon
- 2 tablespoons olive oil
- 2 garlic cloves, minced
- 1 tablespoon cumin, ground
- A pinch of salt and black pepper
- 2 tablespoons chives, chopped

Directions:

In a large sous vide bag, mix the turkey with the onion, lemon juice and the other ingredients, seal the bag and cook in the water bath at 180 degrees F for 50 minutes. Divide everything between plates and serve with a side salad.

Nutrition: calories 214, fat 14, fiber 2, carbs 6, protein 15

Chicken and Red Beans

Preparation time: 10 minutes | Cooking time: 1 hour | Servings: 4

Ingredients:

- 1 pound chicken breasts, skinless, boneless and cubed
- 1 tablespoon olive oil
- 1 cup canned red kidney beans, drained and rinsed
- ½ cup tomato sauce
- 1 red onion, sliced
- 1 tablespoon chives, chopped
- ½ teaspoon chili powder

Directions:

In a large sous vide bag, mix the chicken with the oil, beans and the other ingredients, seal the bag and cook in the water bath at 175 degrees F for 1 hour. Divide the mix between plates and serve.

Nutrition: calories 231, fat 12, fiber 4, carbs 7, protein 15

Rosemary Chicken

Preparation time: 10 minutes | Cooking time: 1 hour | Servings: 4

Ingredients:

- 2 pounds chicken breast, skinless, boneless and cubed
- 2 tablespoons olive oil
- Juice of 1 lime
- 1 tablespoon rosemary, chopped
- 2 garlic cloves, minced
- 1 teaspoon chili powder

Directions:

In a large sous vide bag, mix the chicken with the oil and the other ingredients, seal the bag and cook in the water bath at 175 degrees F for 1 hour. Divide everything between plates and serve.

Nutrition: calories 263, fat 12, fiber 5, carbs 7, protein 16

Chicken and Peppers

Preparation time: 10 minutes | Cooking time: 1 hour | Servings: 4

Ingredients:

- 2 tablespoons olive oil
- 1 red bell pepper, cut into strips
- 1 green bell pepper, cut into strips
- 1 orange bell pepper, cut into strips
- 2 pound chicken breasts, skinless, boneless and roughly cubed
- ½ cup scallions, chopped
- ½ cup chicken stock
- ½ teaspoon oregano, dried
- A pinch of salt and black pepper
- 1 tablespoon cilantro, chopped

Directions:

In a large sous vide bag, mix the chicken with the oil, peppers and the other ingredients, seal the bag and cook in the water bath at 180 degrees F for 1 hour. Divide the mix into bowls and serve.

Nutrition: calories 242, fat 14, fiber 3, carbs 7, protein 14

Turkey and Quinoa

Preparation time: 10 minutes | Cooking time: 1 hour | Servings: 4

Ingredients:
- 2 pounds turkey breasts, skinless, boneless and cubed
- 2 tablespoons avocado oil
- 1 cup quinoa, cooked
- 1 cup chicken stock
- 2 spring onions, chopped
- ½ teaspoon garam masala
- ½ teaspoon sweet paprika
- ½ teaspoon chili powder
- ½ teaspoon turmeric powder
- A pinch of salt and black pepper

Directions:
In a sous vide bag, mix the turkey with the oil, quinoa and the other ingredients, seal the bag and cook in the water bath at 170 degrees F for 1 hour. Divide everything between plates and serve.

Nutrition: calories 232, fat 12, fiber 2, carbs 6, protein 15

Spiced Chicken Wings

Preparation time: 10 minutes | Cooking time: 1 hour | Servings: 4

Ingredients:
- 1 pound chicken wings, halved
- 1 tablespoon lime zest, grated
- ½ tablespoon lime juice
- 1 teaspoon nutmeg, ground
- ½ teaspoon cumin, ground
- ½ teaspoon cinnamon powder
- 1 red chili pepper, chopped
- 2 tablespoons olive oil
- A pinch of salt and black pepper

Directions:
In a large sous vide bag, mix the chicken wings with the nutmeg and the other ingredients, toss, seal the bag and cook in the water bath at 180 degrees F for 1 hour. Divide the mix between plates and serve.

Nutrition: calories 263, fat 14, fiber 4, carbs 6, protein 18

Turkey with Mushrooms

Preparation time: 10 minutes | Cooking time: 1 hour | Servings: 4

Ingredients:
- 1 pound turkey breast, skinless, boneless and sliced
- 1 cup mushrooms, halved
- 1 tablespoon balsamic vinegar
- 2 tablespoons lemon juice
- 1 tablespoon olive oil
- 1 teaspoon chili powder
- ¼ cup cilantro, chopped

Directions:
In a large sous vide bag, mix the turkey with the mushrooms and the other ingredients, seal the bag, cook in the water bath at 175 degrees F for 1 hour, divide everything between plates and serve.

Nutrition: calories 262, fat 16, fiber 2, carbs 8, protein 16

Turkey with Lime Sauce

Preparation time: 10 minutes | Cooking time: 1 hour | Servings: 4

Ingredients:
- 1 tablespoon avocado oil
- Juice of 1 lime
- 1 tablespoon chives, chopped
- 1 tablespoon lime zest, grated
- 1 pound turkey breast, skinless, boneless and roughly cubed
- 2 spring onions, chopped
- A pinch of salt and black pepper

Directions:
In a sous vide bag, mix the turkey with the lime juice and the other ingredients, seal the bag and cook in the water bath at 180 degrees F for 1 hour. Divide everything between plates and serve.

Nutrition: calories 283, fat 16, fiber 2, carbs 6, protein 17

Turkey with Lentils

Preparation time: 10 minutes | Cooking time: 50 minutes | Servings: 4

Ingredients:
- 2 tablespoons olive oil
- 1 cup canned lentils, drained and rinsed
- 2 pounds turkey breast, boneless, skinless and roughly cubed
- ½ cup chicken stock
- ½ teaspoon sweet paprika
- ½ teaspoon chili powder
- ½ teaspoon cumin, ground
- A pinch of salt and black pepper
- 1 tablespoon parsley, chopped

Directions:
In a large sous vide bag, mix the turkey with the lentils, oil and the other ingredients, seal the bag and cook in the water bath at 175 degrees F for 50 minutes. Divide the mix between plates and serve.

Nutrition: calories 291, fat 17, fiber 3, carbs 7, protein 16

Chicken and Leeks

Preparation time: 10 minutes | Cooking time: 1 hour | Servings: 4

Ingredients:
- 2 pounds chicken breast, skinless, boneless and cubed
- 2 tablespoons avocado oil
- 1 cup leeks, sliced
- 2 spring onions, chopped
- Juice of ½ lemon
- ½ teaspoon hot paprika
- ½ cup chicken stock
- ½ teaspoon cumin, ground
- A pinch of salt and black pepper
- 1 tablespoon chives, chopped

Directions:
Divide the chicken, leeks and the other ingredients into 2 sous vide bags, seal them, submerge in the water bath, cook at 180 degrees F for 1 hour, divide everything between plates and serve.

Nutrition: calories 226, fat 9, fiber 1, carbs 6, protein 12

Turmeric Duck

Preparation time: 10 minutes | Cooking time: 1 hour and 10 minutes | Servings: 4

Ingredients:
- 2 spring onions, chopped
- 2 pounds duck breast, skinless, boneless and sliced
- 1 teaspoon turmeric powder
- 2 garlic cloves, minced
- 1 tablespoon lime juice
- 1 tablespoon lime zest, grated
- 2 tablespoons olive oil
- A pinch of salt and black pepper
- 1 tablespoon oregano, chopped

Directions:
In a large sous vide bag, mix the duck with the spring onions, turmeric and the other ingredients, seal the bag and cook in the water bath at 180 degrees F for 1 hour and 10 minutes. Divide the mix between plates and serve.

Nutrition: calories 283, fat 11, fiber 2, carbs 8, protein 15

Chicken and Cauliflower

Preparation time: 10 minutes | Cooking time: 1 hour | Servings: 4

Ingredients:

- 1 pound chicken breasts, skinless, boneless and cubed
- 1 cup cauliflower florets
- ½ cup chicken stock
- 1 red onion, sliced
- Juice of 1 lime
- 1 tablespoon olive oil
- A pinch of salt and black pepper
- 1 teaspoon sweet paprika
- 1 tablespoon chives, chopped

Directions:

In a large sous vide bag, mix the chicken with the cauliflower, stock and the other ingredients, seal the bag, submerge in the water bath and cook at 185 degrees F for 1 hour. Divide the mix between plates and serve.

Nutrition: calories 221, fat 12, fiber 2, carbs 5, protein 17

Chicken with Hot Red Chard

Preparation time: 10 minutes | Cooking time: 50 minutes | Servings: 4

Ingredients:

- 1 tablespoon olive oil
- 2 pounds chicken breast, skinless, boneless and sliced
- 1 teaspoon hot paprika
- 2 red chilies, minced
- 1 cup red chard, torn
- 1 red onion, chopped
- 2 garlic cloves, minced
- 1 tablespoon lime juice
- A pinch of salt and black pepper
- ¼ cup chicken stock
- ½ tablespoon parsley, chopped

Directions:

In a large sous vide bag, mix the chicken with the chard, chilies and the other ingredients, seal the bag, submerge in the water bath, cook at 185 degrees F for 50 minutes, divide the mix between plates and serve.

Nutrition: calories 227, fat 12, fiber 3, carbs 7, protein 18

Creamy Chicken

Preparation time: 10 minutes | Cooking time: 50 minutes | Servings: 4

Ingredients:

- 1 pound chicken breast, skinless, boneless and cubed
- 1 tablespoon olive oil
- 1 teaspoon garam masala
- 1 cup coconut cream
- ½ teaspoon oregano, dried
- ½ teaspoon coriander, ground
- 1 yellow onion, chopped
- A pinch of salt and black pepper
- 1 tablespoon chives, chopped

Directions:

In a large sous vide bag, mix the chicken with the oil, cream and the other ingredients, seal the bag, cook in the water oven at 180 degrees F for 50 minutes, divide everything between plates and serve.

Nutrition: calories 293, fat 15, fiber 4, carbs 6, protein 14

Turkey with Chickpeas

Preparation time: 10 minutes | Cooking time: 50 minutes | Servings: 4

Ingredients:
- 1 pound turkey breasts, skinless, boneless and cubed
- 1 tablespoon olive oil
- Juice of ½ lemon
- 1 cup canned chickpeas, drained and rinsed
- ½ cup chicken stock
- 1 red onion, sliced
- ½ teaspoon sweet paprika
- A pinch of salt and black pepper
- 1 teaspoon chili powder
- 1 tablespoon parsley, chopped

Directions:
In a large sous vide bag, mix the turkey with the oil, lemon juice and the other ingredients, seal the bag, submerge in the water bath, cook at 175 degrees F for 50 minutes, divide the mix between plates and serve.

Nutrition: calories 223, fat 9, fiber 2, carbs 4, protein 11

Masala Turkey

Preparation time: 10 minutes | Cooking time: 1 hour | Servings: 4

Ingredients:
- 1 pound turkey breasts, skinless, boneless and roughly cubed
- 1 teaspoon garam masala
- 1 cup heavy cream
- ½ teaspoon curry powder
- 2 scallions, chopped
- 1 tablespoon olive oil
- 1 tablespoon parsley, chopped

Directions:
In a large sous vide bag, mix the turkey with the garam masala, cream and the other ingredients, seal the bag, submerge in the water bath, cook at 180 degrees F for 1 hour, divide the mix into bowls and serve.

Nutrition: calories 210, fat 11, fiber 2, carbs 7, protein 14

Turkey with Pomegranate Mix

Preparation time: 10 minutes | Cooking time: 50 minutes | Servings: 4

Ingredients:
- 1 pound turkey breast, skinless, boneless and cut into strips
- 1 cup pomegranate seeds
- Juice of 1 lime
- 1 tablespoon soy sauce
- 4 scallions, chopped
- 1 tablespoon olive oil
- 1 green chili pepper, minced
- 1 tablespoon sweet paprika
- A pinch of salt and black pepper
- 1 tablespoon chives, chopped

Directions:
In a sous vide bag, mix the turkey with the pomegranate seeds, lime juice and the other ingredients, seal the bag, submerge in the water bath, cook at 180 degrees F for 50 minutes, divide everything into bowls and serve.

Nutrition: calories 263, fat 8, fiber 2, carbs 7, protein 12

Chicken with Tomato and Kale

Preparation time: 10 minute | Cooking time: 1 hour | Servings: 4

Ingredients:
- 1 pound chicken breasts, skinless, boneless and cubed
- 1 cup cherry tomatoes, halved
- 1 tablespoon balsamic vinegar
- 1 tablespoon lemon zest, grated
- 1 cup baby kale
- 2 tablespoons olive oil
- 2 garlic cloves, minced
- 1 tablespoon oregano, chopped

Directions:
In a sous vide bag, mix the chicken with the tomatoes, kale and the other ingredients, seal the bag, cook in the water bath at 180 degrees F for 1 hour, divide everything between plates and serve.

Nutrition: calories 220, fat 8, fiber 2, carbs 7, protein 15

Ground Chicken and Veggies Mix

Preparation time: 10 minutes | Cooking time: 1 hour and 10 minutes | Servings: 4

Ingredients:
- 1 pound chicken breasts, skinless, boneless and ground
- 1 zucchini, cubed
- 1 eggplant, cubed
- 1 cup cherry tomatoes, halved
- 1 tablespoon balsamic vinegar
- 1 tablespoon lime zest, grated
- 1 cup roasted red peppers, cut into strips
- 1 teaspoon chili powder
- 2 tablespoon olive oil
- ¼ cup sweet chili sauce
- A pinch of salt and black pepper
- 1 tablespoon chives, chopped

Directions:
In a large sous vide bag, combine the ground chicken with the zucchini, eggplant and the other ingredients, toss, seal the bag, submerge in the water bath and cook at 165 degrees F for 1 hour and 10 minutes. Divide everything into bowls and serve.

Nutrition: calories 282, fat 12, fiber 2, carbs 6, protein 18

Chicken and Yogurt Sauce

Preparation time: 10 minutes | Cooking time: 1 hour | Servings: 4

Ingredients:
- 1 pound chicken breasts, skinless, boneless and sliced
- 2 cups Greek yogurt
- 2 garlic cloves, minced
- 2 tablespoons olive oil
- A pinch of salt and black pepper
- ½ teaspoon turmeric powder
- ½ teaspoon coriander, ground
- ½ teaspoon cumin, ground
- ¼ cup dill, chopped

Directions:
In a large sous vide bag, mix the chicken with the yogurt, garlic and the other ingredients, seal the bag, cook in the water bath at 180 degrees F for 1 hour, divide everything into bowls and serve.

Nutrition: calories 285, fat 16, fiber 4, carbs 8, protein 18

Duck and Plums Mix

Preparation time: 10 minutes | Cooking time: 1 hour | Servings: 4

Ingredients:
- 1 pound duck breasts, skinless, boneless and cubed
- 1 cup plums, stoned and halved
- 1 tablespoon balsamic vinegar
- 2 tablespoons lime zest, grated
- 2 tablespoons lime juice
- 3 scallions, chopped
- 1 tablespoon olive oil
- A pinch of salt and black pepper
- 1 tablespoon chives, chopped

Directions:
In a sous vide bag, mix the duck with the plums, balsamic vinegar and the other ingredients, seal the bag, submerge in the water bath, cook at 180 degrees F for 1 hour, divide everything into bowls and serve.

Nutrition: calories 292, fat 17, fiber 2, carbs 7, protein 16

Chicken Wings and Tomato Sauce

Preparation time: 10 minutes | Cooking time: 1 hour | Servings: 4

Ingredients:
- 1 pound chicken wings, halved
- 1 cup tomato sauce
- ½ teaspoon sweet paprika
- ½ teaspoon chili powder
- ½ teaspoon cumin, ground
- A pinch of salt and black pepper
- 3 scallions, chopped
- 2 tablespoons olive oil
- ¼ cup basil, chopped

Directions:
In a large sous vide bag, mix the chicken wings with the tomato sauce, paprika and the other ingredients, seal the bag, submerge in the water bath, cook at 175 degrees F for 1 hour, divide everything between plates and serve.

Nutrition: calories 224, fat 11, fiber 2, carbs 9, protein 11

Cayenne Turkey and Green Beans

Preparation time: 10 minutes | Cooking time: 1 hour and 10 minutes | Servings: 4

Ingredients:
- 2 pounds turkey breast, skinless, boneless and cubed
- 1 red onion, sliced
- 1 cup green beans, trimmed and halved
- 2 garlic cloves, minced
- 1 tablespoon avocado oil
- A pinch of salt and black pepper
- 1 teaspoon cayenne pepper
- ½ cup white wine
- 1 tablespoon chives, chopped chives, chopped

Directions:
In a large sous vide bag, mix the turkey with the green beans, onion and the other ingredients, seal the bag, submerge into the preheated water oven and cook at 170 degrees F for 1 hour and 10 minutes Divide everything between plates and serve.

Nutrition: calories 229, fat 9, fiber 4, carbs 7, protein 16

Oregano Turkey

Preparation time: 10 minutes | Cooking time: 50 minutes | Servings: 4

Ingredients:
- 2 pounds turkey breast, skinless, boneless and cubed
- 2 tablespoons avocado oil
- 3 garlic cloves, minced
- 2 tablespoons oregano, chopped
- ½ cup white wine
- A pinch of salt and black pepper
- 1 teaspoon rosemary, dried

Directions:
In a sous vide bag, mix the turkey with the oil, oregano and the other ingredients, seal the bag, submerge in the water oven and cook at 170 degrees F for 50 minutes Divide the mix between plates and serve.

Nutrition: calories 183, fat 2.5, fiber 1.2, carbs 1.5, protein 13.4

Allspice Turkey

Preparation time: 10 minutes | Cooking time: 50 minutes | Servings: 4

Ingredients:
- 2 pounds turkey breasts, skinless, boneless and cubed
- 1 red onion, chopped
- ½ teaspoon rosemary, dried
- ¼ cup red wine
- 2 tablespoons avocado oil
- 1 teaspoon allspice, ground
- 1 tablespoon chives, chopped

Directions:
In a large sous vide bag, combine the turkey with the onion, allspice and the other ingredients, seal the bag, cook in the water oven at 180 degrees F for 50 minutes, divide the mix between plates and serve.

Nutrition: calories 238, fat 9.7, fiber 1, carbs 2.9, protein 33.3

Chicken with Okra

Preparation time: 10 minutes | Cooking time: 1 hour | Servings: 4

Ingredients:
- 2 pounds chicken breast, skinless, boneless and cubed
- 1 red onion, chopped
- 1 cup okra, sliced
- 2 tablespoons olive oil
- 2 tablespoons lime juice
- 1 tablespoon balsamic vinegar
- A pinch of salt and black pepper
- ½ teaspoon turmeric powder
- 1 tablespoon oregano, chopped

Directions:
In a large sous vide bag, mix the chicken with the onion, okra and the other ingredients, seal the bag, submerge in the water bath and cook at 180 degrees F for 1 hour. Divide everything between plates and serve.

Nutrition: calories 256, fat 12.6, fiber 0.6, carbs 1.2, protein 33.2

Cinnamon Chicken

Preparation time: 10 minutes | Cooking time: 1 hour | Servings: 4

Ingredients:
- 2 pounds chicken breasts, skinless, boneless and sliced
- 1 tablespoon cinnamon powder
- 2 tablespoons lemon juice
- ¼ cup chicken stock
- 2 tablespoons avocado oil
- 3 scallions, chopped
- A pinch of salt and black pepper
- 1 teaspoon chili powder
- 2 tablespoons cilantro, chopped

Directions:
In a sous vide bag, mix the chicken with the cinnamon, lemon juice, stock and the other ingredients, toss, seal the bag and cook in the water oven at 170 degrees F for 1 hour. Divide the mix between plates and serve.

Nutrition: calories 364, fat 23.2, fiber 2.3, carbs 5.1, protein 35.4

Turkey Meatballs and Sauce

Preparation time: 10 minutes | Cooking time: 55 minutes | Servings: 4

Ingredients:
- 1 pound turkey breasts, skinless, boneless and ground
- 2 eggs, whisked
- 1 red onion, sliced
- A pinch of salt and black pepper
- 1 tablespoon almond flour
- 2 tablespoons oregano, chopped
- 1 cup tomato sauce

Directions:
In a bowl, combine the turkey with the onion, eggs, flour salt and pepper, stir and shape medium meatballs out of this mix. In a sous vide bag, mix the meatballs with the oregano and sauce, seal the bag and cook in the water bath at 170 degrees F for 55 minutes. Divide the mix between plates and serve.

Nutrition: calories 300, fat 15.8, fiber 2, carbs 5.2, protein 33.9

Chicken and Bulgur

Preparation time: 10 minutes | Cooking time: 1 hour | Servings: 4

Ingredients:
- 1 pound chicken breast, skinless, boneless and cubed
- 1 cup bulgur
- 1 cup chicken stock
- A pinch of salt and black pepper
- ½ teaspoon coriander, ground
- 1 teaspoon turmeric powder
- 1 tablespoon chives, chopped

Directions:
In a sous vide bag, mix the chicken with the bulgur, stock and the other ingredients, seal the bag and cook in the water bath at 170 degrees F for 1 hour. Divide the mix between plates and serve.

Nutrition: calories 360, fat 22.1, fiber 1.4, carbs 4.3, protein 34.5

Turkey and Tomatoes

Preparation time: 10 minutes | Cooking time: 1 hour | Servings: 4

Ingredients:
- 2 pounds turkey breasts, skinless, boneless and cubed
- ½ pound cherry tomatoes, halved
- Juice of 1 lime
- 1 tablespoon balsamic vinegar
- 1 tablespoon avocado oil
- ½ teaspoon smoked paprika
- A pinch of salt and black pepper
- 1 tablespoon cilantro, chopped

Directions:
In a sous vide bag, mix the turkey with the tomatoes, lime juice and the other ingredients, seal the bag and cook in the water bath at 180 degrees F for 1 hour. Divide between plates and serve.

Nutrition: calories 362, fat 16.1, fiber 4.4, carbs 5.4, protein 36.4

Turkey with Spinach and Kale

Preparation time: 10 minutes | Cooking time: 1 hour | Servings: 4

Ingredients:
- 2 pounds turkey breasts, skinless, boneless and cubed
- 2 tablespoons olive oil
- 1 cup baby spinach
- 1 cup baby kale
- Juice of 1 lime
- ¼ cup white wine
- 4 garlic cloves, minced
- 1 tablespoon lime zest, grated
- A pinch of salt and black pepper
- 1 tablespoon parsley, chopped

Directions:
In a sous vide bag, mix the turkey with the oil, spinach and the other ingredients, seal the bag, cook in the water bath at 175 degrees F for 1 hour, divide everything between plates and serve.

Nutrition: calories 243, fat 9, fiber 1.6, carbs 5.4, protein 34.1

Turkey and Spring Onions

Preparation time: 10 minutes | Cooking time: 50 minutes | Servings: 4

Ingredients:
- 2 pounds turkey breast, skinless, boneless and cubed
- 1 cup spring onions, chopped
- ¼ cup white wine
- ½ teaspoon sweet paprika
- ½ teaspoon chili powder
- 2 tablespoons avocado oil
- 1 tablespoon parsley, chopped
- A pinch of salt and black pepper

Directions:
In a large sous vide bag, mix the turkey with the spring onions, wine and the other ingredients, seal the bag, submerge in the water bath, cook at 175 degrees F for 50 minutes, divide the mix between plates and serve.

Nutrition: calories 222, fat 6.7, fiber 1.6, carbs 4.8, protein 34.4

Chicken and Lime Red Cabbage

Preparation time: 10 minutes | Cooking time: 1 hour | Servings: 4

Ingredients:
- 1 pound chicken breasts, skinless, boneless and cubed
- 1 cup red cabbage, shredded
- Juice of 1 lime
- Zest of 1 lime, grated
- 2 tablespoons olive oil
- 2 tablespoons balsamic vinegar
- A pinch of salt and black pepper
- 1 tablespoon chives, chopped
- 1 tablespoon rosemary, chopped

Directions:
In a large sous vide bag, mix the chicken with the cabbage, lime juice and the other ingredients, seal the bag, submerge in the water bath, cook at 180 degrees F for 1 hour, divide between plates and serve.

Nutrition: calories 264, fat 13.2, fiber 0.7, carbs 1.9, protein 33.2

Sous Vide Meat Recipes

Turmeric Pork Chops

Preparation time: 10 minutes | Cooking time: 1 hour and 30 minutes | Servings: 4

Ingredients:
- 2 pound pork chops
- 1 tablespoon balsamic vinegar
- ½ cup red wine
- 2 tablespoons avocado oil
- ½ teaspoon turmeric powder
- 1 red onion, sliced
- Salt and black pepper to the taste
- 2 tablespoons parsley, chopped

Directions:
In a sous vide bag, mix the pork chops with the vinegar, wine and the other ingredients, toss well, seal the bag and cook in the water oven at 186 degrees F for 1 hour and 30 minutes. Divide everything between plates and serve.

Nutrition: calories 254, fat 12, fiber 2, carbs 6, protein 16

Garlic Pork Chops

Preparation time: 10 minutes | Cooking time: 1 hour and 20 minutes | Servings: 4

Ingredients:
- 2 pounds pork chops
- Juice of 1 lemon
- 4 garlic cloves, minced
- 2 tablespoons avocado oil
- 1 tablespoon rosemary, chopped
- ½ teaspoon chili powder
- A pinch of salt and black pepper

Directions:
Divide the pork chops and the other ingredients into sous vide bags, seal them, cook in the water oven at 186 degrees F for 1 hour and 20 minutes, divide everything between plates and serve.

Nutrition: calories 243, fat 15, fiber 3, carbs 6, protein 20

Creamy Pork

Preparation time: 10 minutes | Cooking time: 1 hour and 20 minutes | Servings: 4

Ingredients:
- 2 pounds pork stew meat, cubed
- 2 tablespoons avocado oil
- 1 cup heavy cream
- 4 spring onions, chopped
- ½ teaspoon garam masala
- ½ teaspoon coriander, ground
- 2 garlic cloves, minced
- A pinch of salt and black pepper

Directions:
In a large sous vide bag, mix the pork with the oil, cream and the other ingredients, seal the bag, submerge in the water bath and cook at 180 degrees F for 1 hour and 20 minutes. Divide everything between plates and serve.

Nutrition: calories 263, fat 14, fiber 3, carbs 6, protein 16

Italian Lamb Chops

Preparation time: 10 minutes | Cooking time: 1 hour and 20 minutes | Servings: 4

Ingredients:
- 2 pounds lamb chops
- 3 scallions, chopped
- ½ cup red wine
- 1 teaspoon Italian seasoning
- ½ teaspoon chili powder
- 2 tablespoons avocado oil
- 1 tablespoon chives, chopped
- A pinch of salt and black pepper

Directions:
In a large sous vide bag, mix the lamb chops with the scallions, wine and the other ingredients, seal the bag, submerge in the water bath, cook at 186 degrees F for 1 hour and 20 minutes, divide the mix between plates and serve.

Nutrition: calories 264, fat 14, fiber 4, carbs 7, protein 15

Chives Lamb

Preparation time: 10 minutes | Cooking time: 1 hour and 20 minutes | Servings: 4

Ingredients:

- 2 pounds lamb meat, roughly cubed
- 1 red onion, sliced
- ½ cup red wine
- 1 tablespoon chives, chopped
- 1 tablespoon lime juice
- 2 scallions, chopped
- 2 tablespoons avocado oil
- 2 garlic cloves, minced
- A pinch of salt and black pepper

Directions:

In a large sous vide bag, mix the lamb with the onion, wine and the other ingredients, seal the bag, submerge in the water bath, cook at 180 degrees F for 1 hour and 20 minutes, divide the mix between plates and serve.

Nutrition: calories 263, fat 12, fiber 4, carbs 6, protein 16

Oregano Pork

Preparation time: 10 minutes | Cooking time: 1 hour and 30 minutes | Servings: 4

Ingredients:

- 2 pounds pork shoulder, sliced
- 1 cup red wine
- 1 tablespoon oregano, chopped
- 2 garlic cloves, minced
- 1 tablespoon avocado oil
- 1 red onion, chopped
- 1 tablespoon lime juice
- A pinch of salt and black pepper
- ½ teaspoon chili powder

Directions:

In a large sous vide bag, mix the pork slices with the wine, oregano and the other ingredients, toss, seal the bag, cook in the water bath at 186 degrees F for 1 hour and 30 minutes, divide the mix between plates and serve right away.

Nutrition: calories 263, fat 14, fiber 4, carbs 6, protein 18

Pork Chops and Green Beans

Preparation time: 10 minutes | Cooking time: 1 hour and 20 minutes | Servings: 4

Ingredients:

- 2 pounds pork chops
- 1 cup green beans, trimmed and halved
- 1 tablespoon lime zest, grated
- 1 tablespoon balsamic vinegar
- 1 tablespoon lime juice
- 1 tablespoon avocado oil
- ½ teaspoon rosemary, dried
- A pinch of salt and black pepper
- 1 tablespoon chives, chopped

Directions:

In a large sous vide bag, mix the pork chops with the green beans, lime zest and the other ingredients, seal the bag, submerge in the water bath, cook at 185 degrees F for 1 hour and 20 minutes, divide the mix between plates and serve.

Nutrition: calories 264, fat 14, fiber 4, carbs 6, protein 17

Basil Lamb

Preparation time: 10 minutes | *Cooking time:* 1 hour and 10 minutes | *Servings:* 4

Ingredients:
- 2 tablespoons avocado oil
- 2 pounds lamb chops
- 1 tablespoon basil, chopped
- 2 tablespoons soy sauce
- 1 red onion, chopped
- 2 tablespoons garlic, minced
- ¼ cup red wine
- A pinch of salt and black pepper

Directions:

In a large sous vide bag, mix the lamb chops with the basil, oil and the other ingredients, seal the bag, cook in the water bath at 180 degrees F for 1 hour and 10 minutes, divide the mix between plates and serve.

Nutrition: calories 263, fat 14, fiber 3, carbs 7, protein 20

Hot Beef

Preparation time: 10 minutes | *Cooking time:* 1 hour and 20 minutes | *Servings:* 4

Ingredients:
- 1 tablespoon olive oil
- 2 pounds beef stew meat, cubed
- 1 red chili pepper, chopped
- 1 teaspoon chili powder
- ½ teaspoon red pepper flakes, crushed
- A pinch of salt and black pepper
- Juice of 1 lime
- 2 garlic cloves, minced
- A pinch of salt and black pepper
- ¼ tablespoon rosemary, chopped

Directions:

In a large sous vide bag, mix the beef with the oil, chili pepper and the other ingredients, seal the bag, submerge in the water bath, cook at 180 degrees F for 1 hour and 20 minutes, divide the mix between plates and serve.

Nutrition: calories 263, fat 14, fiber 5, carbs 7, protein 15

Mint Lamb

Preparation time: 10 minutes | *Cooking time:* 1 hour and 20 minutes | *Servings:* 4

Ingredients:
- 2 pounds lamb chops
- 2 tablespoons mint, chopped
- 1 tablespoon balsamic vinegar
- 1 tablespoon avocado oil
- 1 red onion, chopped
- ¼ cup red wine
- ½ teaspoon chili powder
- A pinch of salt and black pepper

Directions:

In a large sous vide bag, mix the lamb chops with the mint, balsamic vinegar and the other ingredients, seal the bag, submerge in the water bath, cook at 186 degrees F for 1 hour and 20 minutes, divide everything between plates and serve.

Nutrition: calories 253, fat 14, fiber 3, carbs 7, protein 17

Lamb and Zucchini Mix

Preparation time: 10 minutes | *Cooking time:* 1 hour and 10 minutes | *Servings:* 4

Ingredients:
- 2 tablespoons avocado oil
- 2 zucchinis, cubed
- 1 pound lamb stew meat, cubed
- 2 tablespoons lime juice
- 1 tablespoon oregano, chopped
- 2 tablespoons balsamic vinegar
- ½ teaspoon sweet paprika
- 1 red onion, chopped
- A pinch of salt and black pepper

Directions:

In a large sous vide bag mix the zucchinis with the lamb and the other ingredients, seal the bag, submerge in the water bath, cook at 175 degrees F for 1 hour and 10 minutes, divide the mix between plates and serve.

Nutrition: calories 276, fat 14, fiber 3, carbs 7, protein 20

Beef and Artichokes

Preparation time: 10 minutes | Cooking time: 1 hour | Servings: 4

Ingredients:

- 2 pounds beef stew meat, cubed
- 2 cups canned artichoke hearts, drained
- Juice of ½ lemon
- ¼ cup tomato passata
- 2 tablespoons avocado oil
- 1 red onion, chopped
- 2 teaspoons sweet paprika
- 1 tablespoon chives, chopped

Directions:

In a large sous vide bag, mix the beef with the artichokes, lemon juice and the other ingredients, seal the bag, submerge in the water bath, cook at 180 degrees F for 1 hour, divide the mix between plates and serve.

Nutrition: calories 287, fat 16, fiber 4, carbs 6, protein 20

Pork and Mushrooms

Preparation time: 10 minutes | Cooking time: 1 hour and 20 minutes | Servings: 4

Ingredients:

- 2 pounds pork stew meat, cubed
- 1 cup brown mushrooms, halved
- 2 spring onions, chopped
- 2 tablespoons balsamic vinegar
- 1 red onion, chopped
- 1 tablespoon lemon juice
- 1 tablespoon lemon zest, grated
- 2 tablespoon olive oil
- ½ teaspoon sweet paprika
- A pinch of salt and black pepper
- 1 tablespoon cilantro, chopped

Directions:

In a large sous vide bag, mix the pork with the mushrooms, spring onions and the other ingredients, seal the bag, cook in the water bath at 180 degrees F for 1 hour and 20 minutes, divide the mix between plates and serve.

Nutrition: calories 264, fat 8, fiber 3, carbs 6, protein 17

Pork and Tomatoes

Preparation time: 10 minutes | Cooking time: 1 hour and 30 minutes | Servings: 4

Ingredients:

- 2 pounds pork stew meat, cubed
- 2 tablespoons avocado oil
- 1 pound cherry tomatoes, halved
- 3 garlic cloves, minced
- 2 spring onions, chopped
- 1 teaspoon chili powder
- Juice of 1 lime
- A pinch of salt and black pepper
- 1 tablespoon chives, chopped

Directions:

In a large sous vide bag, mix the pork with the oil, cherry tomatoes and the other ingredients, seal the bag, submerge in the water bath, cook at 180 degrees F for 1 hour and 30 minutes, divide between plates and serve.

Nutrition: calories 275, fat 13, fiber 4, carbs 7, protein 20

Allspice Lamb

Preparation time: 10 minutes | Cooking time: 1 hour and 30 minutes | Servings: 4

Ingredients:

- 1 pound lamb stew meat, roughly cubed
- 1 teaspoon allspice, ground
- 2 tablespoons olive oil
- Juice of 1 lime
- 1 yellow onion, chopped
- ½ teaspoon chili powder
- 4 garlic cloves, minced
- ¼ cup red wine
- A pinch of salt and black pepper

Directions:

In a large sous vide bag, mix the lamb with the allspice, oil and the other ingredients, seal the bag, submerge in the water bath and cook at 187 degrees F for 1 hour and 30 minutes. Divide the mix between plates and serve.

Nutrition: calories 263, fat 12, fiber 4, carbs 7, protein 12

Pork and Fennel

Preparation time: 10 minutes | Cooking time: 1 hour and 20 minutes | Servings: 4

Ingredients:

- 2 pounds pork stew meat, roughly cubed
- 2 fennel bulbs, sliced
- 1 tablespoon soy sauce
- 1 tablespoon brown sugar
- 1 tablespoon lemon juice
- 2 tablespoons avocado oil
- 4 garlic cloves, minced
- ¼ cup red wine
- A pinch of salt and black pepper
- 1 tablespoon chives, chopped

Directions:

In a large sous vide bag, mix the pork with the fennel, soy sauce and the other ingredients, seal the bag, submerge in the water bath and cook at 185 degrees F for 1 hour and 20 minutes Divide the mix between plates and serve.

Nutrition: calories 263, fat 12, fiber 3, carbs 7, protein 10

Creamy Lamb

Preparation time: 10 minutes | Cooking time: 1 hour | Servings: 4

Ingredients:

- 2 pounds lamb chops
- 1 tablespoon lime juice
- 1 teaspoon turmeric powder
- 2 tablespoons avocado oil
- 1 cup heavy cream
- 1 yellow onion, chopped
- A pinch of salt and black pepper
- 1 tablespoon oregano, chopped

Directions:

In a large sous vide bag, mix the lamb chops with the lime juice, cream and the other ingredients, seal the bag, submerge in the water oven, cook at 180 degrees F for 1 hour, divide the mix into bowls and serve.

Nutrition: calories 233, fat 7, fiber 2, carbs 6, protein 12

Paprika Lamb

Preparation time: 10 minutes | Cooking time: 1 hour | Servings: 4

Ingredients:
- 2 pounds lamb chops
- 1 tablespoon sweet paprika
- ½ teaspoon rosemary, dried
- Juice of 1 lime
- 2 tablespoons avocado oil
- ½ cup beef stock
- A pinch of salt and black pepper
- 2 tablespoons chives, chopped

Directions:
In a sous vide bag, mix the lamb chops with the paprika, rosemary and the other ingredients, seal the bag, submerge in the water oven and cook at 180 degrees F for 1 hour Divide the mix between plates and serve.

Nutrition: calories 235, fat 12, fiber 5, carbs 7, protein 10

Beef and Berries

Preparation time: 10 minutes | Cooking time: 1 hour and 20 minutes | Servings: 4

Ingredients:
- 2 pounds beef stew meat
- 1 cup blackberries, pureed
- 1 tablespoon lime juice
- ½ teaspoon chili powder
- 2 tablespoons olive oil
- 1 teaspoon sweet paprika
- 1 tablespoon chives, chopped
- A pinch of salt and black pepper

Directions:
In a large sous vide bag, mix the beef stew meat with the blackberries, lime juice and the other ingredients, seal the bag, submerge in the water oven and cook at 180 degrees F for 1 hour and 20 minutes, divide the mix between plates and serve.

Nutrition: calories 211, fat 9, fiber 2, carbs 6, protein 12

Pesto Lamb

Preparation time: 10 minutes | Cooking time: 1 hour and 10 minutes | Servings: 4

Ingredients:
- 2 pounds lamb chops
- 2 tablespoons basil pesto
- Juice of 1 lime
- 1 red onion, chopped
- 2 tablespoons olive oil
- ½ teaspoon curry powder
- A pinch of salt and black pepper
- 1 tablespoon cilantro, chopped

Directions:
In a sous vide bag, combine the lamb chops with the pesto, lime juice and the other ingredients, seal the bag, submerge in the water oven and cook at 187 degrees F for 1 hour and 10 minutes. Divide everything between plates and serve.

Nutrition: calories 254, fat 12, fiber 3, carbs 6, protein 16

Pork and Lentils Mix

Preparation time: 10 minutes | Cooking time: 1 hour and 30 minutes | Servings: 4

Ingredients:
- 2 pounds pork stew meat, cubed
- 1 cup canned lentils, drained and rinsed
- 2 tablespoons avocado oil
- 2 spring onions, chopped
- ½ teaspoon rosemary, dried
- ¼ cup tomato sauce
- A pinch of salt and black pepper
- 1 tablespoon parsley, chopped

Directions:
In a large sous vide bag, mix the pork with the lentils, oil and the other ingredients, seal the bag, submerge in the water oven, cook at 180 degrees F for 1 hour and 30 minutes, divide the mix between plates and serve.

Nutrition: calories 232, fat 10, fiber 5, carbs 7, protein 11

Lamb and Potatoes

Preparation time: 10 minutes | Cooking time: 1 hour and 30 minutes | Servings: 4

Ingredients:
- 2 pounds lamb stew meat, cubed
- 2 gold potatoes, peeled and cut into wedges
- Juice of 1 lime
- 1 teaspoon sweet paprika
- ½ teaspoon coriander, ground
- 2 tablespoons avocado oil
- 2 tablespoons chives, chopped
- 1 tablespoon balsamic vinegar
- A pinch of salt and black pepper
- ½ cup beef stock

Directions:
In a large sous vide bag, mix the lamb with the potatoes, lime juice and the other ingredients, seal the bag, submerge in the water oven and cook at 180 degrees F for 1 hour and 30 minutes. Divide the mix into bowls and serve.

Nutrition: calories 243, fat 11, fiber 4, carbs 6, protein 10

Spiced Beef and Peppers

Preparation time: 10 minutes | Cooking time: 1 hour and 30 minutes | Servings: 4

Ingredients:
- 2 pounds beef stew meat, cubed
- 2 tablespoons avocado oil
- 2 red bell peppers, cut into strips
- Juice of ½ lemon
- ½ teaspoon nutmeg, ground
- ½ teaspoon cinnamon powder
- ½ cup beef stock
- 3 garlic cloves, minced
- A pinch of salt and black pepper
- 1 tablespoon parsley, chopped

Directions:
In a large sous vide bag, mix the beef with the oil, peppers and the other ingredients, seal the bag, submerge in the water oven and cook at 187 degrees F for 1 hour and 30 minutes. Divide the mix between plates and serve.

Nutrition: calories 232, fat 12, fiber 4, carbs 6, protein 9

Rosemary Beef

Preparation time: 10 minutes | Cooking time: 1 hour and 40 minutes | Servings: 4

Ingredients:
- 2 pounds beef roast, sliced
- 2 tablespoons rosemary, chopped
- 2 tablespoons balsamic vinegar
- 2 tablespoons avocado oil
- 1 red onion, chopped
- 1 tablespoon garlic, minced
- A pinch of salt and black pepper
- 1 tablespoon chives, chopped

Directions:
In a large sous vide bag, mix the beef roast with the rosemary, vinegar and the other ingredients, seal the bag, submerge in the water oven, cook at 189 degrees F for 1 hour and 40 minutes, divide the mix between plates and serve.

Nutrition: calories 274, fat 9, fiber 5, carbs 6, protein 12

Lamb and Corn

Preparation time: 10 minutes | Cooking time: 1 hour and 30 minutes | Servings: 4

Ingredients:
- 4 lamb chops
- 1 cup corn
- 2 tablespoons balsamic vinegar
- 1 tablespoon lime juice
- 2 scallions, chopped
- ¼ cup heavy cream
- 2 tablespoons avocado oil
- A pinch of salt and black pepper
- 1 teaspoon chili powder
- 1 tablespoon cilantro, chopped

Directions:
In a large sous vide bag, combine the lamb chops with the corn, vinegar and the other ingredients, seal the bag, submerge in the water oven, cook at 178 degrees F for 1 hour and 30 minutes, divide everything between plates and serve.

Nutrition: calories 232, fat 9, fiber 3, carbs 6, protein 10

Sage Beef

Preparation time: 10 minutes | Cooking time: 1 hour and 20 minutes | Servings: 4

Ingredients:
- 2 pounds beef roast, sliced
- 2 tablespoons soy sauce
- 1 tablespoon sage, chopped
- ¼ cup red wine
- 2 tablespoons olive oil
- 1 red onion, sliced
- ½ teaspoon chili powder
- A pinch of salt and black pepper

Directions:
In a large sous vide bag, combine the roast with the soy sauce, sage and the other ingredients, seal the bag, submerge in the water oven, cook at 180 degrees F for 1 hour and 20 minutes, divide between plates and serve with a side salad.

Nutrition: calories 200, fat 11, fiber 3, carbs 6, protein 15

Lemon Chops and Peas

Preparation time: 10 minutes | Cooking time: 1 hour and 20 minutes | Servings: 4

Ingredients:
- 2 pounds pork chops
- 1 cup fresh peas
- Juice of ½ lemon
- Zest of 1 lemon, grated
- 2 tablespoons olive oil
- ½ cup beef stock
- A pinch of salt and black pepper
- 1 tablespoon chives, chopped

Directions:
In a large sous vide bag, mix the pork chops with the peas, lemon juice and the other ingredients, seal the bag, submerge in the water bath, cook at 180 degrees F for 1 hour and 20 minutes, divide everything between plates and serve.

Nutrition: calories 210, fat 5, fiber 3, carbs 8, protein 12

Parsley Pork

Preparation time: 10 minutes | Cooking time: 1 hour and 30 minutes | Servings: 4

Ingredients:
- 2 pounds pork stew meat, roughly cubed
- 2 tablespoons olive oil
- 2 tablespoons parsley, chopped
- ½ cup white wine
- 2 scallions, chopped
- Juice of 1 lime
- ½ teaspoon coriander, ground
- Salt and black pepper to the taste

Directions:
In a large sous vide bag, mix the pork with the oil, parsley and the other ingredients, seal the bag, submerge in the water oven and cook at 180 degrees F for 1 hour and 30 minutes. Divide the mix between plates and serve right away.

Nutrition: calories 248, fat 11, fiber 3, carbs 6, protein 15

Beef and Sprouts

Preparation time: 10 minutes | Cooking time: 1 hour and 20 minutes | Servings: 4

Ingredients:
- 2 pounds beef stew meat
- 2 tablespoons avocado oil
- 2 tablespoons balsamic vinegar
- 1 cup Brussels sprouts, trimmed and halved
- ½ teaspoon chili powder
- A pinch of salt and black pepper
- 1 tablespoon cilantro, chopped

Directions:
In a sous vide bag, mix the beef with the oil, vinegar and the other ingredients, seal the bag, submerge in the water oven and cook at 180 degrees F for 1 hour and 20 minutes. Divide everything between plates and serve.

Nutrition: calories 233, fat 9, fiber 3, carbs 7, protein 14

Lamb and Avocado Mix

Preparation time: 10 minutes | Cooking time: 1 hour and 10 minutes | Servings: 4

Ingredients:
- 2 pounds lamb stew, roughly cubed
- 2 tablespoons avocado oil
- 1 cup avocado, peeled, pitted and cubed
- 1 tablespoon chives, chopped
- 2 scallions, chopped
- ½ teaspoon coriander, ground
- 1 teaspoon chili powder
- A pinch of salt and black pepper

Directions:
In a large sous vide bag, mix the lamb with the avocado, oil and the other ingredients, seal the bag, submerge in the water oven, cook at 180 degrees F for 1 hour and 10 minutes, divide the mix between plates and serve.

Nutrition: calories 227, fat 14, fiber 4, carbs 6, protein 16

Beef and Corn

Preparation time: 10 minutes | Cooking time: 1 hour and 30 minutes | Servings: 4

Ingredients:
- 2 pounds beef stew meat, cubed
- 2 cups corn
- 1 red onion, chopped
- 1 tablespoon balsamic vinegar
- 1 tablespoon lime juice
- 1 tablespoon olive oil
- 1 teaspoon hot paprika
- 1 tablespoon chives, chopped

Directions:
In a sous vide bag, mix the beef with the corn, onion and the other ingredients, seal the bag, submerge in the water bath and cook at 180 degrees F for 1 hour and 30 minutes. Divide the mix between plates and serve.

Nutrition: calories 236, fat 12, fiber 2, carbs 7, protein 15

Pork and Olives

Preparation time: 10 minutes | Cooking time: 1 hour and 30 minutes | Servings: 4

Ingredients:
- 2 pounds pork stew meat, roughly cubed
- 1 teaspoon coriander, ground
- ½ teaspoon turmeric powder
- ¼ cup red wine
- 1 cup black olives, pitted and halved
- 2 tablespoons lemon juice
- 2 tablespoons olive oil
- A pinch of salt and black pepper

Directions:
In a large sous vide bag, mix the pork with the coriander, turmeric and the other ingredients, seal the bag, submerge in the water oven and cook at 186 degrees F for 1 hour and 30 minutes. Divide the mix between plates and serve.

Nutrition: 273, fat 12, fiber 4, carbs 7, protein 17

Lamb and Cucumber Mix

***Preparation time:** 10 minutes* | ***Cooking time:** 1 hour and 30 minutes* | ***Servings:** 4*

Ingredients:
- 2 pounds lamb stew meat, roughly cubed
- 2 tablespoons olive oil
- 1 cup cucumbers, cubed
- 1 teaspoon cumin, ground
- ¼ cup beef stock
- 4 garlic cloves, minced
- A pinch of salt and black pepper
- 1 tablespoon cilantro, chopped

Directions:
In a large sous vide bag mix the lamb with the oil, cucumber and the other ingredients, seal the bag, cook in the water oven at 180 degrees F for 1 hour and 30 minutes, divide the mix between plates and serve.

Nutrition: calories 244, fat 12, fiber 2, carbs 5, protein 16

Ground Lamb and Carrots Mix

***Preparation time:** 10 minutes* | ***Cooking time:** 1 hour* | ***Servings:** 4*

Ingredients:
- 2 pounds lamb stew meat, ground
- 1 tablespoon balsamic vinegar
- 1 red onion, sliced
- 2 tablespoons olive oil
- 3 carrots, peeled and grated
- 1 parsnip, peeled and sliced
- ¼ cup red wine
- 1 tablespoon chives, chopped
- A pinch of salt and black pepper

Directions:
In a large sous vide bag, mix the lamb with the vinegar, onion and the other ingredients, seal the bag, submerge in the water oven, cook at 175 degrees F for 1 hour, divide the mix into bowls and serve.

Nutrition: calories 254, fat 14, fiber 3, carbs 6, protein 17

Lamb and Capers

***Preparation time:** 10 minutes* | ***Cooking time:** 1 hour and 10 minutes* | ***Servings:** 4*

Ingredients:
- 2 pounds lamb stew meat, cubed
- 1 red onion, sliced
- 2 tablespoons capers, drained
- Juice of 1 lemon
- ½ teaspoon chili pepper
- 1 green bell pepper, cut into strips
- 2 tablespoons olive oil
- ½ teaspoon red pepper flakes, crushed
- A pinch of salt and black pepper
- 1 tablespoon cilantro, chopped

Directions:
In a large sous vide bag, mix the lamb with the onion, capers and the other ingredients, seal the bag, submerge in the water bath, cook at 180 degrees F for 1 hour and 10 minutes, divide the mix between plate sand serve.

Nutrition: calories 263, fat 14, fiber 3, carbs 6, protein 20

Beef and Spicy Zucchinis

***Preparation time:** 10 minutes | **Cooking time:** 1 hour and 10 minutes | **Servings:** 4*

Ingredients:

- 2 pounds beef stew meat, cubed
- 2 zucchinis, cubed
- 1 teaspoon chili powder
- ½ teaspoon hot paprika
- 1 red onion, sliced
- 2 tablespoons avocado oil
- ¼ cup beef stock
- A pinch of salt and black pepper
- 1 teaspoon cayenne pepper
- 1 tablespoon chives, chopped

Directions:

In a large sous vide bag, mix the beef with the zucchinis, chili powder and the other ingredients, seal the bag, cook in the water bath at 175 degrees F for 1 hour and 10 minutes, divide mix between plates and serve.

Nutrition: calories 283, fat 13, fiber 4, carbs 6, protein 16

Pork with Tomatoes and Potatoes

***Preparation time:** 10 minutes | **Cooking time:** 1 hour and 40 minutes | **Servings:** 4*

Ingredients:

- 2 pounds pork stew meat, roughly cubed
- 1 cup cherry tomatoes, halved
- ½ pound gold potatoes, peeled and cut into wedges
- 1 teaspoon sweet paprika
- Juice of 1 lime
- 1 red onion, chopped
- 2 tablespoons avocado oil
- 3 garlic cloves, minced
- 1 tablespoon chives, chopped

Directions:

In a large sous vide bag, mix the pork with the tomatoes, potatoes and the other ingredients, seal the bag, submerge in the water bath, cook at 180 degrees F for 1 hour and 40 minutes, divide the mix between plates and serve.

Nutrition: calories 253, fat 14, fiber 2, carbs 6, protein 18

Lamb and Savoy Cabbage Mix

***Preparation time:** 10 minutes | **Cooking time:** 1 hour and 20 minutes | **Servings:** 4*

Ingredients:

- 2 pounds lamb shoulder, cubed
- 2 tablespoons olive oil
- 1 cup Savoy cabbage, shredded
- 1 tablespoon balsamic vinegar
- 2 spring onions, chopped
- 1 tablespoon balsamic vinegar
- A pinch of salt and black pepper
- Juice of 1 lime
- 1 tablespoon chives, chopped

Directions:

In a large sous vide bag, mix the lamb with the cabbage, oil and the other ingredients, seal the bag, submerge in the water bath, cook at 180 degrees F for 1 hour and 20 minutes, divide everything between plates and serve.

Nutrition: calories 264, fat 14, fiber 3, carbs 6, protein 17

Beef with Carrots and Cabbage

Preparation time: 10 minutes | Cooking time: 1 hour and 30 minutes | Servings: 4

Ingredients:

- 2 tablespoons olive oil
- 2 carrots, peeled and sliced
- 1 cup red cabbage, shredded
- Juice of 1 lime
- 2 tablespoons balsamic vinegar
- 2 pounds beef stew meat, roughly cubed
- 1 red onion, chopped
- A pinch of salt and black pepper
- ½ teaspoon cumin, ground
- 1 tablespoon chives, chopped

Directions:
In a sous vide bag, mix the beef with the oil, carrots and the other ingredients, seal the bag, submerge in the water oven and cook at 186 degrees F for 1 hour and 30 minutes. Divide the mix into bowls and serve.

Nutrition: calories 273, fat 13, fiber 2, carbs 6, protein 15

Orange Lamb

Preparation time: 10 minutes | Cooking time: 1 hour | Servings: 4

Ingredients:

- 2 pounds lamb chops
- 2 tablespoons olive oil
- Juice of 2 oranges
- 2 tablespoons orange zest, grated
- ½ teaspoon turmeric powder
- A pinch of salt and black pepper
- 1 tablespoon chives, chopped

Directions:
In a large sous vide bag, mix the lamb chops with the oil, orange juice and the other ingredients, seal the bag, submerge in the water bath, cook at 180 degrees F for 1 hour, divide between plates and serve.

Nutrition: calories 274, fat 14, fiber 2, carbs 6, protein 16

Ginger Pork

Preparation time: 10 minutes | Cooking time: 1 hour and 10 minutes | Servings: 4

Ingredients:

- 2 pounds pork shoulder, boneless and cubed
- 2 spring onions, chopped
- 1 tablespoon ginger, grated
- ½ teaspoon chili powder
- ½ teaspoon coriander, ground
- A pinch of salt and black pepper
- ¼ cup beef stock
- 1 tablespoon cilantro, chopped

Directions:
In a sous vide bag, mix the pork with the ginger, spring onions and the other ingredients, seal the bag, submerge in the water bath, cook at 175 degrees F for 1 hour and 10 minutes, divide the mix between plates and serve with a side salad.

Nutrition: calories 264, fat 14, fiber 2, carbs 8, protein 12

Beef and Swiss Chard

Preparation time: 10 minutes | Cooking time: 1 hour and 10 minutes | Servings: 4

Ingredients:

- 2 pounds beef stew meat, roughly cubed
- 2 scallions, chopped
- 1 cup red chard, torn
- Juice of 1 lime
- 1 tablespoon olive oil
- 1 teaspoon hot paprika
- ½ teaspoon turmeric powder
- 1 tablespoon chives, chopped
- A pinch of salt and black pepper

Directions:

In a large sous vide bag, mix the beef with the scallions, chard and the other ingredients, seal the bag, submerge in the water bath, cook at 176 degrees F for 1 hour and 10 minutes, divide the mix between plates and serve with a side salad.

Nutrition: calories 200, fat 9, fiber 2, carbs 6, protein 12

Nutmeg Pork Roast

Preparation time: 10 minutes | Cooking time: 1 hour and 40 minutes | Servings: 4

Ingredients:

- 2 pounds pork roast, sliced
- 1 teaspoon nutmeg, ground
- Juice of ½ lemon
- ½ tablespoon lemon zest, grated
- 2 tablespoons olive oil
- A pinch of salt and black pepper
- ½ cup red wine
- 1 tablespoon chives, chopped

Directions:

In a large sous vide bag, mix the pork roast with the nutmeg, lemon juice and the other ingredients, seal the bag, submerge in the water bath, cook at 180 degrees F for 1 hour and 40 minutes, divide roast between plates and serve with a side salad.

Nutrition: calories 234, fat 11, fiber 3, carbs 7, protein 15

Lamb with Ginger Artichokes

Preparation time: 10 minutes | Cooking time: 1 hour and 10 minutes | Servings: 4

Ingredients:

- 2 pounds lamb meat, cubed
- 1 cup canned artichoke hearts, drained and quartered
- 1 tablespoon ginger, grated
- 1 red onion, sliced
- Juice of ½ lime
- ½ teaspoon chili powder
- ½ teaspoon turmeric powder
- 1 cup beef stock
- 2 tablespoons olive oil
- 1 tablespoon parsley, chopped

Directions:

In a large sous vide bag, mix the lamb with the artichokes, ginger, and the other ingredients, seal the bag, submerge in the water bath, cook at 180 degrees F for 1 hour and 10 minutes, divide the mix between plates and serve.

Nutrition: calories 273, fat 14, fiber 2, carbs 6, protein 15

Balsamic Pork Chops

Preparation time: 10 minutes | Cooking time: 1 hour and 20 minutes | Servings: 4

Ingredients:
- 1 pound pork chops
- 2 tablespoons balsamic vinegar
- 1 tablespoon olive oil
- 4 garlic cloves, minced
- ¼ cup red wine
- A pinch of salt and black pepper
- 1 tablespoon chives, chopped

Directions:
In a large sous vide bag, mix the pork chops with the vinegar, oil and the other ingredients, seal the bag, submerge in the water bath, cook at 184 degrees F for 1 hour and 20 minutes, divide everything between plates and serve.

Nutrition: calories 292, fat 12, fiber 3, carbs 7, protein 16

Pork and Creamy Scallions Sauce

Preparation time: 10 minutes | Cooking time: 1 hour and 20 minutes | Servings: 4

Ingredients:
- 2 pounds pork stew meat, cubed
- 1 cup heavy cream
- ½ cup scallions, chopped
- Juice of 1 lime
- 1 teaspoon turmeric powder
- ½ teaspoon garam masala
- 2 tablespoons olive oil
- 1 tablespoon chives, chopped
- A pinch of salt and black pepper

Directions:
In a large sous vide bag, mix the pork with the cream, scallions, lime juice and the other ingredients, seal the bag, submerge in the water bath, cook at 180 degrees F for 1 hour and 20 minutes, divide everything into bowls and serve.

Nutrition: calories 277, fat 14, fiber 3, carbs 7, protein 17

Almond Beef

Preparation time: 10 minutes | Cooking time: 1 hour and 15 minutes | Servings: 4

Ingredients:
- 2 pounds beef stew meat, cubed
- 2 tablespoons avocado oil
- 1 tablespoon almond butter
- 1 tablespoon almonds, chopped
- ½ cup beef stock
- ½ teaspoon rosemary, dried
- A pinch of salt and black pepper
- 1 tablespoon chives, chopped

Directions:
In a large sous vide bag, mix the beef with the oil, almond butter and the other ingredients, seal the bag, submerge in the water bath, cook at 180 degrees F for 1 hour and 15 minutes, divide everything between plates and serve.

Nutrition: calories 274, fat 12, fiber 4, carbs 7, protein 16

Pork, Capers and Green Beans

Preparation time: 10 minutes | Cooking time: 1 hour and 10 minutes | Servings: 4

Ingredients:
- 2 pounds pork chops
- 1 tablespoon capers, drained
- 1 cup green beans, halved
- Juice of ½ lemon
- 2 tablespoons olive oil
- 2 garlic cloves, minced
- 2 scallions, chopped
- A pinch of salt and black pepper
- 1 tablespoon chives, chopped

Directions:
In a large sous vide bag, mix the pork chops with the capers, green beans and the other ingredients, seal the bag, submerge in the water bath, cook at 187 degrees F for 1 hour and 10 minutes, divide the mix between plates and serve.

Nutrition: calories 269, fat 12, fiber 3, carbs 5, protein 16

Beef and Beets

Preparation time: 10 minutes | Cooking time: 1 hour and 35 minutes | Servings: 4

Ingredients:

- 2 pounds beef stew meat, cubed
- 2 beets, peeled and cut into wedges
- 1 red onion, chopped
- 2 tablespoons balsamic vinegar
- 2 tablespoons olive oil
- 2 garlic cloves, minced
- A pinch of salt and black pepper
- ½ teaspoon chili powder
- 1 tablespoon cilantro, chopped

Directions:

In a large sous vide bag, mix the beef with the beets, onion and the other ingredients, seal the bag, submerge in the water bath, cook at 180 degrees F for 1 hour and 35 minutes, divide everything between plates and serve.

Nutrition: calories 293, fat 14, fiber 4, carbs 6, protein 18

Lamb and Broccoli

Preparation time: 10 minutes | Cooking time: 1 hour and 30 minutes | Servings: 4

Ingredients:

- 2 spring onions, chopped
- 2 pounds lamb chops
- 1 cup broccoli florets
- 2 tablespoons olive oil
- 2 tablespoons lime zest, grated
- Juice of ½ lime
- 1 tablespoon chives, chopped
- A pinch of salt and black pepper
- 1 tablespoon cilantro, chopped

Directions:

In a large sous vide bag, mix the lamb chops with the spring onions, broccoli and the other ingredients, seal the bag, cook in the water bath at 175 degrees F for 1 hour and 30 minutes, divide the mix between plates and serve.

Nutrition: calories 263, fat 12, fiber 3, carbs 6, protein 13

Lamb and Radish Mix

Preparation time: 10 minutes | Cooking time: 1 hour and 30 minutes | Servings: 4

Ingredients:

- 2 pounds lamb shoulder, cubed
- 1 cup radishes, halved
- 2 tablespoons avocado oil
- 1 tablespoon lemon juice
- 1 tablespoon lemon zest, grated
- 2 spring onions, chopped
- ½ teaspoon rosemary, dried
- ¼ cup beef stock
- 2 garlic cloves, minced
- Salt and black pepper to the taste

Directions:

In a large sous vide bag, mix the lamb with the radishes, oil and the other ingredients, seal the bag, cook in the water oven at 175 degrees F for 1 hour and 30 minutes, divide everything between plates and serve.

Nutrition: calories 454, fat 26.5, fiber 0.3, carbs 1.1, protein 35.6

Citrus Lamb Mix

Preparation time: 10 minutes | *Cooking time:* 1 hour and 30 minutes | *Servings:* 6

Ingredients:
- 2 pounds lamb chops
- Juice of 1 orange
- Juice of 1 lime
- Zest of 1 orange, grated
- 1 teaspoon nutmeg, ground
- 2 spring onions, chopped
- ½ teaspoon chili powder
- 1 tablespoon olive oil
- 2 garlic cloves, minced
- A pinch of salt and black pepper
- 1 tablespoon chives, chopped

Directions:
In a large sous vide bag, mix the lamb chops with the orange juice, lime juice and the other ingredients, seal the bag, submerge in the water bath, cook at 180 degrees F for 1 hour and 30 minutes, divide between plates and serve with a side salad.

Nutrition: calories 352, fat 26.5, fiber 0.3, carbs 0.7, protein 26.5

Pork and Red Onions Mix

Preparation time: 10 minutes | *Cooking time:* 1 hour and 30 minutes | *Servings:* 4

Ingredients:
- 2 pounds pork shoulder, cubed
- 2 tablespoons olive oil
- 2 big red onions, sliced
- 2 tablespoons balsamic vinegar
- 1 teaspoon chili powder
- 2 tablespoons chives, chopped
- 2 garlic cloves, minced
- ½ cup beef stock
- A pinch of salt and black pepper

Directions:
In a large sous vide bag, mix the pork with the oil, onions and the other ingredients, seal the bag, submerge in the water bath, cook at 180 degrees F for 1 hour and 30 minutes, divide everything between plates and serve right away.

Nutrition: calories 373, fat 25, fiber 1.6, carbs 6.9, protein 28.8

Pork and Walnuts Mix

Preparation time: 10 minutes | *Cooking time:* 1 hour and 20 minutes | *Servings:* 4

Ingredients:
- 2 pound pork stew meat, cubed
- 2 tablespoons olive oil
- 2 tablespoons balsamic vinegar
- 1 tablespoon walnuts, chopped
- 2 tablespoons cilantro, chopped
- 1 tablespoon lime juice
- 2 garlic cloves, minced
- A pinch of salt and black pepper

Directions:
In a large sous vide bag, mix the pork with the oil, vinegar, and the other ingredients, seal the bag, submerge in the water bath, cook at 180 degrees F for 1 hour and 20 minutes, divide the mix between plates and serve.

Nutrition: calories 285, fat 14.6, fiber 0.6, carbs 3.1, protein 33.9

Pork and Pumpkin Mix

Preparation time: 10 minutes | Cooking time: 1 hour and 20 minutes | Servings: 4

Ingredients:
- 2 pounds pork stew meat, cubed
- 1 tablespoon olive oil
- 1 cup pumpkin, peeled and roughly cubed
- Juice of 1 lime
- ½ teaspoons garlic powder
- ½ teaspoon chili powder
- ½ teaspoon cumin, ground
- 2 scallions, chopped
- A pinch of salt and black pepper
- ½ cup beef stock
- 1 tablespoon cilantro, chopped

Directions:

In a large sous vide bag, mix the pork with the oil, pumpkin and the other ingredients, seal the bag, submerge in the water bath, cook at 180 degrees F for 1 hour and 20 minutes, divide the mix between plates and serve.

Nutrition: calories 353, fat 17.4, fiber 0.4, carbs 1.2, protein 34.2

Pork with Peppers and Avocado

Preparation time: 10 minutes | Cooking time: 1 hour and 20 minutes | Servings: 4

Ingredients:
- 2 pounds pork shoulder, cubed
- 2 spring onions, chopped
- 2 red bell peppers, cut into strips
- 1 cup avocado, peeled, pitted and halved
- ½ pound baby spinach
- 1 cup beef stock
- ½ teaspoon sweet paprika
- ½ teaspoon chili powder
- 1 tablespoon avocado oil
- A pinch of salt and black pepper
- 1 tablespoon cilantro, chopped

Directions:

In a large sous vide bag, mix the pork with the onions, bell peppers and the other ingredients, seal the bag, submerge in the water bath, cook at 180 degrees F for 1 hour and 20 minutes, divide the mix between plates and serve.

Nutrition: calories 384, fat 26.5, fiber 1.8, carbs 5, protein 28.4

Ground Beef with Beets and Radishes

Preparation time: 10 minutes | Cooking time: 1 hour | Servings: 4

Ingredients:
- 2 pounds beef stew meat, ground
- 2 beets, peeled and cubed
- 1 cup radishes, sliced
- 1 teaspoon sweet paprika
- ½ teaspoon chili powder
- ½ tablespoon lemon zest, grated
- Juice of ½ lemon
- 1 tablespoon avocado oil
- A pinch of salt and black pepper
- 2 garlic cloves, minced
- 1 tablespoons chives, chopped

Directions:

In a sous vide bag, mix the beef with the beets, radishes and the other ingredients, seal the bag, submerge in the water bath, cook at 180 degrees F for 1 hour, divide the mix into bowls and serve.

Nutrition: calories 367, fat 24.5, fiber 1.3, carbs 6.8, protein 28.2

Orange Pork and Veggies

Preparation time: 10 minutes | Cooking time: 1 hour and 20 minutes | Servings: 4

Ingredients:

- 2 tablespoons avocado oil
- 2 pounds pork chops
- 1 orange, peeled and cut into segments
- 1 zucchini, cubed
- 1 eggplants, cubed
- 1 carrot, peeled and sliced
- 1 cup green beans, trimmed and halved
- ½ cup orange juice
- 2 tablespoons oregano, chopped
- A pinch of salt and black pepper

Directions:

In a large sous vide bag, mix the pork chops with the oil, orange and the other ingredients, seal the bag, submerge in the water bath, cook at 180 degrees F for 1 hour and 20 minutes, divide the mix between plates and serve.

Nutrition: calories 272, fat 14.5, fiber 0.1, carbs 0.3, protein 33.3

Oregano and Chili Lamb

Preparation time: 10 minutes | Cooking time: 1 hour and 20 minutes | Servings: 4

Ingredients:

- 1 pound lamb chops
- 2 red chilies, minced
- 2 tablespoons oregano, chopped
- 2 tablespoons balsamic vinegar
- 2 tablespoons olive oil
- 1 cup beef stock
- ½ teaspoon chili powder
- 2 tablespoons chives, chopped
- A pinch of salt and black pepper

Directions:

In a large sous vide bag, mix the lamb chops with the oregano, chilies and the other ingredients, seal the bag, submerge in the water bath, cook at 175 degrees F for 1 hour and 20 minutes, divide the mix between plates and serve.

Nutrition: calories 393, fat 13, fiber 0.1, carbs 0.2, protein 27.2

Pork and Pears Mix

Preparation time: 10 minutes | Cooking time: 1 hour and 20 minutes | Servings: 4

Ingredients:

- 2 pounds pork shoulder, cubed
- 2 pears, cored and cut into wedges
- 2 tablespoons balsamic vinegar
- ¼ cup red wine
- 1 tablespoon avocado oil
- ½ teaspoon coriander, ground
- A pinch of red pepper flakes, crushed
- 1 tablespoon chives, chopped
- 1 tablespoon cilantro, chopped
- A pinch of salt and black pepper

Directions:

In a large sous vide bag, mix the pork with the pears, vinegar and the other ingredients, seal the bag submerge in the water oven and cook at 178 degrees F for 1 hour and 20 minutes. Divide everything between plates and serve.

Nutrition: calories 396, fat 26.4, fiber 2.3, carbs 5.5, protein 28.5

Sous Vide Vegetable Recipes

Lime Artichokes

***Preparation time:** 5 minutes | **Cooking time:** 35 minutes | **Servings:** 4*

Ingredients:
- 4 artichokes, trimmed and halved
- 1 tablespoon lime juice
- 2 tablespoons balsamic vinegar
- ½ teaspoon coriander, ground
- A pinch of salt and black pepper

Directions:
In a large sous vide bag, mix the artichokes with the lime juice and the other ingredients, seal the bag, submerge in the water bath, cook at 160 degrees F for 35 minutes, divide between plates and serve.

Nutrition: calories 56, fat 1.8, fiber 0.4, carbs 0.5, protein 5.6

Basil Green Beans

***Preparation time:** 10 minutes | **Cooking time:** 35 minutes | **Servings:** 4*

Ingredients:
- 1 pound green beans, trimmed
- 1 tablespoon soy sauce
- 1 tablespoon butter, melted
- Juice of ½ lime
- 2 tablespoons basil, chopped
- A pinch of salt and black pepper
- A pinch of red pepper flakes
- A pinch of salt and black pepper

Directions:
In a sous vide bag, mix the green beans with the soy sauce, butter and the other ingredients, seal the bag, submerge in the water bath, cook at 174 degrees F for 35 minutes, divide the between plates and serve.

Nutrition: calories 10, fat 1.1, fiber 0.8, carbs 1.6, protein 0.6

Buttery Leeks

***Preparation time:** 5 minutes | **Cooking time:** 25 minutes | **Servings:** 4*

Ingredients:
- 2 leeks, sliced
- 2 tablespoons lime juice
- 2 tablespoons butter, melted
- 1 tablespoon dill, chopped
- ½ teaspoon coriander, ground
- A pinch of salt and black pepper

Directions:
In a sous vide bag, mix the leeks with the melted butter and the other ingredients, seal the bag, submerge in the water oven, cook at 170 degrees F for 25 minutes, divide the mix between plates and serve.

Nutrition: calories 148, fat 7.8, fiber 2.9, carbs 5.4, protein 5.5

Green Beans and Capers

***Preparation time:** 5 minutes | **Cooking time:** 30 minutes | **Servings:** 4*

Ingredients:
- 1 pound green beans, trimmed and halved
- 1 tablespoon balsamic vinegar
- ½ teaspoon chili powder
- Juice of ½ lemon
- 1 tablespoon capers, drained
- 1 tablespoon sweet paprika
- 1 tablespoon basil, chopped
- 2 garlic cloves, chopped

Directions:
In a sous vide bag, mix the green beans with the capers, vinegar and the other ingredients, seal the bag, submerge in the water bath, cook at 164 degrees F for 30 minutes, divide the mix between plates, and serve.

Nutrition: calories 106, fat 1.9, fiber 0.2, carbs 0.5, protein 7.8

Balsamic Tomatoes

Preparation time: 5 minutes | Cooking time: 30 minutes | Servings: 4

Ingredients:
- 1 pound cherry tomatoes, halved
- 2 tablespoons balsamic vinegar
- 2 tablespoons avocado oil
- 1 tablespoon basil, chopped
- ½ teaspoon chili powder
- ½ teaspoon sweet paprika
- A pinch of salt and black pepper
- 1 tablespoon chives, chopped

Directions:

In a sous vide bag, mix the tomatoes with the vinegar, oil and the other ingredients, seal the bag, submerge in the water bath, cook at 167 degrees F for 30 minutes, divide mix between plates and serve.

Nutrition: calories 42, fat 1.2, fiber 0.7, carbs 1, protein 3.5

Mustard Asparagus

Preparation time: 5 minutes | Cooking time: 30 minutes | Servings: 4

Ingredients:
- 1 pound asparagus, trimmed
- 2 tablespoons avocado oil
- 2 tablespoons mustard
- 2 tablespoons lime juice
- A pinch of salt and black pepper
- 1 teaspoon garlic powder
- 1 tablespoon basil, chopped

Directions:

In a sous vide bag, mix the asparagus with the oil, mustard and the other ingredients, seal the bag, submerge in the water bath, cook at 170 degrees F for 30 minutes, divide between plates and serve.

Nutrition: calories 102, fat 7.5, fiber 3, carbs 6.1, protein 3.4

Green Beans and Corn

Preparation time: 5 minutes | Cooking time: 30 minutes | Servings: 4

Ingredients:
- 1 pound green beans, trimmed and halved
- 1 cup corn
- 1 tablespoon balsamic vinegar
- Juice of ½ lime
- 2 tablespoons oregano, chopped
- A pinch of salt and black pepper
- ½ cup chicken stock

Directions:

In a sous vide bag, mix the green beans with the corn, vinegar and the other ingredients, seal the bag, cook in the water bath at 165 degrees F for 30 minutes, divide everything between plates and serve.

Nutrition: calories 121, fat 11.5, fiber 1.8, carbs 4.1, protein 1.9

Balsamic Radishes

Preparation time: 5 minutes | Cooking time: 30 minutes | Servings: 4

Ingredients:
- 1 pound radishes, halved
- 2 tablespoons balsamic vinegar
- ½ teaspoon garam masala
- ½ cup chicken stock
- 1 tablespoon chives, chopped
- 1 teaspoon chili powder

Directions:

In a sous vide bag, mix the radishes with the vinegar, masala and the other ingredients, seal the bag, submerge in the water bath, cook at 165 degrees F for 30 minutes, divide the mix between plates and serve.

Nutrition: calories 45, fat 0.6, fiber 0.1, carbs 0.4, protein 2

Parsley Artichokes

Preparation time: 5 minutes | Cooking time: 30 minutes | Servings: 4

Ingredients:
- 4 artichokes, trimmed and halved
- 2 teaspoons lemon zest, grated
- 1 tablespoon lemon juice
- 1 teaspoon chili powder
- A pinch of salt and black pepper
- 1 tablespoon parsley, chopped

Directions:

In a sous vide bag, mix the artichokes with the lemon juice and the other ingredients, seal the bag, submerge in the water bath, cook at 170 degrees F for 30 minutes, divide the mix between plates, and serve.

Nutrition: calories 82, fat 2.5, fiber 1.9, carbs 2.1, protein 5.6

Balsamic Zucchini Mix

Preparation time: 10 minutes | Cooking time: 30 minutes | Servings: 4

Ingredients:
- 1 pound zucchinis, roughly cubed
- 2 tablespoons balsamic vinegar
- 1 tablespoon capers, drained
- A pinch of salt and black pepper
- 2 garlic cloves, minced
- 1 tablespoon dill, chopped
- ½ teaspoon chili powder

Directions:

In a sous vide bag, mix the zucchinis with the vinegar and the other ingredients, seal the bag, cook in the water bath at 165 degrees F for 30 minutes, divide everything between plates and serve.

Nutrition: calories 46, fat 1.7, fiber 0.1, carbs 0.6, protein 2.7

Garlic Brussels Sprouts

Preparation time: 10 minutes | Cooking time: 35 minutes | Servings: 4

Ingredients:
- 1 pound Brussels sprouts, trimmed and halved
- Juice of 1 lemon
- 3 garlic cloves, minced
- ½ teaspoon coriander, ground
- ½ teaspoon sweet paprika
- A pinch of salt and black pepper
- 1 tablespoon rosemary, chopped

Directions:

In a sous vide bag, mix the sprouts with the lemon juice, garlic and the other ingredients, seal the bag, cook in the water bath at 167 degrees F for 35 minutes, divide the mix between plates and serve.

Nutrition: calories 71, fat 2.1, fiber 1.1, carbs 1.3, protein 4.4

Creamy Bell Peppers

Preparation time: 10 minutes | Cooking time: 30 minutes | Servings: 4

Ingredients:
- 1 pound red bell peppers, cut into wedges
- 1 cup heavy cream
- 1 teaspoon turmeric powder
- ½ teaspoon coriander, ground
- 1 tablespoon lime juice
- 1 tablespoon chives, chopped

Directions:

In a sous vide bag, mix the peppers with the cream, turmeric and the other ingredients, seal the bag, submerge in the water bath, cook at 180 degrees F fro 30 minutes, divide the mix between plates and serve.

Nutrition: calories 70, fat 1.8, fiber 1.1, carbs 1.4, protein 0.6

Cayenne Broccoli

Preparation time: 5 minutes | *Cooking time:* 25 minutes | *Servings:* 4

Ingredients:
- 1 pound broccoli florets
- ½ cup chicken stock
- Juice of 1 lime
- A pinch of cayenne pepper
- A pinch of salt and black pepper
- 1 tablespoon chives, chopped

Directions:
In a sous vide bag, mix the broccoli with the lime juice, cayenne and the other ingredients, seal the bag, submerge in the water bath, cook at 165 degrees F for 25 minutes, divide the mix between plates and serve.

Nutrition: calories 63, fat 5.7, fiber 0.4, carbs 2.8, protein 0.7

Nutmeg Brussels Sprouts

Preparation time: 5 minutes | *Cooking time:* 35 minutes | *Servings:* 4

Ingredients:
- 1 pound Brussels sprouts, halved
- 2 tablespoons balsamic vinegar
- 2 tablespoons olive oil
- 1 teaspoon nutmeg, ground
- 1 tablespoon chives, chopped

Directions:
In a sous vide bag, mix the sprouts with the oil and the other ingredients, seal the bag, cook in the water oven at 165 degrees F for 35 minutes, divide the mix between plates and serve.

Nutrition: calories 68, fat 4.2, fiber 2.3, carbs 3.4, protein 2.4

Garlic Kale

Preparation time: 5 minutes | *Cooking time:* 20 minutes | *Servings:* 4

Ingredients:
- 1 pound baby kale
- 3 garlic cloves, minced
- 2 tablespoons olive oil
- A pinch of salt and black pepper
- 1 teaspoon sweet paprika
- 1 teaspoon chives, chopped

Directions:
In a sous vide bag, mix the kale with the garlic, oil and the other ingredients, seal the bag, submerge in the water oven, cook at 160 degrees F for 20 minutes, divide the mix between plates and serve.

Nutrition: calories 32, fat 3.4, fiber 2.3, carbs 2.9, protein 2.3

Chives Radish

Preparation time: 10 minutes | *Cooking time:* 25 minutes | *Servings:* 4

Ingredients:
- 1 pound radishes, sliced
- 1 tablespoon olive oil
- 1 tablespoon lime juice
- 1 teaspoon chili powder
- A pinch of salt and black pepper
- 1 tablespoon chives, minced

Directions:
In a sous vide bag, mix the radishes with the oil, lime juice and the other ingredients, seal the bag, cook in the water oven at 165 degrees F for 25 minutes, divide mix between plates and serve.

Nutrition: calories 38, fat 1.5, fiber 0.2, carbs 0.4, protein 2.5

Dill Tomatoes

Preparation time: 10 minutes | Cooking time: 20 minutes | Servings: 4

Ingredients:
- 2 pounds tomatoes, cut into wedges
- 1 tablespoon lemon zest, grated
- A pinch of salt and black pepper
- 1 tablespoon dill, chopped
- 1 teaspoon rosemary, dried
- 1 teaspoon chili powder

Directions:

In a sous vide bag, mix the tomatoes with the lemon zest and the other ingredients, seal the bag, submerge in the water oven, cook at 170 degrees F for 20 minutes, divide the mix between plates and serve.

Nutrition: calories 161, fat 10.1, fiber 3.1, carbs 4.5, protein 9.6

Green Beans Sauté

Preparation time: 10 minutes | Cooking time: 25 minutes | Servings: 4

Ingredients:
- 1 pound green beans, trimmed
- 1 tablespoon soy sauce
- 2 tablespoons olive oil
- 2 spring onions, chopped
- ½ teaspoon coriander, ground
- A pinch of salt and black pepper
- 2 tablespoons garlic, minced
- 1 tablespoon dill, chopped

Directions:

In a sous vide bag, mix the green beans with the soy sauce, oil and the other ingredients, seal the bag, cook in the water oven at 165 degrees F for 25 minutes, divide the mix between plates and serve.

Nutrition: calories 165, fat 14.5, fiber 2.8, carbs 6.4, protein 2.7

Garlic Spinach

Preparation time: 10 minutes | Cooking time: 15 minutes | Servings: 4

Ingredients:
- 1 pound baby spinach
- Juice of 1 lime
- 1 tablespoon olive oil
- 4 garlic cloves, minced
- A pinch of salt and black pepper
- 1 teaspoon chili powder

Directions:

In a sous vide bag, mix the spinach with the lime juice and the other ingredients, seal the bag, cook in the water bath at 160 degrees F for 15 minutes, divide the mix between plates and serve.

Nutrition: calories 95, fat 3.7, fiber 1.9, carbs 2.4, protein 3.8

Creamy Zucchini

Preparation time: 10 minutes | Cooking time: 25 minutes | Servings: 4

Ingredients:
- 2 tablespoons rosemary, chopped
- 1 pound zucchinis, cut into wedges
- 2 tablespoons lime juice
- 1 tablespoon olive oil
- A pinch of salt and black pepper
- 1 cup heavy cream
- ½ teaspoon rosemary, dried
- 1 tablespoon dill, chopped

Directions:

In a sous vide bag, mix the zucchinis with the rosemary and the other ingredients, seal the bag, submerge in the water bath, cook at 160 degrees F for 25 minutes, divide the mix between plates and serve.

Nutrition: calories 181, fat 11.8, fiber 4.2, carbs 5.9, protein 3.6

Spicy Eggplant

Preparation time: 10 minutes | Cooking time: 25 minutes | Servings: 4

Ingredients:
- 1 pound eggplants, sliced
- ¼ cup lemon juice
- 2 tablespoons olive oil
- ½ teaspoon hot paprika
- 1 red chili pepper, minced
- 1 tablespoon chili powder
- A pinch of salt and black pepper

Directions:
In a large sous vide bag, mix the eggplants with the lemon juice, oil and the other ingredients, seal the bag, submerge in the water bath, cook at 170 degrees F for 25 minutes, divide the mix between plates and serve.

Nutrition: calories 65, fat 1.5, fiber 0.3, carbs 0.9, protein 2.8

Pesto Tomato Mix

Preparation time: 10 minutes | Cooking time: 20 minutes | Servings: 4

Ingredients:
- 1 pound cherry tomatoes, halved
- 2 tablespoons olive oil
- 2 tablespoons basil pesto
- ½ teaspoon sweet paprika
- 1 teaspoon garlic, minced
- A pinch of salt and black pepper
- 1 tablespoon chives, chopped

Directions:
In a sous vide bag, mix the tomatoes with the pesto, oil and the other ingredients, seal the bag, cook in the water bath at 167 degrees F for 20 minutes, divide the mix between plates and serve.

Nutrition: calories 25, fat 1.9, fiber 0.5, carbs 1.4, protein 1.4

Cabbage Sauté

Preparation time: 10 minutes | Cooking time: 25 minutes | Servings: 4

Ingredients:
- 1 pound red cabbage, shredded
- 1 tablespoon lime juice
- 2 tablespoons olive oil
- 1 teaspoon sweet paprika
- A pinch of salt and black pepper
- ¼ cup chicken stock
- 1 tablespoon dill, chopped

Directions:
In a sous vide bag, mix the cabbage with the lime juice, oil and the other ingredients, seal the bag, cook in the water bath at 170 degrees F for 25 minutes, divide the mix between plates and serve.

Nutrition: calories 36, fat 1.4, fiber 0.2, carbs 0.4, protein 2

Zucchini and Tomato Mix

Preparation time: 10 minutes | Cooking time: 30 minutes | Servings: 4

Ingredients:
- 2 cups zucchinis, sliced
- 1 cup cherry tomatoes, halved
- 2 tablespoons olive oil
- 2 tablespoons balsamic vinegar
- A pinch of salt and black pepper
- 2 tablespoons parsley, chopped

Directions:
In a sous vide bag, mix the zucchinis with the tomatoes and the other ingredients, seal the bag, submerge in the water bath, cook at 160 degrees F for 30 minutes, divide the mix between plates and serve.

Nutrition: calories 41, fat 1.2, fiber 0.2, carbs 0.6, protein 2.4

Paprika Okra

Preparation time: 10 minutes | Cooking time: 25 minutes | Servings: 4

Ingredients:
- 2 cups okra
- 1 teaspoon sweet paprika
- 1 tablespoon olive oil
- 1 tablespoon lemon juice
- A pinch of salt and black pepper
- 1 tablespoon balsamic vinegar
- 1 tablespoon chives, chopped

Directions:

In a sous vide bag, mix the okra with the lemon juice, paprika and the other ingredients, seal the bag, cook in the water bath at 160 degrees F for 25 minutes, divide the mix between plates and serve.

Nutrition: calories 26, fat 1.2, fiber 0.2, carbs 0.7, protein 1.4

Chili Collard Greens

Preparation time: 10 minutes | Cooking time: 20 minutes | Servings: 4

Ingredients:
- 1 pound collard greens, trimmed
- 2 tablespoons balsamic vinegar
- ½ teaspoon chili powder
- 1 red chili pepper, minced
- 2 tablespoons olive oil
- 1 tablespoon sweet paprika
- A pinch of salt and black pepper
- 1 tablespoon cilantro, chopped

Directions:

In a sous vide bag, mix the collard greens with the vinegar, chili powder and the other ingredients, seal the bag, cook in the water bath at 160 degrees F for 20 minutes, divide the mix between plates and serve.

Nutrition: calories 151, fat 12.2, fiber 4.3, carbs 6.8, protein 4

Beet and Radish Mix

Preparation time: 10 minutes | Cooking time: 35 minutes | Servings: 4

Ingredients:
- 1 pound radishes, halved
- ½ pound beets, peeled and cut into wedges
- 2 tablespoons olive oil
- 2 tablespoons balsamic vinegar
- 1 tablespoon chives, chopped
- A pinch of salt and black pepper

Directions:

In a sous vide bag, mix the radishes with the beets, oil and the rest of the ingredients, seal the bag, cook in the water oven at 167 degrees F for 35 minutes, divide the mix between plates and serve.

Nutrition: calories 61, fat 1.3, fiber 0.8, carbs 1, protein 3.2

Cilantro Hot Artichokes

Preparation time: 10 minutes | Cooking time: 30 minutes | Servings: 4

Ingredients:
- ½ cup canned artichoke hearts, drained and chopped
- 2 red chilies, minced
- ½ teaspoon hot paprika
- 1 tablespoon cilantro, chopped
- 2 tablespoons olive oil
- 2 tablespoons balsamic vinegar
- A pinch of red pepper flakes, crushed
- A pinch of salt and black pepper

Directions:

In a large sous vide bag, mix the artichoke hearts with the chilies and the other ingredients, seal the bag, cook in the water bath at 170 degrees F for 30 minutes, divide the mix between plates and serve.

Nutrition: calories 141, fat 1.5, fiber 0.2, carbs 1.2, protein 7.3

Dill Endives

Preparation time: 10 minutes | Cooking time: 25 minutes | Servings: 4

Ingredients:
- 2 endives, halved
- 2 tablespoons olive oil
- 2 tablespoons lime juice
- A pinch of salt and black pepper
- 1 tablespoon dill, chopped
- ½ teaspoon cumin, ground
- ½ teaspoon coriander, ground

Directions:
In a sous vide bag, mix the endives with the oil, lime juice and the other ingredients, seal the bag, cook in the water bath at 170 degrees F for 25 minutes, divide the mix between plates and serve.

Nutrition: calories 96, fat 1.4, fiber 0.8, carbs 1, protein 5.6

Lime Fennel

Preparation time: 10 minutes | Cooking time: 25 minutes | Servings: 4

Ingredients:
- 2 fennel bulbs, sliced
- Juice of 1 lime
- 1 tablespoon lime zest, grated
- 2 tablespoons avocado oil
- ½ teaspoon coriander, ground
- A pinch of salt and black pepper
- 1 teaspoon chili powder
- 1 tablespoon rosemary, chopped

Directions:
In a sous vide bag, mix the fennel with the lime juice, zest and the other ingredients, seal the bag, cook in the water bath at 167 degrees F for 25 minutes, divide the mix between plates and serve.

Nutrition: calories 41, fat 1.4, fiber 0.1, carbs 0.5, protein 2.3

Paprika Olives Mix

Preparation time: 10 minutes | Cooking time: 15 minutes | Servings: 4

Ingredients:
- 2 cups kalamata olives, pitted
- A pinch of salt and black pepper
- 2 tablespoons olive oil
- ½ teaspoon sweet paprika
- ½ teaspoon rosemary, dried
- Juice of 1 lime
- 2 tablespoons parsley, chopped

Directions:
In a sous vide bag, mix the olives with the oil, paprika and the other ingredients, seal the bag, cook in the water bath at 165 degrees F for 15 minutes, divide the mix between plates and serve.

Nutrition: calories 64, fat 4, fiber 2.8, carbs 3, protein 1.4

Olives and Tomatoes

Preparation time: 10 minutes | Cooking time: 30 minutes | Servings: 4

Ingredients:
- 1 cup black olives, pitted and halved
- 1 cup green olives, pitted and halved
- 1 pound cherry tomatoes, halved
- 2 tablespoons avocado oil
- 1 tablespoon lemon juice
- 2 spring onions, chopped
- A pinch of salt and black pepper
- 1 tablespoon chives, chopped

Directions:
In a sous vide bag, mix the olives with the tomatoes, oil and the other ingredients, seal the bag, cook in the water bath at 165 degrees F for 30 minutes, divide the mix between plates and serve.

Nutrition: calories 99, fat 3.7, fiber 2.3, carbs 3, protein 4

Eggplant and Okra Mix

Preparation time: 5 minutes | Cooking time: 25 minutes | Servings: 4

Ingredients:
- 1 pound eggplants, peeled and cubed
- 1 cup okra, sliced
- 2 tablespoons avocado oil
- ½ teaspoon turmeric powder
- ½ teaspoon sweet paprika
- Juice of ½ lemon
- 2 garlic cloves, minced
- A pinch of salt and black pepper
- 1 tablespoon chives, chopped
- 1 teaspoon cumin, ground

Directions:
In a sous vide bag, mix the eggplant with the okra, oil and the other ingredients, seal the bag, cook in the water bath at 165 degrees F for 25 minutes, divide the mix between plates and serve.

Nutrition: calories 94, fat 1.5, fiber 0.4, carbs 1, protein 4.5

Beets and Olives

Preparation time: 10 minutes | Cooking time: 35 minutes | Servings: 4

Ingredients:
- 1 pound beets, peeled and cubed
- 1 cup kalamata olives, pitted and halved
- 1 cup black olives, pitted and halved
- 1 teaspoon coriander, ground
- ½ teaspoon hot paprika
- 1 tablespoon avocado oil
- 1 shallot, minced
- A pinch of salt and black pepper
- ¼ cup chicken stock

Directions:
In a sous vide bag, mix the beets with the olives, coriander and the other ingredients, seal the bag, cook in the water bath at 170 degrees F for 35 minutes, divide the mix between plates and serve.

Nutrition: calories 83, fat 4.4, fiber 2.3, carbs 3.4, protein 2

Lemon Bok Choy

Preparation time: 10 minutes | Cooking time: 20 minutes | Servings: 4

Ingredients:
- 1 pound bok choy, roughly torn
- 2 tablespoons balsamic vinegar
- 1 tablespoon olive oil
- ½ teaspoon sweet paprika
- A pinch of salt and black pepper
- ¼ cup lemon juice
- 1 tablespoon chives, chopped

Directions:
In a sous vide bag, mix the bok choy with the vinegar, oil and the other ingredients, seal the bag, cook in the water bath at 170 degrees F for 20 minutes, divide the mix between plates and serve.

Nutrition: calories 34, fat 1, fiber 0.2, carbs 0.5, protein 1.3

Ginger Bok Choy Mix

Preparation time: 10 minutes | Cooking time: 20 minutes | Servings: 4

Ingredients:
- 1 pound bok choy, torn
- 1 cup cherry tomatoes, halved
- 2 tablespoons lime juice
- 2 tablespoons olive oil
- 1 tablespoon ginger, grated
- 1 tablespoon chives, chopped

Directions:
In a sous vide bag, mix the bok choy with the tomatoes and the other ingredients, seal the bag, cook in the water bath at 160 degrees F for 20 minutes, divide the mix between plates and serve.

Nutrition: calories 62, fat 4.1, fiber 2.3, carbs 3, protein 2.5

Spicy Cabbage with Kale

Preparation time: 10 minutes | Cooking time: 30 minutes | Servings: 4

Ingredients:
- 1 pound red cabbage, shredded
- 2 cups baby kale
- Juice of 1 lime
- ½ teaspoon hot paprika
- ½ teaspoon chili powder
- 2 garlic cloves, chopped
- 1 tablespoon olive oil
- 1 tablespoon cilantro, chopped

Directions:

In a sous vide bag, mix the cabbage with the kale, lime juice and the other ingredients, seal the bag, cook in the water bath at 165 degrees F for 30 minutes,, divide the mix between plates and serve.

Nutrition: calories 63, fat 3.5, fiber 2, carbs 3.1, protein 2

Mint Eggplant

Preparation time: 10 minutes | Cooking time: 20 minutes | Servings: 4

Ingredients:
- 1 pound eggplants, roughly cubed
- 2 tablespoons olive oil
- ½ teaspoon sweet paprika
- Juice of 1 lime
- 1 tablespoon mint, chopped
- 2 spring onions, chopped
- A pinch of salt and black pepper

Directions:

In a sous vide bag, mix the eggplants with the mint, oil and the other ingredients, seal the bag, cook in the water bath at 175 degrees F for 20 minutes, divide the mix into bowls and serve.

Nutrition: calories 76, fat 3.7, fiber 0.5, carbs 1.2, protein 0.5

Broccoli and Tomatoes

Preparation time: 10 minutes | Cooking time: 30 minutes | Servings: 4

Ingredients:
- 1 pound broccoli florets
- ½ pound cherry tomatoes, halved
- 1 teaspoon sweet paprika
- 1 tablespoon olive oil
- 2 shallots, chopped
- A pinch of salt and black pepper

Directions:

In a sous vide bag, mix the broccoli with the tomatoes and the other ingredients, seal the bag, coo in the water oven at 164 degrees F for 30 minutes, divide between plates and serve.

Nutrition: calories 81, fat 4.2, fiber 2.3, carbs 3.5, protein 3.8

Balsamic Pearl Onions

Preparation time: 10 minutes | Cooking time: 20 minutes | Servings: 4

Ingredients:
- 1 pound pearl onions, peeled
- 4 garlic cloves, chopped
- Juice of ½ lime
- 1 tablespoon balsamic vinegar
- A pinch of salt and black pepper
- ¼ teaspoon red pepper flakes
- 1 tablespoon chives, chopped

Directions:

In a sous vide bag, mix the pearl onions with the garlic, lime juice and the other ingredients, seal the bag, cook in the water oven at 165 degrees F for 20 minutes, divide the mix between plates and serve.

Nutrition: calories 34, fat 1.2, fiber 0.4, carbs 0.4, protein 2.5

Coconut Cabbage

***Preparation time:** 10 minutes | **Cooking time:** 30 minutes | **Servings:** 4*

Ingredients:
- ½ cup coconut cream
- Juice of ½ lime
- 1 pound red cabbage, cut into wedges
- 2 tablespoons balsamic vinegar
- 1 teaspoon rosemary, dried
- A pinch of salt and black pepper
- 2 tablespoons cilantro, chopped

Directions:

In a large sous vide bag, mix the cabbage with the cream, lime juice and the other ingredients, seal the bag, cook in the water oven at 170 degrees F for 30 minutes, divide the mix between plates and serve.

Nutrition: calories 118, fat 6.8, fiber 2.9, carbs 5.1, protein 1.5

Turmeric Brussels Sprouts

***Preparation time:** 10 minutes | **Cooking time:** 30 minutes | **Servings:** 4*

Ingredients:
- 2 pounds Brussels sprouts, halved
- 1 teaspoon turmeric powder
- Zest of 1 lime, grated
- ½ cup chicken stock
- A pinch of salt and black pepper
- 2 tablespoons ghee, melted
- 2 tablespoons chives, chopped

Directions:

In a sous vide bag, mix the sprouts with the turmeric, lime zest and the other ingredients, seal the bag, cook in the water bath at 170 degrees F for 30 minutes, divide between plates and serve.

Nutrition: calories 166, fat 7.3, fiber 3.4, carbs 4.4, protein 7.8

Lemon Cauliflower

***Preparation time:** 5 minutes | **Cooking time:** 30 minutes | **Servings:** 4*

Ingredients:
- 2 pounds cauliflower florets
- 2 tablespoons soy sauce
- 1 tablespoon olive oil
- 1 tablespoon lemon juice
- 1 tablespoon lemon zest, grated
- ½ cup chicken stock
- A pinch of salt and black pepper

Directions:

In a large sous vide bag, mix the cauliflower with the soy sauce, oil and the other ingredients, seal the bag, cook in the water bath at 170 degrees F for 30 minutes, divide the mix between plates and serve.

Nutrition: calories 81, fat 1.2, fiber 0.5, carbs 1, protein 6.5

Bok Choy and Cauliflower Mix

***Preparation time:** 5 minutes | **Cooking time:** 35 minutes | **Servings:** 4*

Ingredients:
- 2 cups bok choy, torn
- 2 cups cauliflower florets
- 1 tablespoon olive oil
- ½ teaspoon cumin, ground
- ½ teaspoon garlic powder
- ½ teaspoon sweet paprika
- ½ cup chicken stock
- 2 tablespoons chives, chopped
- 1 tablespoon tomato sauce

Directions:

In a sous vide bag, mix the bok choy with the cauliflower, oil and the other ingredients, seal the bag, submerge in the water bath, cook at 174 degrees F for 35 minutes, divide the mix between plates and serve.

Nutrition: calories 24, fat 1.6, fiber 0.6, carbs 1, protein 2.5

Nutmeg Fennel and Tomatoes

Preparation time: 5 minutes | *Cooking time:* 35 minutes | *Servings:* 4

Ingredients:
- 2 fennel bulbs, sliced
- 1 pound cherry tomatoes, halved
- ½ teaspoon nutmeg, ground
- 2 tablespoons olive oil
- 1 tablespoon soy sauce
- 2 tablespoons lemon juice
- ¼ cup veggie stock
- A pinch of salt and black pepper

Directions:

In a sous vide bag, mix the fennel with the cherry tomatoes, nutmeg and the other ingredients, seal the bag, cook in the water oven at 170 degrees F for 35 minutes, divide the mix between plates and serve.

Nutrition: calories 243, fat 20.4, fiber 4.3, carbs 5.7, protein 4.2

Green Beans and Avocado Mix

Preparation time: 10 minutes | *Cooking time:* 25 minutes | *Servings:* 4

Ingredients:
- 1 pound green beans, trimmed
- 1 cup avocado, peeled, pitted and cubed
- 1 tablespoon olive oil
- Juice of 1 lime
- 1 green onion, sliced
- 1 tablespoon mint, chopped
- A pinch of salt and black pepper
- 1 tablespoon chives, chopped

Directions:

In a sous vide bag, mix the green beans with the avocado, oil and the other ingredients, seal the bag, submerge in the water oven and cook at 170 degrees F for 25 minutes Divide the mix between plates and serve.

Nutrition: calories 40, fat 1.2, fiber 0.4, carbs 0.6, protein 2.4

Green Beans and Pine Nuts Mix

Preparation time: 10 minutes | *Cooking time:* 25 minutes | *Servings:* 4

Ingredients:
- 1 pound green beans, trimmed
- 2 tablespoons pine nuts, toasted
- 1 tablespoon balsamic vinegar
- 2 tablespoons olive oil
- A pinch of salt and black pepper
- 2 tablespoons almonds, chopped
- 1 tablespoon chives, chopped
- ¼ cup chicken stock

Directions:

In a sous vide bag, mix the green beans with the pine nuts, vinegar and the other ingredients, seal the bag, submerge in the water bath, cook at 170 degrees F for 25 minutes, divide the mix between plates and serve.

Nutrition: calories 56, fat 1.7, fiber 0.5, carbs 1, protein 2.9

Mustard Roasted Peppers

Preparation time: 10 minutes | *Cooking time:* 30 minutes | *Servings:* 4

Ingredients:
- 2 cups roasted red peppers, cut into strips
- 2 tablespoons mustard
- 2 tablespoons olive oil
- 1 tablespoon balsamic vinegar
- 2 garlic cloves, minced
- A pinch of salt and black pepper
- ¼ cup chicken stock
- 1 bunch parsley, chopped

Directions:

In a large sous vide bag, mix the peppers with the mustard, oil and the other ingredients, seal the bag, cook in the water bath at 166 degrees F for 30 minutes, divide the mix between plates and serve.

Nutrition: calories 25, fat 1, fiber 0.1, carbs 0.5, protein 1

Peppers and Green Beans

Preparation time: 10 minutes | Cooking time: 35 minutes | Servings: 4

Ingredients:
- 2 red bell peppers, cut into wedges
- 1 pound green beans, trimmed and halved
- 2 tablespoons soy sauce
- Juice of ½ lime
- A pinch of salt and black pepper
- 2 garlic cloves, minced
- 1 cup black olives, pitted and halved

Directions:

In a sous vide bag, mix the peppers with the green beans, soy sauce and the other ingredients, seal the bag, submerge in the water bath, cook at 180 degrees F for 35 minutes, divide the mix between plates and serve.

Nutrition: calories 70, fat 3.9, fiber 2.8, carbs 3.2, protein 1.6

Lemon Okra

Preparation time: 10 minutes | Cooking time: 35 minutes | Servings: 4

Ingredients:
- 2 cups okra
- Juice of 1 lemon
- 2 tablespoons balsamic vinegar
- 1 tablespoon olive oil
- A pinch of salt and black pepper
- 1 cup canned tomatoes, crushed
- 1 bunch parsley, chopped
- 2 garlic cloves, crushed

Directions:

In a sous vide bag, mix the okra with the lemon juice, vinegar and the other ingredients, seal the bag, cook in the water oven at 160 degrees F for 35 minutes, divide the mix between plates and serve.

Nutrition: calories 94, fat 1.4, fiber 0.2, carbs 0.6, protein 5.3

Ginger Radish and Spring Onions

Preparation time: 10 minutes | Cooking time: 30 minutes | Servings: 4

Ingredients:
- 1 pound radishes, halved
- 4 spring onions, chopped
- 2 tablespoons balsamic vinegar
- Juice of ½ lime
- 3 garlic cloves, minced
- 1 tablespoon olive oil
- ½ inch ginger, grated
- 1 tablespoon chives, chopped

Directions:

In a large sous vide bag, mix the radishes with the spring onions, vinegar and the other ingredients, seal the bag, submerge in the water bath, cook at 165 degrees F for 30 minutes, divide the mix between plates and serve as a side dish.

Nutrition: calories 83, fat 4.4, fiber 2.1, carbs 3.3, protein 2.6

Broccoli and Zucchini Mix

Preparation time: 10 minutes | Cooking time: 30 minutes | Servings: 4

Ingredients:
- 1 pound zucchinis, roughly cubed
- 2 cups broccoli florets
- 2 tablespoons balsamic vinegar
- ½ teaspoon sweet paprika
- ¼ cup chicken stock
- A pinch of salt and black pepper
- 2 tablespoons olive oil
- 1 tablespoon chives, chopped

Directions:

Divide the zucchinis, broccoli, vinegar and the other ingredients, into sous vide bags, seal them, submerge in the preheated water bath, cook at 170 degrees F for 30 minutes, divide the mix between plates and serve.

Nutrition: calories 112, fat 7.5, fiber 2.4, carbs 4.5, protein 4

Broccoli and Rice

Preparation time: 10 minutes | Cooking time: 45 minutes | Servings: 4

Ingredients:
- 1 cup wild rice
- 1 cup chicken stock
- 1 cup broccoli florets
- 1 tablespoon olive oil
- ½ teaspoon sweet paprika
- ½ teaspoon rosemary, dried
- Juice of ½ lime
- 2 shallots, chopped
- A pinch of salt and black pepper
- 1 tablespoon cilantro, chopped

Directions:

In a large sous vide bag, mix the rice with the stock and the other ingredients, seal the bag, submerge in the water bath, cook at 170 degrees F for 45 minutes, divide the mix between plates and serve.

Nutrition: calories 149, fat 12.1, fiber 3, carbs 7.8, protein 5.2

Coconut Broccoli Mix

Preparation time: 10 minutes | Cooking time: 35 minutes | Servings: 4

Ingredients:
- 2 tablespoons avocado oil
- 1 pound broccoli florets
- 3 garlic cloves, minced
- ½ cup coconut cream
- Zest of 1 lime, grated
- 1 tablespoon dill, chopped
- A pinch of salt and black pepper

Directions:

In a sous vide bag, mix the broccoli with the oil, garlic and the other ingredients, seal the bag, cook in the water bath at 170 degrees F for 35 minutes, divide the mix between plates and serve.

Nutrition: calories 170, fat 14, fiber 3.8, carbs 6.5, protein 4.3

Balsamic Mushroom Mix

Preparation time: 10 minutes | Cooking time: 30 minutes | Servings: 4

Ingredients:
- 2 tablespoons olive oil
- 1 pound brown mushrooms, halved
- 1 tablespoon soy sauce
- 1 tablespoon lime juice
- ½ teaspoon rosemary, dried
- ½ teaspoon garam masala
- A pinch of salt and black pepper
- ¼ cup chicken stock
- 1 tablespoon dill, chopped

Directions:

In a large sous vide bag, mix the mushrooms with the oil, soy sauce and the other ingredients, seal the bag, cook in the water bath at 175 degrees F for 30 minutes, divide the mix between plates and serve.

Nutrition: calories 41, fat 4.3, fiber 1.9, carbs 3.5, protein 3.9

Mushroom and Tomatoes Sauté

Preparation time: 10 minutes | Cooking time: 35 minutes | Servings: 4

Ingredients:
- 2 tablespoons olive oil
- 1 pound cherry tomatoes, halved
- ½ pound mushrooms, halved
- ¼ cup red wine
- ½ teaspoon rosemary, dried
- ½ teaspoon coriander, ground
- ½ teaspoon chili powder
- 2 spring onions, chopped
- A pinch of salt and black pepper
- 1 tablespoon chives, chopped

Directions:

In a sous vide bag, mix the tomatoes with the mushrooms, oil and the other ingredients, seal the bag, submerge in the water bath, cook at 170 degrees F for 35 minutes, divide the mix between plates and serve.

Nutrition: calories 60, fat 4.6, fiber 1.4, carbs 3.2, protein 3.6

Balsamic Walnuts and Radish Mix

Preparation time: 5 minutes | Cooking time: 35 minutes | Servings: 4

Ingredients:
- ¼ cup walnuts
- 1 pound radishes, halved
- 2 tablespoons olive oil
- ½ teaspoon sweet paprika
- A pinch of salt and black pepper
- 1 tablespoon balsamic vinegar
- 1 tablespoon chives, chopped

Directions:

In a sous vide bag, mix the radishes with the walnuts, oil and the other ingredients, seal the bag, submerge in the water bath, cook at 170 degrees F for 35 minutes, divide the mix between plates and serve.

Nutrition: calories 13, fat 1.2, fiber 0.2, carbs 0.3, protein 0.5

Paprika Avocado and Mushrooms

Preparation time: 10 minutes | Cooking time: 30 minutes | Servings: 4

Ingredients:
- 1 pound white mushrooms, halved
- 1 cup avocado, peeled, pitted and cubed
- ½ cup black olives, pitted and halved
- Juice of 1 lime
- ½ teaspoon sweet paprika
- A pinch of salt and black pepper
- ¼ cup veggie stock
- 1 tablespoon rosemary, chopped
- 1 tablespoon avocado oil

Directions:

In a sous vide bag, mix the mushrooms with the avocado, olives and the other ingredients, seal the bag, submerge in the water bath, cook at 170 degrees F for 30 minutes, divide the mix between plates and serve.

Nutrition: calories 14, fat 2.3, fiber 1.3, carbs 2.1, protein 0.5

Coconut Tomatoes and Spinach

Preparation time: 10 minutes | Cooking time: 30 minutes | Servings: 4

Ingredients:
- 1 pound baby spinach
- ½ pound cherry tomatoes, halved
- ½ cup coconut flesh, unsweetened and shredded
- 1 tablespoon avocado oil
- ¼ cup coconut cream
- 1 teaspoon chili powder
- A pinch of salt and black pepper
- 1 tablespoon chives, chopped

Directions:

In a sous vide bag, mix the spinach with the tomatoes, coconut and the other ingredients, seal the bag, cook in the water bath at 165 degrees F for 30 minutes, divide the mix between plates and serve.

Nutrition: calories 41, fat 3.9, fiber 1, carbs 1.9, protein 0.6

Chili Okra and Radishes

Preparation time: 10 minutes | Cooking time: 30 minutes | Servings: 4

Ingredients:
- 1 pound radishes, halved
- 2 cups okra, sliced
- 1 cup cherry tomatoes, halved
- 2 tablespoons balsamic vinegar
- 2 tablespoons avocado oil
- 2 teaspoons chili paste
- 1 tablespoon cilantro, chopped

Directions:

In a large sous vide bag, mix the radishes with the okra, tomatoes and the other ingredients, seal the bag, submerge in the water bath, cook at 175 degrees F for 30 minutes, divide everything between plates and serve.

Nutrition: calories 84, fat 2.4, fiber 2, carbs 6, protein 4.2

Sous Vide Dessert Recipes

Coffee Cream

Preparation time: 2 hours | Cooking time: 20 minutes | Servings: 6

Ingredients:
- 4 eggs, whisked
- Zest of 1 lime, grated
- 2 tablespoons coffee powder
- 3 tablespoons brown sugar
- 2 cups coconut cream

Directions:
In a blender, combine the eggs with the lime zest and the other ingredients, pulse well, pour this into a sous vide bag, seal, submerge in the preheated water oven and cook at 140 degrees F for 20 minutes. Transfer this mix to a container and cool down for 2 hours before serving.

Nutrition: calories 172, fat 2, fiber 1, carbs 4, protein 2

Turmeric and Lime Crème Brule

Preparation time: 1 hour | Cooking time: 1 hour and 10 minutes | Servings: 4

Ingredients:
- 1-quart heavy cream
- 4 tablespoons brown sugar
- ½ teaspoon turmeric powder
- ½ tablespoon lime zest, grated
- 8 egg yolks

Directions:
Heat up a pan with the cream over medium heat, add the lime zest and turmeric, cook for 10 minutes, take off the heat and cool down for 1 hour. Heat up the pot with the cream over medium-high heat and take it off heat again. In a bowl, mix the egg yolks with the sugar and the turmeric cream, whisk well, pour this into a large sous vide bag, seal the bag, introduce it in the preheated water oven and cook at 185 degrees F for 1 hour. Divide into bowls and serve cold.

Nutrition: calories 232, fat 4, fiber 5, carbs 8, protein 4

Walnuts Pudding

Preparation time: 10 minutes | Cooking time: 40 minutes | Servings: 4

Ingredients:
- 1 teaspoon butter, melted
- 2 eggs, whisked
- 3 tablespoons brown sugar
- ½ cup walnuts, chopped
- ¼ cup lemon juice
- 1/3 cup coconut milk
- ¼ cup coconut flour

Directions:
In a bowl, mix the eggs with the sugar, and the other ingredients except the butter and whisk well. Grease 4 ramekins with the butter, divide the pudding mix in each and cover the ramekins with some tin foil. Place ramekins in your sous vide machine, fill it with water until it reaches halfway up the side of the ramekins, cook at 185 degrees F for 40 minutes and serve cold.

Nutrition: calories 192, fat 3, fiber 6, carbs 9, protein 6

Cinnamon Apples

Preparation time: 10 minutes | Cooking time: 40 minutes | Servings: 4

Ingredients:
- 1 pound apples, cored and cut into wedges
- 1 teaspoon cinnamon powder
- ½ teaspoon nutmeg, ground
- 3 tablespoons sugar

Directions:
In a sous vide bag, combine the apples with the cinnamon and the other ingredients, seal the bag, submerge it in the preheated water oven and cook at 176 degrees F for 40 minutes. Divide the mix into bowls and serve them as a dessert.

Nutrition: calories 177, fat 3, fiber 7, carbs 8, protein 3

Vanilla Pudding

Preparation time: 10 minutes | Cooking time: 30 minutes | Servings: 4

Ingredients:
- 1 cup heavy cream
- 1/3 cup milk
- 1 tablespoon sugar
- 3 eggs, whisked
- ½ teaspoon nutmeg, ground
- ¼ teaspoon vanilla extract

Directions:

In a bowl, mix the cream with the milk and the other ingredients, whisk and divide the pudding into 4 ramekins. Put the ramekins in your water oven, fill the oven with water halfway up the sides of the ramekins, cook at 180 degrees F for 30 minutes and serve the puddings cold.

Nutrition: calories 200, fat 2, fiber 5, carbs 7, protein 5

Grapes Bowls

Preparation time: 10 minutes | Cooking time: 40 minutes | Servings: 4

Ingredients:
- 2 cups grapes
- ½ cup heavy cream
- 2 tablespoons sugar
- 1 teaspoon nutmeg, ground

Directions:

In a sous vide bag, combine the grapes with the cream and the other ingredients, seal the bag, submerge in the preheated water oven and cook at 176 degrees F for 40 minutes. Divide into bowls and serve.

Nutrition: calories 162, fat 3, fiber 3, carbs 5, protein 3

Grapes and Rice Pudding

Preparation time: 10 minutes | Cooking time: 1 hour and 30 minutes | Servings: 4

Ingredients:
- 1 cup white rice
- 2 cups almond milk
- 1 cup grapes, halved
- 3 tablespoons sugar
- 1 tablespoon vanilla extract

Directions:

In a sous vide bag, combine the rice with the milk and the other ingredients, seal the bag, submerge in the preheated water oven and cook at 180 degrees F for 1 hour and 30 minutes. Divide into bowls and serve.

Nutrition: calories 162, fat 4, fiber 6, carbs 8, protein 4

Raisins Pudding

Preparation time: 10 minutes | Cooking time: 1 hour | Servings: 4

Ingredients:
- 3 tablespoons sugar
- 1 cup raisins
- ½ cup white rice
- 2 cups almond milk
- 2 tablespoons almonds, chopped
- 1 teaspoon cardamom powder
- 2 tablespoons ghee, melted

Directions:

In a sous vide bag, combine the rice with the raisins, milk and the other ingredients, seal the bag, submerge in the water bath, cook at 174 degrees F for 1 hour, divide into bowls and serve as a dessert.

Nutrition: calories 172, fat 4, fiber 2, carbs 6, protein 5

Orange Bowls

***Preparation time:** 10 minutes | **Cooking time:** 25 minutes | **Servings:** 2*

Ingredients:
- 2 oranges, peeled and cut into wedges
- 1 teaspoon vanilla extract
- ½ cup grapes, halved
- Juice of 1 orange
- 1 tablespoon dried lavender buds
- 2 tablespoons sugar

Directions:
In a sous vide bag, combine the oranges with the grapes and the other ingredients, seal the bag, submerge in the preheated water oven and cook at 185 degrees F for 25 minutes. Divide into bowls and serve cold.

Nutrition: calories 181, fat 2, fiber 2, carbs 5, protein 4

Almond Cheesecake

***Preparation time:** 10 minutes | **Cooking time:** 1 hour and 30 minutes | **Servings:** 4*

Ingredients:
- 2 tablespoons butter, melted
- ¼ cup graham crackers, crushed
- ½ tablespoon brown sugar
- Cooking spray

For the filling:
- 12 ounces cream cheese
- 3 tablespoon sugar
- ½ cup almonds, chopped
- ¼ cup coconut cream
- 2 eggs, whisked
- Zest of 1 lime, grated
- 2 tablespoons lime juice

Directions:
In a bowl, combine the butter with the crackers and brown sugar and stir well. Grease 4 ramekins with the cooking spray and press the crackers layer on the bottom of each. In a bowl, mix the cream cheese with the almonds and the other ingredients for the filling and blend using your mixer. Divide this in each ramekin, cover them with tin foil, place them in your water oven, add water to cover the ramekins halfway and cook at 175 degrees F for 1 hour and 30 minutes. Serve cold.

Nutrition: calories 192, fat 2, fiber 5, carbs 7, protein 3

Cocoa Strawberries Cream

***Preparation time:** 10 minutes | **Cooking time:** 25 minutes | **Servings:** 6*

Ingredients:
- 2 tablespoons sugar
- 4 eggs, whisked
- 1 cup strawberries, halved
- 1/3 cup cocoa powder
- ¼ cup heavy cream

Directions:
In a blender, mix the eggs with the berries and the other ingredients, pulse well, pour into a sous vide bag, seal, submerge in the water oven and cook at 165 degrees F for 25 minutes. Divide this into dessert bowls and serve.

Nutrition: calories 161, fat 2, fiber 3, carbs 6, protein 3

Caramel Apples Mix

***Preparation time:** 10 minutes | **Cooking time:** 50 minutes | **Servings:** 4*

Ingredients:
- 2 tablespoons butter, melted
- 4 apples, cored and halved
- 1 teaspoon cinnamon powder
- 1 cup heavy cream
- ½ cup caramel syrup

Directions:
In a sous vide bag, mix the apples with the butter and the other ingredients, seal the bag, submerge in the preheated water oven and cook at 175 degrees F for 50 minutes. Divide into bowls and serve warm,

Nutrition: calories 200, fat 3, fiber 5, carbs 7, protein 2

Avocado and Strawberries Bowls

Preparation time: *10 minutes* | ***Cooking time:*** *20 minutes* | ***Servings:*** *2*

Ingredients:
- 2 cups strawberries, halved
- 1 cup avocado, peeled, pitted and halved
- 1 cup coconut cream
- ½ teaspoon vanilla extract
- 2 tablespoons sugar

Directions:

In a sous vide bag, combine the berries with the avocado, cream and the other ingredients, seal the bag, submerge it in the preheated water oven and cook at 170 degrees F for 20 minutes. Divide into bowls and serve.

Nutrition: calories 155, fat 2, fiber 5, carbs 8, protein 4

Blackberries Cream

Preparation time: *10 minutes* | ***Cooking time:*** *40 minutes* | ***Servings:*** *4*

Ingredients:
- 2 cups blackberries
- 3 eggs, whisked
- 2 tablespoons butter, melted
- 1 tablespoon sugar
- ½ teaspoon vanilla extract
- ¼ teaspoon cinnamon powder

Directions:

In a blender, mix the berries with the eggs and the other ingredients, pulse well, transfer to a sous vide bag, seal, submerge it in the preheated water oven and cook at 185 degrees F for 40 minutes. Divide into bowls and serve really cold.

Nutrition: calories 162, fat 4, fiber 4, carbs 5, protein 5

Lemon Compote

Preparation time: *10 minutes* | ***Cooking time:*** *45 minutes* | ***Servings:*** *6*

Ingredients:
- ½ cup sugar
- Juice of 2 lemons
- Zest of 2 lemons, grated
- 1 cup water
- 1 lemon, peeled and chopped
- ½ teaspoon vanilla extract

Directions:

In a sous vide bag, combine the lemon juice with the sugar and the other ingredients, seal the bag, submerge it in the preheated water oven and cook at 180 degrees F for 45 minutes Divide into bowls and serve for dessert.

Nutrition: calories 132, fat 2, fiber 3, carbs 4, protein 3

Apple Compote

Preparation time: *10 minutes* | ***Cooking time:*** *40 minutes* | ***Servings:*** *4*

Ingredients:
- ½ pound apples, cored and cut into wedges
- 4 tablespoons sugar
- 1 cup water
- 1 tablespoon lemon zest, grated
- ½ teaspoon vanilla extract
- 2 teaspoons lemon juice

Directions:

In a sous vide bag, mix the apples with the sugar water and the other ingredients, seal the bag, submerge in the preheated water oven and cook at 183 degrees F for 40 minutes. Divide into bowls and serve.

Nutrition: calories 161, fat 2, fiber 5, carbs 5, protein 3

Orange Jam

***Preparation time:** 15 minutes | **Cooking time:** 40 minutes | **Servings:** 8*

Ingredients:
- 3 cups oranges, peeled and cut into wedges
- ½ teaspoon vanilla powder
- ¼ cup sugar
- Zest of 1 orange, grated
- 1 cup water

Directions:
In a sous vide bag, mix the oranges with the sugar and the other ingredients, seal the bag, submerge it in the preheated water oven and cook at 140 degrees F for 40 minutes. Transfer the jam to jars, seal and serve.

Nutrition: calories 100, fat 1, fiber 1, carbs 2, protein 4

Avocado Cream

***Preparation time:** 2 hours | **Cooking time:** 20 minutes | **Servings:** 6*

Ingredients:
- 1 teaspoon gelatin
- 8 ounces cream cheese
- 1 cup avocado, peeled, pitted and mashed
- 2 tablespoons water
- ½ tablespoon lemon juice
- 2 tablespoons sugar
- ½ cup heavy cream

Directions:
In a blender, combine the cream cheese with the avocado and the other ingredients and pulse well Divide this into 6 ramekins, cover with tin foil. introduce them all in your water oven, add water to cover the ramekins halfway and cook the pie at 183 degrees F for 20 minute Keep the cream in the fridge for 2 hours before serving.

Nutrition: calories 234, fat 3, fiber 2, carbs 6, protein 7

Chocolate Cream Cheese Ramekins

***Preparation time:** 3 hours | **Cooking time:** 30 minutes | **Servings:** 4*

Ingredients:
- 1 tablespoon vanilla extract
- 4 tablespoons butter, melted
- 1 cup dark chocolate, melted
- 4 tablespoons heavy cream
- 2 cups cream cheese
- ½ cup sugar
- 1 teaspoon vanilla extract
- Cooking spray

Directions:
Grease 4 ramekins with the cooking spray In a bowl, mix the melted butter with the chocolate and the other ingredients, whisk and divide into the ramekins. Cover the ramekins with tin foil, add water to the oven halfway to the sides of the ramekins and cook at 160 degrees F for 30 minutes. Keep the cream into the fridge for 3 hours before serving.

Nutrition: calories 210, fat 43, fiber 3, carbs 7, protein 7

Coconut Raspberry Bowls

***Preparation time:** 10 minutes | **Cooking time:** 30 minutes | **Servings:** 6*

Ingredients:
- ½ cup coconut butter, melted
- 1 cup coconut cream
- 3 tablespoons sugar
- ½ teaspoon vanilla extract
- ½ teaspoon ginger, powder
- 1 cup raspberries

Directions:
In a sous vide bag, mix the cream with the raspberries, butter and the other ingredients, seal the bag, submerge in the preheated water oven and cook at 185 degrees F for 30 minutes. Divide into bowls and serve cold.

Nutrition: calories 234, fat 22, fiber 2, carbs 7, protein 2

Mascarpone and Plums Cream

***Preparation time:** 10 minutes | **Cooking time:** 30 minutes | **Servings:** 4*

Ingredients:
- 1 cup heavy cream
- 2 tablespoons sugar
- 1 cup plums, chopped
- 2 tablespoons lemon juice
- 8 ounces mascarpone cheese

Directions:

In a bowl, mix the cream with the mascarpone and the other ingredients, whisk, transfer to a sous vide bag, seal, it, submerge in the preheated water oven and cook at 180 degrees F for 30 minutes. Divide into bowls and keep in the fridge until you serve.

Nutrition: calories 265, fat 7, fiber 6, carbs 12, protein 4

Maple and Plums Pudding

***Preparation time:** 10 minutes | **Cooking time:** 40 minutes | **Servings:** 2*

Ingredients:
- 2 tablespoons water
- 1 tablespoon gelatin
- 3 tablespoons maple syrup
- 2 tablespoons sugar
- 1 cup plums, stones removed and chopped
- 2 tablespoons cocoa powder
- 1 cup coconut milk
- ½ cup heavy cream

Directions:

In a bowl, mix the gelatin with the water, maple syrup and the other ingredients, whisk well, divide into 2 ramekins, put them in your water oven, add water to cover the ramekins halfway and cook them at 180 degrees F for 40 minutes. Serve cold.

Nutrition: calories 140, fat 2, fiber 2, carbs 4, protein 4

Almond Blueberries Ramekins

***Preparation time:** 10 minutes | **Cooking time:** 20 minutes | **Servings:** 4*

Ingredients:
- 2 cups almond milk
- 1 teaspoon vanilla extract
- ½ teaspoon nutmeg, ground
- 2 tablespoons sugar
- 2 cups blueberries
- 2 tablespoons walnuts, chopped

Directions:

In a bowl, mix the milk with the blueberries and the other ingredients, whisk well, divide into ramekins, put them in the water bath, add water to cover the ramekins halfway and cook at 170 degrees F for 20 minutes. Cool the mix down before serving.

Nutrition: calories 210, fat 3, fiber 4, carbs 6, protein 7

Carrot and Rice Pudding

***Preparation time:** 10 minutes | **Cooking time:** 45 minutes | **Servings:** 4*

Ingredients:
- 2 cups coconut milk
- 2 tablespoons sugar
- 1 cup white rice
- ½ cup carrots, peeled and grated
- 3 egg yolks
- ½ teaspoon vanilla extract

Directions:

In a sous vide bag, mix the rice with the milk and the other ingredients, seal the bag, submerge into your water oven, cook at 1 degrees F for 45 minutes, divide into bowls and serve.

Nutrition: calories 140, fat 2, fiber 3, carbs 6, protein 2

Cardamom Pudding

Preparation time: 10 minutes | *Cooking time:* 30 minutes | *Servings:* 2

Ingredients:
- 3 tablespoons sugar
- 1 cup rice
- 2 cups coconut milk
- ½ teaspoon cardamom, ground

Directions:

In a sous vide bag, mix the rice with the milk and the other ingredients, seal the bag, submerge in the water oven and cook at 170 degrees F for 30 minutes. Serve the rice pudding cold.

Nutrition: calories 150, fat 1, fiber 2, carbs 5, protein 6

Nuts Custard

Preparation time: 10 minutes | *Cooking time:* 35 minutes | *Servings:* 6

Ingredients:
- 2 cups almond milk
- 2 tablespoons walnuts, chopped
- 2 tablespoons macadamia nuts, chopped
- 4 tablespoons lemon zest, grated
- 4 eggs, whisked
- 2 tablespoons sugar
- 2 tablespoons lemon juice

Directions:

In a blender, mix the walnuts with the macadamia nuts, milk and the other ingredients, pulse well, pour into ramekins and place them in your water oven. Add water to cover the ramekins halfway and cook at 180 degrees F for 35 minutes. Leave the custard to cool down before serving.

Nutrition: calories 120, fat 6, fiber 2, carbs 5, protein 7

Creamy Berries Bowls

Preparation time: 10 minutes | *Cooking time:* 30 minutes | *Servings:* 4

Ingredients:
- 3 tablespoons walnuts, chopped
- 2 cups heavy cream
- ½ cup blackberries
- ½ cup blueberries
- ½ cup raspberries
- 2 tablespoons sugar

Directions:

In a sous vide bag, mix the berries with the cream and the other ingredients, seal the bag, submerge in the water bath and cook at 160 degrees F for 30 minutes. Divide into bowls and serve.

Nutrition: calories 135, fat 34, fiber 2, carbs 6, protein 2

Sweet Coconut Mix

Preparation time: 10 minutes | *Cooking time:* 40 minutes | *Servings:* 4

Ingredients:
- 2 cups coconut cream
- 1 cup coconut flesh, shredded
- 2 tablespoons sugar
- 1 apple, cored and cubed
- 1 cup strawberries

Directions:

In a sous vide bag, mix the coconut with the cream and the other ingredients, seal the bag, submerge it in the preheated water oven and cook at 170 degrees F for 40 minutes. Divide this mix into bowls and serve cold.

Nutrition: calories 162, fat 4, fiber 1, carbs 5, protein 4

Carrot Custard

Preparation time: 10 minutes | Cooking time: 40 minutes | Servings: 4

Ingredients:
- 1 tablespoon gelatin
- ¼ cup warm water
- 1 cup heavy cream
- 1 cup coconut cream
- 1 cup carrots, peeled and grated
- ½ teaspoon vanilla extract
- 1 teaspoon cinnamon powder
- 3 tablespoons sugar

Directions:
In a bowl, mix the cream with the gelatin, water and the other ingredients, whisk really well, divide custard into ramekins, cover them with tin foil, place them in your water oven, add water to cover the ramekins halfway and cook at 167 degrees F for 40 minutes. Serve the custard cold.

Nutrition: calories 200, fat 2, fiber 1, carbs 3, protein 5

Pears Jam

Preparation time: 10 minutes | Cooking time: 1 hour | Servings: 8

Ingredients:
- 2 pounds pears, cored and roughly cubed
- 1 cup water
- 3 tablespoons sugar
- ½ teaspoon nutmeg, ground
- ½ teaspoon vanilla extract
- 1 tablespoon cinnamon powder

Directions:
In a sous vide bag, combine the pears with the water, sugar and the other ingredients, toss, seal the bag, submerge in the preheated water oven and cook at 183 degrees F for 1 hour. Transfer the jam to a large bowl, blend it a bit using an immersion blender, divide into smaller bowls and serve cold.

Nutrition: calories 140, fat 0, fiber 2, carbs 7, protein 4

Strawberries Compote

Preparation time: 10 minutes | Cooking time: 30 minutes | Servings: 4

Ingredients:
- 2 cups strawberries, chopped
- Juice of 1 lime
- Zest of 1 lime, grated
- 3 tablespoons sugar
- 1 cup water

Directions:
In a sous vide bag, mix the berries with the water and the other ingredients, seal the bag, submerge it in the preheated water oven and cook at 183 degrees F for 30 minutes. Divide into cups and serve cold.

Nutrition: calories 200, fat 1, fiber 3, carbs 12, protein 3

Cinnamon Nectarines Bowls

Preparation time: 10 minutes | Cooking time: 40 minutes | Servings: 4

Ingredients:
- 1 pound nectarines, stones removed and halved
- 2 tablespoons sugar
- 1 cup almond milk
- ½ teaspoon vanilla extract
- ½ teaspoon cinnamon powder
- 1 teaspoon almond extract

Directions:
In a sous vide bag, mix the nectarines with the milk, sugar and the other ingredients, seal the bag, submerge in the preheated water oven and cook at 183 degrees F for 40 minutes. Divide into bowls and serve them cold.

Nutrition: calories 152, fat 2, fiber 2, carbs 4, protein 3

Rhubarb Compote

Preparation time: 10 minutes | Cooking time: 35 minutes | Servings: 4

Ingredients:
- 2 cups rhubarb, roughly sliced
- 2 tablespoons sugar
- 1 teaspoon cinnamon powder
- 1 teaspoon vanilla extract
- 1 cup water

Directions:
In a sous vide bag, mix the rhubarb with the sugar and the other ingredients, seal the bag, submerge in the preheated water oven and cook at 183 degrees F for 35 minutes Divide into bowls and serve cold.

Nutrition: calories 120, fat 2, fiber 2, carbs 6, protein 2

Apples and Berries Compote

Preparation time: 10 minutes | Cooking time: 40 minutes | Servings: 4

Ingredients:
- 4 apples, cored and roughly chopped
- 2 cups water
- 1 cup strawberries
- 3 tablespoon sugar
- 1 teaspoon cinnamon powder

Directions:
In a sous vide bag, mix the apples with the berries and the other ingredients, seal the bag, submerge in the preheated water oven and cook at 170 degrees F for 40 minutes. Divide into bowls and serve cold.

Nutrition: calories 142, fat 2, fiber 2, carbs 6, protein 2

Minty Apples Compote

Preparation time: 10 minutes | Cooking time: 30 minutes | Servings: 4

Ingredients:
- 4 apples, cored and cut into wedges
- 3 tablespoon sugar
- ½ teaspoon vanilla extract
- ½ cup water
- 1 tablespoon mint, chopped

Directions:
In a sous vide bag, combine the apples with the sugar and the other ingredients, seal, submerge in the preheated water oven and cook at 180 degrees F for 30 minutes Divide into bowls and serve cold.

Nutrition: calories 101, fat 1, fiber 1, carbs 8, protein 1

Figs and Grapes Compote

Preparation time: 10 minutes | Cooking time: 30 minutes | Servings: 4

Ingredients:
- 1 cup apple juice
- 1 cup grapes, halved
- 1 pound figs
- ½ cup water
- 4 tablespoons sugar

Directions:
In a sous vide bag, combine the apple juice with the grapes and the other ingredients, seal the bag, submerge it in the preheated water oven and cook at 170 degrees F for 30 minutes. Divide this into bowls and serve cold.

Nutrition: calories 130, fat 0, fiber 1, carbs 9, protein 1

Sweet Pumpkin Bowls

Preparation time: 10 minutes | Cooking time: 40 minutes | Servings: 4

Ingredients:
- 1 tablespoon sugar
- 2 cups pumpkin, peeled and roughly cubed
- 1 tablespoon butter, melted
- ½ teaspoon cinnamon powder
- ½ cup coconut cream

Directions:
In a sous vide bag, mix the pumpkin with the sugar, butter and the other ingredients, toss, seal the bag, submerge it in the preheated water oven and cook at 182 degrees F for 40 minutes. Divide into bowls and serve warm.

Nutrition: calories 120, fat 1, fiber 1, carbs 2, protein 2

Pecan Plums Bowls

Preparation time: 10 minutes | Cooking time: 35 minutes | Servings: 4

Ingredients:
- 1 pound plums, stoned and halved
- ½ cups pecans, chopped
- 1 cup heavy cream
- ½ teaspoon vanilla extract
- Juice of 1 lime
- 2 tablespoons sugar
- ½ teaspoon cinnamon powder

Directions:
In a sous vide bag, mix the plums with the pecans, cream and the other ingredients, toss, seal the bag, submerge in the preheated water oven and cook at 183 degrees F for 35 minutes. Divide into bowls and serve.

Nutrition: calories 152, fat 2, fiber 2, carbs 8, protein 7

Blackberry and Rhubarb Jam

Preparation time: 10 minutes | Cooking time: 50 minutes | Servings: 4

Ingredients:
- 1 pound blackberries
- 2 cups rhubarb, chopped
- 2 cups water
- Juice of 1 lime
- 1 cup sugar

Directions:
In a sous vide bag, mix the berries with the rhubarb and the other ingredients, whisk, seal the bag, submerge it in the preheated water oven and cook at 185 degrees F for 1 hour. Divide into cups and serve cold.

Nutrition: calories 100, fat 2, fiber 3, carbs 8, protein 3

Black Currant Marmalade

Preparation time: 2 hours | Cooking time: 1 hour | Servings: 8

Ingredients:
- ½ pound blueberries
- 4 ounces black currant
- 2 cups sugar
- Juice of 1 lemon
- Zest of 1 lemon, grated
- 2 tablespoon water

Directions:
In a sous vide bag, mix the berries with the currant and the other ingredients, whisk, seal the bag, submerge it in the preheated water oven and cook at 180 degrees F for 1 hour. Divide into bowls and keep in the fridge for 2 hours before serving.

Nutrition: calories 100, fat 2, fiber 3, carbs 7, protein 3

Lime Jam

Preparation time: 10 minutes | Cooking time: 45 minutes | Servings: 8

Ingredients:
- 2 tablespoons lime zest, grated
- 2 tablespoons lime juice
- 1 cup sugar
- 1 cup water
- 1 tablespoon ginger, grated

Directions:
In a sous vide bag, mix the lime juice with the sugar and the other ingredients, seal the bag, submerge it in the preheated water oven and cook at 160 degrees F for 45 minutes. Divide into bowls and serve cold.

Nutrition: calories 162, fat 2, fiber 3, carbs 8, protein 4

Creamy Pears

Preparation time: 10 minutes | Cooking time: 50 minutes | Servings: 6

Ingredients:
- 1 pound, cored and cut into quarters
- 1 cup heavy cream
- ¼ cup apple juice
- 1 teaspoon cinnamon powder
- ½ teaspoon nutmeg, ground

Directions:
In a sous vide bag, mix the pears with the cream and the other ingredients, seal the bag, submerge it in the preheated water oven and cook at 180 degrees F for 50 minutes. Divide into bowls and serve cold.

Nutrition: calories 100, fat 2, fiber 2, carbs 6, protein 4

Peaches Bowls

Preparation time: 10 minutes | Cooking time: 30 minutes | Servings: 6

Ingredients:
- 6 peaches, cored and cut into quarters
- 3 tablespoons sugar
- ½ teaspoon cinnamon powder
- 1 teaspoon vanilla extract
- 1 cup heavy cream

Directions:
In a sous vide bag, mix the peaches with the sugar and the other ingredients, seal the bag, submerge it in the preheated water bath and cook at 183 degrees F for 30 minutes. Divide into bowls and serve.

Nutrition: calories 125, fat 3, fiber 5, carbs 6, protein 4

Avocado and Figs Bowls

Preparation time: 10 minutes | Cooking time: 40 minutes | Servings: 4

Ingredients:
- 1 cup heavy cream
- 1 cup avocado, peeled, pitted and cubed
- 1 pound figs, halved
- ½ cup coconut milk
- ½ cup sugar
- ½ teaspoon ginger, ground

Directions:
In a sous vide bag, mix the avocado with the figs and the other ingredients, toss, seal the bag, submerge it in the preheated water oven and cook at 170 degrees F for 40 minutes. Divide into bowls and serve cold.

Nutrition: calories 121, fat 2, fiber 2, carbs 6, protein 4

Peach Jelly

Preparation time: 10 minutes | Cooking time: 40 minutes | Servings: 4

Ingredients:
- 4 pears, cored and cubed
- Juice of 1 lemon
- 2 cups currant jelly
- 3 tablespoons sugar
- ½ teaspoon almond extract
- ½ teaspoon vanilla extract

Directions:

In a sous vide bag, mix the pears with the jelly and the other ingredients, seal the bag, shake it a bit, submerge it in the preheated water oven and cook at 180 degrees F for 40 minutes. Divide everything into dessert bowls and serve cold.

Nutrition: calories 182, fat 3, fiber 1, carbs 2, protein 3

Cocoa Berries Cream

Preparation time: 5 minutes | Cooking time: 35 minutes | Servings: 4

Ingredients:
- 1 cup dark chocolate, chopped
- 1 cup coconut milk
- 2 tablespoons sugar
- 1 tablespoon cocoa powder
- 1 cup blackberries

Directions:

In a blender, mix the chocolate with the milk, berries and the other ingredients, pulse well, divide into 4 ramekins, place the ramekins in your water oven, fill the oven with water halfway up the sides of the ramekins, cover the ramekins with tin foil and cook at 180 degrees F for 35 minutes. Serve warm.

Nutrition: calories 110, fat 3, fiber 2, carbs 4, protein 2

Dates and Cauliflower Rice Pudding

Preparation time: 5 minutes | Cooking time: 45 minutes | Servings: 4

Ingredients:
- ½ cup dates, chopped
- 1 cup cauliflower rice
- 2 cups almond milk
- 2 tablespoons sugar
- ½ teaspoon cinnamon powder
- ½ teaspoon vanilla extract

Directions:

In a sous vide bag, mix the cauliflower with the dates and the other ingredients, seal the bag, submerge in the water oven, and cook at 180 degrees F for 45 minutes. Divide into bowls and serve warm.

Nutrition: calories 174, fat 1, fiber 3, carbs 6, protein 7

Berry and Pumpkin Curd

Preparation time: 10 minutes | Cooking time: 25 minutes | Servings: 4

Ingredients:
- 3 tablespoons sugar
- 1 cup raspberries
- 1 cup pumpkin, peeled and chopped
- 2 egg yolks, whisked
- 2 tablespoons lemon juice
- 2 tablespoons butter, melted

Directions:

In a blender, combine the berries with the pumpkin and the other ingredients and pulse well. Pour this into a sous vide bag, seal it, submerge in the preheated water oven and cook at 180 degrees F for 25 minutes. Transfer the mix to a container and serve cold.

Nutrition: calories 132, fat 1, fiber 5, carbs 7, protein 4

Peach Compote

Preparation time: 10 minutes | Cooking time: 30 minutes | Servings: 4

Ingredients:
- Juice of 1 lime
- Zest of 1 lime, grated
- 3 tablespoons sugar
- 1 pound peaches, stones removed and halved
- 2 cups water

Directions:
In a sous vide bag, combine the peaches with the water and the other ingredients, seal the bag, submerge it in the preheated water oven and cook at 180 degrees F for 30 minutes. Divide into bowls and serve cold.

Nutrition: calories 105, fat 2, fiber 0, carbs 2, protein 2

Tomato Jam

Preparation time: 10 minutes | Cooking time: 25 minutes | Servings: 6

Ingredients:
- 2 pounds tomatoes, peeled and cubed
- 3 tablespoons sugar
- 1 cup water
- ½ teaspoon ginger powder
- 1 tablespoon vinegar

Directions:
In a sous vide bag, mix the tomatoes with the sugar and the other ingredients, seal, submerge in the preheated water oven and cook at 180 degrees F for 25 minutes. Transfer to a blender, pulse a bit, divide into bowls and serve cold.

Nutrition: calories 102, fat 2, fiber 1, carbs 2, protein 6

Dates Espresso Cream

Preparation time: 10 minutes | Cooking time: 30 minutes | Servings: 4

Ingredients:
- 2 cups dates, chopped
- 2 tablespoons brown sugar
- 2 tablespoons espresso powder
- 1 cup heavy cream
- 2 eggs, whisked
- Cooking spray

Directions:
In a blender, combine the espresso powder with the dates and the other ingredients and pulse well. Grease 4 ramekins with the cooking spray, divide the mix in each and cover them with tin foil. Put the ramekins in the water bath, fill it with water halfway and cook at 180 degrees F for 30 minutes. Serve the cream cold.

Nutrition: calories 152, fat 5, fiber 2, carb 6, protein 3

Mango Bowls

Preparation time: 10 minutes | Cooking time: 20 minutes | Servings: 4

Ingredients:
- 1 tablespoon almonds, chopped
- 1 cup mango, peeled and roughly cubed
- 1 cup heavy cream
- 1 teaspoon almond extract
- 1 tablespoon brown sugar

Directions:
In a sous vide bag, mix the mango with the cream and the other ingredients, seal the bag, submerge in the water oven, cook at 170 degrees F for 20 minutes, divide the mix into bowls and serve.

Nutrition: calories 220, fat 4, fiber 2, carbs 4, protein 6

Fruit Salad

***Preparation time:** 10 minutes | **Cooking time:** 20 minutes | **Servings:** 4*

Ingredients:
- 2 tablespoons brown sugar
- 1 cup avocado, peeled, pitted and cubed
- ½ cup mango, peeled and cubed
- 1 cup heavy cream
- 1 cup blackberries
- 1 cup strawberries

Directions:

In a sous vide bag, mix the avocado with the mango and the other ingredients, seal the bag, cook in the water oven and cook at 170 degrees F for 20 minutes. Divide the mix into bowls and serve.

Nutrition: calories 262, fat 7, fiber 2, carbs 5, protein 8

Nuts and Apples Bowls

***Preparation time:** 10 minutes | **Cooking time:** 20 minutes | **Servings:** 4*

Ingredients:
- 2 tablespoons almonds, chopped
- 1 tablespoon pecans, chopped
- 1 tablespoon walnuts, chopped
- 4 apples, cored and halved
- 1 tablespoon brown sugar
- ½ cup heavy cream

Directions:

In a sous vide bag, mix the apples with the sugar, cream and the other ingredients, seal the bag, submerge in the water bath, cook at 180 degrees F for 20 minutes, divide the mix into bowls and serve.

Nutrition: calories 120, fat 2, fiber 2, carbs 4, protein 3

Plums and Peaches Bowls

***Preparation time:** 10 minutes | **Cooking time:** 15 minutes | **Servings:** 4*

Ingredients:
- 2 cups plums, pitted and halved
- 1 cup peaches, stones removed and cubed
- 1 cup heavy cream
- ½ teaspoon vanilla extract
- 3 tablespoons sugar
- 1 teaspoon ginger powder

Directions:

In a sous vide bag, mix the plums with the peaches, cream and the other ingredients, seal the bag, submerge in the water bath, cook at 170 degrees F for 15 minutes, divide the mix into bowls and serve.

Nutrition: calories 162, fat 2, fiber 2, carbs 4, protein 5

Yogurt and Berries Pudding

***Preparation time:** 5 minutes | **Cooking time:** 25 minutes | **Servings:** 4*

Ingredients:
- 1 cup heavy cream
- 2 eggs, whisked
- ½ teaspoon baking soda
- 1 cup Greek yogurt
- 1 cup raspberries
- 3 tablespoons sugar
- ½ teaspoon cinnamon powder

Directions:

In a blender, combine the cream with the eggs, yogurt and the other ingredients, pulse well, transfer to a sous vide bag, submerge in the water oven, cook at 180 degrees F for 25 minutes, divide into bowls and serve.

Nutrition: calories 172, fat 2, fiber 3, carbs 4, protein 5

Strawberries and Ginger Cream

Preparation time: 10 minutes | Cooking time: 30 minutes | Servings: 4

Ingredients:
- 1 cup strawberries, chopped
- 1 cup Greek yogurt
- 2 tablespoons brown sugar
- 1 tablespoon ginger, grated
- ½ teaspoon vanilla extract
- ½ teaspoon almond extract
- 1 cup heavy cream

Directions:

In a blender, combine the berries with the yogurt, sugar and the other ingredients, pulse well and divide into 4 ramekins. Cover the ramekins with tin foil, put them in the water oven, fill it halfway with water, cook at 170 degrees F for 30 minutes and serve cold.

Nutrition: calories 200, fat 5, fiber 3, carbs 4, protein 5

Cinnamon Cream

Preparation time: 10 minutes | Cooking time: 25 minutes | Serving: 4

Ingredients:
- 1 tablespoon cinnamon powder
- 1 cup heavy cream
- ½ teaspoon pumpkin pie spice
- 2 eggs, whisked
- 1 cup Greek yogurt
- 2 tablespoons brown sugar

Directions:

In a bowl, mix the cream with the eggs, cinnamon and the other ingredients, whisk well, transfer to a sous vide bag, seal it, submerge in the water bath, cook at 170 degrees F for 25 minutes, divide into bowls, cool down and serve.

Nutrition: calories 200, fat 5, fiber 2, carbs 5, protein 6

Quinoa Pudding

Preparation time: 10 minutes | Cooking time: 20 minutes | Servings: 4

Ingredients:
- 1 cup quinoa
- 2 cups almond milk
- 2 tablespoons sugar
- 2 tablespoons honey
- ½ teaspoon ginger powder
- 1 teaspoon cinnamon powder

Directions:

In a sous vide bag, mix the quinoa with the sugar, honey and the other ingredients, seal the bag, submerge in the water bath, cook at 180 degree F for 20 minutes divide the pudding into bowls and serve.

Nutrition: calories 172, fat 4, fiber 2, carbs 4, protein 5

Avocado and Quinoa Bowls

Preparation time: 10 minutes | Cooking time: 30 minutes | Servings: 4

Ingredients:
- 1 cup avocado, peeled, pitted and roughly cubed
- 1 cup quinoa
- 2 cups coconut milk
- 2 tablespoons sugar
- ½ teaspoon almond extract

Directions:

In a sous vide bag, mix the quinoa with the milk and the other ingredients, seal the bag, submerge in the water bath, cook at 180 degrees F for 30 minutes, divide into bowls and serve warm.

Nutrition: calories 172, fat 2, fiber 2, carbs 4, protein 6

Conclusion

Sous vide cooking might seem a bit complex and you might think that only certain cooks can do it but this cooking guide you've just discovered proves that this is not true.

The sous vide recipes collection you have just discovered brings to you some of the best, most delicious and rich dishes made using only this cooking method.

You only need a sous vide machine and this special collection in order to create some real culinary feasts. The dishes you'll make will be so tasty, intense and colored and you'll become a real star in the kitchen once you give this futuristic and innovative kitchen tool a chance.

So, what are you still waiting for? Get your own sous vide machine and start cooking in a different and fun way. Make some amazing dishes in no time and enjoy them with your friends and loved ones.

Recipe Index

ALMOND BUTTER
Almond Beef, 133

ALMOND MILK
Lime Coconut Jars, 14
Herbed Ricotta Cheese, 15
Cinnamon Rice Pudding, 16
Almond Oats, 19
Seeds Porridge, 20
Quinoa and Berries Bowls, 26
Banana Oatmeal, 27
Cheddar Eggs, 27
Apple Salad, 29
Grapes and Rice Pudding, 154
Raisins Pudding, 154
Almond Blueberries Ramekins, 158
Nuts Custard, 159
Cinnamon Nectarines Bowls, 160
Dates and Cauliflower Rice Pudding, 164
Quinoa Pudding, 167

ALMONDS
Almond Oats, 19
Lemony Okra, 53
Kale and Spring Onions Mix, 56
Coconut Dip, 82
Almond Beef, 133
Green Beans and Pine Nuts Mix, 149
Raisins Pudding, 154
Almond Cheesecake, 155
Mango Bowls, 165
Nuts and Apples Bowls, 166

APPLE JUICE
Figs and Grapes Compote, 161
Creamy Pears, 163

APPLES
Sweet Coconut Mix, 159
Apple Salad, 29
Roasted Pork and Apples, 40
Apple and Zucchini Mix, 58
Cinnamon Apples, 153
Caramel Apples Mix, 155
Apple Compote, 156
Apples and Berries Compote, 161
Minty Apples Compote, 161
Nuts and Apples Bowls, 166

APPLES (GREEN)
Sprouts Salad, 61
Apple and Shrimp Salsa, 74

ARTICHOKE (CANNED)
Artichoke Dip, 70
Beef and Artichokes, 123
Lamb with Ginger Artichokes, 132
Cilantro Hot Artichokes, 144

ARTICHOKES
Lime Artichokes, 138
Parsley Artichokes, 140

ASPARAGUS
Parsley Asparagus, 51
Chicken and Asparagus, 106
Mustard Asparagus, 139
Eggs and Asparagus, 23
Asparagus, Spinach and Eggs Mix, 16
Tuna and Asparagus, 89

AVOCADO
Smoked Salmon, Avocado and Eggs Mix, 17
Chicken and Eggs, 21
Enchilada Eggs Mix, 25
Chives Avocado Quinoa, 28
Balsamic Avocado and Tomato Salad, 29
Lemon Shrimp and Avocado Bowls, 30
Simple Cabbage and Avocado Mix, 57
Zucchini Salsa, 67
Italian Shrimp Salad, 74
Salmon and Avocado Mix, 85
Mackerel and Avocado Mix, 89
Sea Bass and Avocado, 91
Shrimp, Crab and Avocado Bowls, 98
Chicken and Avocado, 104
Chicken and Salsa, 109
Lamb and Avocado Mix, 128
Pork with Peppers and Avocado, 136
Paprika Avocado and Mushrooms, 152
Avocado and Strawberries Bowls, 156
Avocado Cream, 157
Avocado and Figs Bowls, 163
Fruit Salad, 166
Avocado and Quinoa Bowls, 167
Lime Eggs, Tomato and Avocado Mix, 18

AVOCADO OIL
Eggs, Green Beans and Mushrooms, 17
Bok Choy and Eggs, 22
Tomato Sausage Salad, 23
Eggs, Cheese and Sun-dried Tomatoes Mix, 24
Balsamic Avocado and Tomato Salad, 29
Chickpeas Breakfast Spread, 29
Curry Chicken Thighs, 37
Spring Onion and Soy Chicken, 38
Cranberry Beef, 40

Curry and Coconut Pork Chops, 43
Turmeric Shrimp Mix, 46
Lime Brussels Sprouts, 49
Coconut Endives and Radish, 56
Jalapeno Greens Mix, 61
Rosemary Broccoli Mix, 62
Creamy Tomatoes, 62
Hot Cauliflower, 63
Ginger Green Beans, 63
Italian Shrimp Salad, 74
Cod Salsa, 74
Shrimp and Olives Bowls, 83
Chili Tuna, 84
Paprika Cod, 84
Shrimp and Spinach, 85
Turmeric Tuna, 85
Lemon Cod and Peas, 86
Ginger Cod, 86
Curry Shrimp, 87
Shrimp and Broccoli, 88
Mackerel and Avocado Mix, 89
Tuna and Asparagus, 89
Balsamic Salmon and Beans, 90
Lemon Trout and Cabbage, 90
Chives Cod, 91
Tuna Bites with Pineapple, 91
Shrimp and Eggplant, 92
Garlic Mackerel, 92
Calamari and Mushrooms, 94
Curry Trout and Green Beans, 94
Creole Calamari, 97
Tarragon Trout, 98
Salmon and Kale, 99
Mustard Chicken and Capers, 101
Orange Chicken Mix, 102
Italian Turkey and Carrots, 102
Turkey and Potatoes, 106
Chicken and Asparagus, 106
Paprika Turkey Mix, 108
BBQ Chicken Wings, 109
Chicken and Salsa, 109
Coconut Turkey, 109
Turkey and Quinoa, 111
Turkey with Lime Sauce, 111
Chicken and Leeks, 112
Cayenne Turkey and Green Beans, 116
Oregano Turkey, 117
Allspice Turkey, 117
Cinnamon Chicken, 118
Turkey and Tomatoes, 119
Turkey and Spring Onions, 119
Turmeric Pork Chops, 120
Garlic Pork Chops, 120
Creamy Pork, 120
Italian Lamb Chops, 120

Chives Lamb, 121
Oregano Pork, 121
Pork Chops and Green Beans, 121
Basil Lamb, 122
Mint Lamb, 122
Lamb and Zucchini Mix, 122
Pork and Tomatoes, 123
Pork and Fennel, 124
Creamy Lamb, 124
Paprika Lamb, 125
Pork and Lentils Mix, 125
Lamb and Potatoes, 126
Spiced Beef and Peppers, 126
Rosemary Beef, 126
Lamb and Corn, 127
Beef and Sprouts, 128
Lamb and Avocado Mix, 128
Beef and Spicy Zucchinis, 130
Almond Beef, 133
Pork with Peppers and Avocado, 136
Ground Beef with Beets and Radishes, 136
Orange Pork and Veggies, 137
Pork and Pears Mix, 137
Balsamic Tomatoes, 139
Mustard Asparagus, 139
Lime Fennel, 145
Olives and Tomatoes, 145
Eggplant and Okra Mix, 146
Beets and Olives, 146
Coconut Broccoli Mix, 151
Paprika Avocado and Mushrooms, 152
Coconut Tomatoes and Spinach, 152
Chili Okra and Radishes, 152
Mushroom Salad, 54
Pork with Tomatoes and Potatoes, 130

BACON
Ham and Eggs, 13
Bacon and Radish Scramble, 20
Brussels Sprouts Salad, 20
Bok Choy and Eggs, 22
Shrimp, Eggs and Mushrooms, 24

BANANA
Banana Oatmeal, 27

BEANS (GREEN)
Eggs, Green Beans and Mushrooms, 17
Green Beans, Kale and Eggs, 26
Green Beans Salad, 47
Orange Green Beans, 49
Green Beans and Walnuts Mix, 57
Ginger Green Beans, 63
Cod and Green Beans, 85
Curry Trout and Green Beans, 94

Chicken and Green Beans, 103
Turkey Medley, 104
Cayenne Turkey and Green Beans, 116
Pork Chops and Green Beans, 121
Pork, Capers and Green Beans, 133
Orange Pork and Veggies, 137
Basil Green Beans, 138
Green Beans and Capers, 138
Green Beans and Corn, 139
Green Beans Sauté, 142
Green Beans and Avocado Mix, 149
Green Beans and Pine Nuts Mix, 149
Peppers and Green Beans, 150

BEANS BLACK (CANNED)
Black Beans Mix, 64
Balsamic Salmon and Beans, 90

BEANS RED (CANNED)
Chicken and Red Beans, 110

BEEF
Ground Beef and Eggs Ramekins, 18
Lemony and Parsley Beef, 40
Cranberry Beef, 40
Beef and Yogurt Mix, 42
Beef and Tomato Mix, 46
Spicy Meatballs, 69
Stuffed Peppers, 77
Chinese Beef Bites, 78
Hot Beef, 122
Beef and Artichokes, 123
Paprika Lamb, 125
Beef and Berries, 125
Lamb and Potatoes, 126
Spiced Beef and Peppers, 126
Rosemary Beef, 126
Sage Beef, 127
Lemon Chops and Peas, 127
Beef and Sprouts, 128
Beef and Corn, 128
Lamb and Cucumber Mix, 129
Beef and Spicy Zucchinis, 130
Beef and Spicy Zucchinis, 130
Beef with Carrots and Cabbage, 131
Ginger Pork, 131
Beef and Swiss Chard, 132
Almond Beef, 133
Almond Beef, 133
Beef and Beets, 134
Lamb and Radish Mix, 134
Pork and Red Onions Mix, 135
Pork and Pumpkin Mix, 136
Ground Beef with Beets and Radishes, 136
Oregano and Chili Lamb, 137

BEETS
Beet Cream Soup, 38
Glazed Beets, 48
Spicy Beets and Okra, 55
Tuna Salad, 75
Beet Salsa, 80
Beef and Beets, 134
Ground Beef with Beets and Radishes, 136
Beet and Radish Mix, 144
Beets and Olives, 146
Balsamic Beet Salad, 48

BELL PEPPER
Stuffed Peppers, 77

BELL PEPPER (GREEN)
Pepper Eggs Mix, 16
Chicken, Shrimp and Rice, 32
Chicken Soup, 39
Chicken Salad, 77
Chicken and Peppers, 110
Lamb and Capers, 129

BELL PEPPER (ORANGE)
Chicken and Peppers, 110

BELL PEPPER (RED)
Pepper Eggs Mix, 16
Sausage Ramekins, 17
Kale, Sausage and Eggs, 24
Oregano Eggs, 26
Chicken Soup, 39
Turmeric Veggies and Rice, 44
Chicken and Peppers, 110
Peppers Stew, 47
Peppers and Eggplant Mix, 50
Peppers and Seeds Mix, 51
Peppers Salsa, 66
Spiced Beef and Peppers, 126
Pork with Peppers and Avocado, 136
Creamy Bell Peppers, 140
Peppers and Green Beans, 150
Ginger Tomatoes Eggs, 21
Ginger Broccoli and Radish Mix, 58
Spicy Lentils Bowls, 81
Ground Chicken and Veggies Mix, 115
Mustard Roasted Peppers, 149

BLACKBERRIES
Berry Coconut Mix, 14
Walnut and Berries Bowls, 28
Beef and Berries, 125
Blackberries Cream, 156
Creamy Berries Bowls, 159
Blackberry and Rhubarb Jam, 162

Cocoa Berries Cream, 164
Fruit Salad, 166
Quinoa and Berries Bowls, 26
Pork and Blueberries Mix, 33
Almond Blueberries Ramekins, 158
Creamy Berries Bowls, 159
Black Currant Marmalade, 162

BOK CHOY
Bok Choy and Veggies Bowls, 22
Bok Choy and Eggs, 22
Lemon Bok Choy, 146
Ginger Bok Choy Mix, 146
Bok Choy and Cauliflower Mix, 148

BROCCOLI
Broccoli Eggs, 21
Mushroom and Broccoli Mix, 52
Cheesy Broccoli, 53
Ginger Broccoli and Radish Mix, 58
Rosemary Broccoli Mix, 62
Tuna Salad, 75
Shrimp and Broccoli, 88
Lamb and Broccoli, 134
Cayenne Broccoli, 141
Broccoli and Tomatoes, 147
Broccoli and Zucchini Mix, 150
Broccoli and Rice, 151
Coconut Broccoli Mix, 151

BRUSSELS SPROUTS
Brussels Sprouts Salad, 20
Lime Brussels Sprouts, 49
Sprouts Salad, 61
Tuna and Brussels Sprouts, 88
Chicken with Brussels Sprouts Mix, 107
Beef and Sprouts, 158
Garlic Brussels Sprouts, 140
Nutmeg Brussels Sprouts, 141
Turmeric Brussels Sprouts, 148

BUTTER
Crab and Eggs Mix, 14
Pepper Eggs Mix, 16
Oregano Scramble, 19
Zucchini Bowls, 23
Italian Squash and Olives Bowls, 25
Lime Lobster, 32
Vanilla and Butter Shrimp, 33
Buttery Pork Tenderloin, 34
Lamb and Pomegranate Mix, 35
Curry Chicken Thighs, 37
Provence Chicken Breast, 37
Turkey Breast and Cranberries, 38
Chili Chicken, 38

Zucchini Cream, 39
Glazed Beets, 48
Orange Green Beans, 49
Buttery Squash Mix, 49
Parmesan Fennel, 49
Creamy Spinach, 52
Creamy Garlic Spinach and Corn, 59
Lemon Greens Mix, 59
Creamy Radish and Corn Mix, 61
Chives Potatoes, 64
Black Beans Mix, 64
Olives Balls, 68
Lemon Mussels, 72
Basil Green Beans, 138
Buttery Leeks, 138
Walnuts Pudding, 153
Almond Cheesecake, 155
Caramel Apples Mix, 155
Blackberries Cream, 156
Chocolate Cream Cheese Ramekins, 157
Sweet Pumpkin Bowls, 162
Berry and Pumpkin Curd, 164

CABBAGE (GREEN)
Simple Cabbage and Avocado Mix, 57

CABBAGE (RED)
Cabbage and Carrots Mix, 56
Lemon Trout and Cabbage, 90
Chicken and Lime Red Cabbage, 119
Beef with Carrots and Cabbage, 131
Cabbage Sauté, 143
Spicy Cabbage with Kale, 147
Coconut Cabbage, 148
Beet Cream Soup, 38

CALAMARI RINGS
Balsamic Calamari and Tomatoes, 30
Calamari, Salmon and Shrimp Bowls, 31
Creamy Calamari, 32
Parsley Calamari Bites, 71
Calamari and Radish Salad, 73
Calamari and Mushrooms, 94
Creole Calamari, 97
Rosemary Calamari, 99

CAPERS
Mustard Salmon Mix, 32
Lamb Fillets and Olives, 36
Cabbage and Carrots Mix, 56
Shrimp and Olives Bowls, 83
Walnuts Bowls, 83
Shrimp and Quinoa, 95
Parsley Cod, 96
Trout and Capers Mix, 97

Mustard Chicken and Capers, 101
Lamb and Capers, 129
Pork, Capers and Green Beans, 133
Green Beans and Capers, 138
Balsamic Zucchini Mix, 140

CARROT
Mushroom Oatmeal, 27
Calamari, Salmon and Shrimp Bowls, 31
Chickpeas Stew, 47
Potato Stew, 47
Turkey and Tomato Sauce, 104
Orange Pork and Veggies, 137
Thyme Pork and Carrots, 34
Beet Cream Soup, 38
Chicken Soup, 39
Balsamic Carrots and Parsnips, 50
Cabbage and Carrots Mix, 56
Balsamic Carrots, 62
Cod and Carrots, 89
Italian Turkey and Carrots, 102
Ground Lamb and Carrots Mix, 129
Beef with Carrots and Cabbage, 131
Carrot and Rice Pudding, 158
Carrot Custard, 160

CAULIFLOWER
Dates and Cauliflower Rice Pudding, 164
Rack of Lamb and Baby Cauliflower Mix, 36
Cauliflower Salad, 48
Olives and Cauliflower, 51
Parsley Cauliflower, 52
Cauliflower and Chard Mix, 58
Hot Cauliflower, 63
Cauliflower Spread, 65
Cauliflower Bowls, 69
Chicken and Cauliflower, 113
Lemon Cauliflower, 148
Bok Choy and Cauliflower Mix, 148

CELERY
Calamari, Salmon and Shrimp Bowls, 31
Chili and Paprika Pork, 42

CHARD (RED)
Lemon Greens Mix, 59
Jalapeno Greens Mix, 61
Chicken with Hot Red Chard, 113
Beef and Swiss Chard, 132

CHEESE (CHEDDAR)
Eggs and Asparagus, 23
Eggs, Cheese and Sun-dried Tomatoes Mix, 24
Cheddar Eggs, 27
Bbq Chicken Meatballs, 76

CHEESE (GOAT)
Cheesy Broccoli, 53
Pearl Onions Bowls, 65

CHEESE (MASCARPONE)
Mascarpone and Plums Cream, 158

CHEESE (MOZZARELLA)
Cheesy Eggs Mix, 13
Shallot Scramble, 13
Mushroom Dip, 78
Coconut Cheese Dip, 66
Artichoke Dip, 70

CHEESE (PARMESAN)
Parmesan Eggs, 14
Spinach Scramble, 15
Asparagus, Spinach and Eggs Mix, 16
Cream Cheese and Spinach Eggs, 17
Tomato Ramekins, 18
Zucchini Bowls, 23
Green Beans, Kale and Eggs, 26
Parmesan Fennel, 49
Turkey Meatballs, 65
Olives Balls, 68
Cauliflower Bowls, 69
Oregano Scramble, 19
Parmesan Chicken Wings, 69

CHICKEN
Chicken and Eggs, 21
Chicken Soup, 39
Chicken, Shrimp and Rice, 32
Sage Cajun Turkey, 37
Curry Chicken Thighs, 37
Provence Chicken Breast, 37
Chili Chicken, 38
Spring Onion and Soy Chicken, 38
Chicken Soup, 39
Cauliflower Soup, 39
Turmeric Veggies and Rice, 44
Chicken and Eggplants, 45
Turkey Hash, 45
Cauliflower Spread, 65
Parmesan Chicken Wings, 69
Clam Bowls, 73
Bbq Chicken Meatballs, 76
Chicken Salad, 77
Chicken Dip, 78
Garlic Chicken Bites, 82
Chili Cod, 90
Shrimp and Rice, 95
Cod, Olives and Zucchinis, 96
Tarragon Trout, 98
Shrimp, Corn and Tomato Bowls, 98

Shrimp, Crab and Avocado Bowls, 98
Salmon and Sweet Potatoes, 99
Salmon with Quinoa and Rice, 100
Pesto Turkey, 101
Mustard Chicken and Capers, 101
Orange Chicken Mix, 102
Italian Turkey and Carrots, 102
Chicken and Green Beans, 103
Duck and Tomatoes, 103
Garlic Chicken Mix, 103
Chicken and Avocado, 104
Chili Chicken, 105
Chili Chicken, 105
Chicken and Mango Mi, 105
Chicken and Asparagus, 106
Chicken and Asparagus, 106
Chicken with Brussels Sprouts Mix, 107
Chicken with Endives, 107
Chicken and Squash Mix, 108
BBQ Chicken Wings, 109
Chicken and Salsa, 109
Chicken and Red Beans, 110
Rosemary Chicken, 110
Chicken and Peppers, 110
Turkey and Quinoa, 111
Spiced Chicken Wings, 111
Turkey with Lentils, 112
Chicken and Leeks, 112
Chicken and Cauliflower, 113
Chicken and Cauliflower, 113
Chicken with Hot Red Chard, 113
Chicken with Hot Red Chard, 113
Creamy Chicken, 113
Turkey with Chickpeas, 114
Chicken with Tomato and Kale, 115
Ground Chicken and Veggies Mix, 115
Chicken and Yogurt Sauce, 115
Chicken Wings and Tomato Sauce, 116
Chicken with Okra, 117
Cinnamon Chicken, 118
Cinnamon Chicken, 118
Chicken and Bulgur, 118
Chicken and Bulgur, 118
Chicken and Lime Red Cabbage, 119
Green Beans and Corn, 139
Balsamic Radishes, 139
Cayenne Broccoli, 141
Cabbage Sauté, 143
Beets and Olives, 146
Turmeric Brussels Sprouts, 148
Lemon Cauliflower, 148
Bok Choy and Cauliflower Mix, 148
Green Beans and Pine Nuts Mix, 149
Mustard Roasted Peppers, 149
Broccoli and Zucchini Mix, 150

Broccoli and Rice, 151
Balsamic Mushroom Mix, 151

CHICKPEAS (CANNED)
Chickpeas Breakfast Spread, 29
Chickpeas Stew, 47
Chickpeas Spread, 82
Turkey with Chickpeas, 114

CHIVES
Cheesy Eggs Mix, 13
Shallot Scramble, 13
Crab and Eggs Mix, 14
Parmesan Eggs, 14
Scrambled Eggs, 15
Spinach Scramble, 15
Herbed Ricotta Cheese, 15
Asparagus, Spinach and Eggs Mix, 16
Sausage Ramekins, 17
Lime Eggs, Tomato and Avocado Mix, 18
Coconut Leeks Mix, 19
Lemon Eggs, 19
Bacon and Radish Scramble, 20
Broccoli Eggs, 21
Ginger Tomatoes Eggs, 21
Bok Choy and Veggies Bowls, 22
Kale, Sausage and Eggs, 24
Enchilada Eggs Mix, 25
Prosciutto and Zucchini Eggs, 25
Eggplant Bowls, 26
Cheddar Eggs, 27
Sweet Potato Mix, 28
Chives Avocado Quinoa, 28
Balsamic Avocado and Tomato Salad, 29
Chickpeas Breakfast Spread, 29
Mustard Salmon Steaks, 30
Shrimp Salad, 30
BBQ Cod Mix, 31
Creamy Calamari, 32
Chicken, Shrimp and Rice, 32
Vanilla and Butter Shrimp, 33
Pork and Blueberries Mix, 33
BBQ and Paprika Ribs, 33
Herbed Pork and Sun dried Tomatoes, 33
Lamb, Leeks and Mushroom Mix, 35
Beet Cream Soup, 38
Cauliflower Soup, 39
Pork Roast and Olives Salsa, 41
Beef and Yogurt Mix, 42
Shrimp and Sweet Potato Bowls, 44
Turmeric Shrimp Mix, 46
Beef and Tomato Mix, 46
Potato Stew, 47
Balsamic Carrots and Parsnips, 50
Thai Eggplant Mix, 50

Cumin Okra, 52
Eggplant and Okra Mix, 53
Lemony Okra, 53
Mushroom Salad, 54
Balsamic Tomato and Pineapple Mix, 55
Kale and Spring Onions Mix, 56
Cauliflower and Chard Mix, 58
Ginger Broccoli and Radish Mix, 58
Creamy Garlic Spinach and Corn, 59
Mustard Greens, Olives and Kale Salad, 60
Mango and Radishes Mix, 61
Creamy Radish and Corn Mix, 61
Rosemary Broccoli Mix, 62
Chives Potatoes, 64
Black Beans Mix, 64
Turkey Meatballs, 65
Coconut Cheese Dip, 66
Peppers Salsa, 66
Crab Dip, 67
Spinach Dip, 68
Cauliflower Bowls, 69
Artichoke Dip, 70
Shrimp Bites, 70
Lemon Oysters, 70
Shrimp and Cucumber Salad, 72
Squid Salad, 72
Calamari and Radish Salad, 73
Octopus and Mango Salad, 73
Clam Bowls, 73
Apple and Shrimp Salsa, 74
Shrimp and Pico De Gallo, 75
Scallops and Radish Salad, 75
Tuna Bites and Mint Sauce, 76
Chicken Salad, 77
Duck and Spinach Salad, 77
Chicken Dip, 78
Shrimp Meatballs, 79
Radish Dip, 79
Sriracha Turkey Bites, 80
Beet Salsa, 80
Fennel and Shrimp Salad, 80
Pesto Radish and Corn Dip, 81
Spicy Lentils Bowls, 81
Chickpeas Spread, 82
Shrimp and Olives Bowls, 83
Mussels Bowls, 83
Walnuts Bowls, 83
Lemon Salmon, 84
Chili Tuna, 84
Shrimp and Spinach, 85
Cod and Green Beans, 85
Turmeric Tuna, 85
Shrimp and Corn, 86
Lemon Cod and Peas, 86
Ginger Cod, 86

Chives Shrimp Mix, 87
Pesto Sea Bass, 87
Shrimp and Pineapple Bowls, 87
Tuna and Brussels Sprouts, 88
Mackerel and Avocado Mix, 89
Tuna and Asparagus, 89
Chili Cod, 90
Lemon Trout and Cabbage, 90
Chives Cod, 91
Tuna Bites with Pineapple, 91
Smoked Salmon and Chives, 92
Shrimp and Eggplant, 92
Garlic Mackerel, 92
Coconut Cod, 92
Honey Cod, 93
Shrimp and Rice, 95
Cod, Olives and Zucchinis, 96
Creamy Salmon Mix, 96
Trout and Capers Mix, 97
Creole Calamari, 97
Clams and Wine Sauce, 97
Shrimp, Corn and Tomato Bowls, 98
Salmon and Sweet Potatoes, 99
Lime Duck and Eggplant Mix, 101
Pesto Turkey, 101
Orange Chicken Mix, 102
Turkey with Sauce, 102
Duck and Tomatoes, 103
Chicken and Avocado, 104
Turkey and Tomato Sauce, 104
Chicken and Mango Mi, 105
Ginger Turkey, 105
Sage Turkey and Olives, 106
Chicken with Endives, 107
Balsamic Turkey, 108
Chicken and Squash Mix, 108
Paprika Turkey Mix, 108
BBQ Chicken Wings, 109
Coconut Turkey, 109
Cumin Turkey, 110
Chicken and Red Beans, 110
Turkey with Lime Sauce, 111
Chicken and Leeks, 112
Chicken and Cauliflower, 113
Creamy Chicken, 113
Turkey with Pomegranate Mix, 114
Ground Chicken and Veggies Mix, 115
Duck and Plums Mix, 116
Cayenne Turkey and Green Beans, 116
Allspice Turkey, 117
Chicken and Bulgur, 118
Chicken and Lime Red Cabbage, 119
Italian Lamb Chops, 120
Chives Lamb, 121
Pork Chops and Green Beans, 121

Beef and Artichokes, 123
Pork and Tomatoes, 123
Creamy Lamb, 124
Paprika Lamb, 125
Beef and Berries, 125
Lamb and Potatoes, 126
Rosemary Beef, 126
Lemon Chops and Peas, 127
Lamb and Avocado Mix, 128
Beef and Corn, 128
Ground Lamb and Carrots Mix, 129
Beef and Spicy Zucchinis, 130
Pork with Tomatoes and Potatoes, 130
Lamb and Savoy Cabbage Mix, 130
Beef with Carrots and Cabbage, 131
Orange Lamb, 131
Beef and Swiss Chard, 132
Nutmeg Pork Roast, 132
Balsamic Pork Chops, 133
Pork and Creamy Scallions Sauce, 133
Almond Beef, 133
Pork, Capers and Green Beans, 133
Lamb and Broccoli, 134
Citrus Lamb Mix, 135
Pork and Red Onions Mix, 135
Ground Beef with Beets and Radishes, 136
Oregano and Chili Lamb, 137
Pork and Pears Mix, 137
Balsamic Tomatoes, 139
Balsamic Radishes, 139
Creamy Bell Peppers, 140
Cayenne Broccoli, 141
Nutmeg Brussels Sprouts, 141
Garlic Kale, 141
Chives Radish, 141
Pesto Tomato Mix, 143
Paprika Okra, 144
Beet and Radish Mix, 144
Olives and Tomatoes, 145
Eggplant and Okra Mix, 146
Lemon Bok Choy, 146
Ginger Bok Choy Mix, 146
Balsamic Pearl Onions, 147
Turmeric Brussels Sprouts, 148
Bok Choy and Cauliflower Mix, 148
Green Beans and Avocado Mix, 149
Green Beans and Pine Nuts Mix, 149
Ginger Radish and Spring Onions, 150
Broccoli and Zucchini Mix, 150
Mushroom and Tomatoes Sauté, 151
Balsamic Walnuts and Radish Mix, 152
Coconut Tomatoes and Spinach, 152

CLAMS
Clam Bowls, 73

Clams and Wine Sauce, 97

COCONUT
Coconut Tomatoes and Spinach, 152
Sweet Coconut Mix, 159

COCONUT BUTTER
Curry and Coconut Pork Chops, 43
Coconut Raspberry Bowls, 157

COCONUT CREAM
Lime Coconut Jars, 14
Coconut Eggs, 16
Almond Oats, 19
Shrimp, Eggs and Mushrooms, 24
Walnut and Berries Bowls, 28
Lamb, Leeks and Mushroom Mix, 35
Zucchini Cream, 39
Buttery Squash Mix, 49
Coconut Endives and Radish, 56
Coconut Cheese Dip, 66
Spinach Dip, 68
Coconut Dip, 82
Curry Shrimp, 87
Coconut Cod, 92
Curry Trout and Green Beans, 94
Coconut Turkey, 109
Creamy Chicken, 113
Coconut Cabbage, 148
Coconut Broccoli Mix, 151
Coconut Tomatoes and Spinach, 152
Coffee Cream, 153
Almond Cheesecake, 155
Avocado and Strawberries Bowls, 156
Coconut Raspberry Bowls, 157
Sweet Coconut Mix, 159
Carrot Custard, 160
Sweet Pumpkin Bowls, 162

COCONUT FLAKES
Berry Coconut Mix, 14
Coconut Dip, 82

COCONUT MILK
Coconut Eggs, 16
Coconut Leeks Mix, 19
Mushroom Oatmeal, 27
Strawberry Bowls, 28
Ginger and Shallot Duck, 37
Walnuts Pudding, 153
Maple and Plums Pudding, 158
Carrot and Rice Pudding, 158
Cardamom Pudding, 159
Avocado and Figs Bowls, 163
Cocoa Berries Cream, 164

Avocado and Quinoa Bowls, 167

COD
BBQ Cod Mix, 31
Cod Salsa, 31
Cod Salsa, 74
Paprika Cod, 84
Cod and Green Beans, 85
Lemon Cod and Peas, 86
Ginger Cod, 86
Cod and Carrots, 89
Chili Cod, 90
Chives Cod, 91
Coconut Cod, 92
Honey Cod, 93
Parsley Cod, 96
Cod, Olives and Zucchinis, 96
Creamy Cod and Zucchinis, 99

COLLARD GREENS
Chili Collard Greens, 144

CORN
Creamy Calamari, 32
Creamy Garlic Spinach and Corn, 59
Creamy Radish and Corn Mix, 61
Creamy Corn, 62
Clam Bowls, 73
Creamy Corn Dip, 76
Pesto Radish and Corn Dip, 81
Shrimp and Corn, 86
Shrimp, Corn and Tomato Bowls, 98
Salmon with Quinoa and Rice, 100
Lamb and Corn, 127
Beef and Corn, 128
Green Beans and Corn, 139

CRAB
Crab and Eggs Mix, 14
Crab Dip, 67
Shrimp, Crab and Avocado Bowls, 98

CRANBERRIES
Turkey Breast and Cranberries, 38
Cranberry Beef, 40

CREAM
Cheesy Eggs Mix, 13
Shallot Scramble, 13
Ham and Eggs, 13
Lime Coconut Jars, 14
Berry Coconut Mix, 14
Asparagus, Spinach and Eggs Mix, 16
Oregano Scramble, 19
Seeds Porridge, 20

Cinnamon Eggs, 20
Lime and Chia Eggs, 21
Broccoli Eggs, 21
Zucchini Bowls, 23
Spinach Frittata, 27
Chickpeas Breakfast Spread, 29
Creamy Calamari, 32
Olives and Cauliflower, 51
Creamy Spinach, 52
Creamy Garlic Spinach and Corn, 59
Creamy Radish and Corn Mix, 61
Creamy Corn, 62
Creamy Tomatoes, 62
Cauliflower Spread, 65
Crab Dip, 67
Artichoke Dip, 70
Clam Bowls, 73
Italian Shrimp Salad, 74
Creamy Corn Dip, 76
Chicken Dip, 78
Radish Dip, 79
Pesto Radish and Corn Dip, 81
Eggplant Dip, 81
Shrimp and Mustard Sauce, 95
Parsley Cod, 96
Creamy Salmon Mix, 96
Creamy Cod and Zucchinis, 99
Turkey with Sauce, 102
Masala Turkey, 114
Creamy Pork, 120
Creamy Lamb, 124
Pork and Creamy Scallions Sauce, 133
Creamy Bell Peppers, 140
Creamy Zucchini, 142
Turmeric and Lime Crème Brule, 153
Vanilla Pudding, 154
Cocoa Strawberries Cream, 155
Caramel Apples Mix, 155
Avocado Cream, 157
Chocolate Cream Cheese Ramekins, 157
Mascarpone and Plums Cream, 158
Maple and Plums Pudding, 158
Creamy Berries Bowls, 159
Carrot Custard, 160
Pecan Plums Bowls, 162
Creamy Pears, 163
Peaches Bowls, 163
Avocado and Figs Bowls, 163
Dates Espresso Cream, 165
Mango Bowls, 165
Fruit Salad, 166
Nuts and Apples Bowls, 166
Plums and Peaches Bowls, 166
Yogurt and Berries Pudding, 166
Strawberries and Ginger Cream, 167

Cinnamon Cream, 167

CREAM CHEESE
Crab and Eggs Mix, 14
Cream Cheese and Spinach Eggs, 17
Crab Dip, 67
Spinach Dip, 68
Stuffed Mushrooms, 68
Artichoke Dip, 70
Creamy Corn Dip, 76
Chicken Dip, 78
Mushroom Dip, 78
Radish Dip, 79
Pesto Radish and Corn Dip, 81
Almond Cheesecake, 155
Avocado Cream, 157
Chocolate Cream Cheese Ramekins, 157

CUCUMBERS
Octopus and Mango Salad, 73
Balsamic Avocado and Tomato Salad, 29
Shrimp and Cucumber Salad, 72
Lamb and Cucumber Mix, 129

DATES
Dates and Cauliflower Rice Pudding, 164
Dates Espresso Cream, 165

DUCK
Ginger and Shallot Duck, 37
Duck and Spinach Salad, 77
Lime Duck and Eggplant Mix, 101
Duck and Tomatoes, 103
Turmeric Duck, 112
Duck and Plums Mix, 116

EGGPLANTS
Turmeric Veggies and Rice, 44
Eggplant Stew, 45
Peppers and Eggplant Mix, 50
Eggplant and Okra Mix, 53
Eggplant and Pearl Onion Mix, 55
Dill Eggplant, 63
Eggplant Dip, 81
Turkey Medley, 104
Ground Chicken and Veggies Mix, 115
Eggplant Bowls, 26
Tomato and Eggplant Stew, 43
Chicken and Eggplants, 45
Thai Eggplant Mix, 50
Shrimp and Eggplant, 92
Lime Duck and Eggplant Mix, 101
Orange Pork and Veggies, 137
Spicy Eggplant, 143
Eggplant and Okra Mix, 146

Mint Eggplant, 147

EGGS
Cinnamon Toast, 13
Cheesy Eggs Mix, 13
Shallot Scramble, 13
Ham and Eggs, 13
Crab and Eggs Mix, 14
Parmesan Eggs, 14
Scrambled Eggs, 15
Pesto Eggs, 15
Spinach Scramble, 15
Coconut Eggs, 16
Pepper Eggs Mix, 16
Sausage Ramekins, 17
Eggs, Green Beans and Mushrooms, 17
Cream Cheese and Spinach Eggs, 17
Smoked Salmon, Avocado and Eggs Mix, 17
Lime Eggs, Tomato and Avocado Mix, 18
Zucchini and Eggs, 18
Ground Beef and Eggs Ramekins, 18
Tomato Ramekins, 18
Coconut Leeks Mix, 19
Lemon Eggs, 19
Oregano Scramble, 19
Bacon and Radish Scramble, 20
Cinnamon Eggs, 20
Chicken and Eggs, 21
Lime and Chia Eggs, 21
Broccoli Eggs, 21
Ginger Tomatoes Eggs, 21
Bok Choy and Eggs, 22
Greens and Eggs, 22
Eggs and Asparagus, 23
Zucchini Bowls, 23
Kale, Sausage and Eggs, 24
Eggs, Cheese and Sun-dried Tomatoes Mix, 24
Shrimp, Eggs and Mushrooms, 24
Enchilada Eggs Mix, 25
Italian Squash and Olives Bowls, 25
Prosciutto and Zucchini Eggs, 25
Green Beans, Kale and Eggs, 26
Oregano Eggs, 26
Eggplant Bowls, 26
Cheddar Eggs, 27
Spinach Frittata, 27
Sweet Potato Mix, 28
Pesto Zucchini Ramekins, 29
Turkey Meatballs, 65
Olives Balls, 68
Spicy Meatballs, 69
Cauliflower Bowls, 69
Bbq Chicken Meatballs, 76
Shrimp Meatballs, 79
Turkey Meatballs and Sauce, 118

Coffee Cream, 153
Turmeric and Lime Crème Brule, 153
Walnuts Pudding, 153
Vanilla Pudding, 154
Almond Cheesecake, 155
Cocoa Strawberries Cream, 155
Blackberries Cream, 156
Carrot and Rice Pudding, 158
Nuts Custard, 159
Berry and Pumpkin Curd, 164
Dates Espresso Cream, 165
Yogurt and Berries Pudding, 166
Cinnamon Cream, 167
Asparagus, Spinach and Eggs Mix, 16

ENDIVES
Coconut Endives and Radish, 56
Chicken with Endives, 107
Dill Endives, 145

FENNEL
Pork and Blueberries Mix, 33
Lamb with Fennel and Tomatoes, 42
Parmesan Fennel, 49
Fennel and Shrimp Salad, 80
Turkey and Fennel, 107
Pork and Fennel, 124
Lime Fennel, 145
Nutmeg Fennel and Tomatoes, 149

FIGS
Figs and Grapes Compote, 161
Avocado and Figs Bowls, 163

GARAM MASALA
Ginger and Shallot Duck, 37
Provence Chicken Breast, 37
Beef and Tomato Mix, 46
Soy Mushrooms, 50
Spicy Collards Greens, 59
Pesto Dip, 82
Shrimp and Corn, 86
Garlic Mackerel, 92
Shrimp and Mustard Sauce, 95
Parsley Cod, 96
Salmon and Sweet Potatoes, 99
Turkey with Sauce, 102
Chicken and Mango Mi, 105
Coconut Turkey, 109
Turkey and Quinoa, 111
Creamy Chicken, 113
Masala Turkey, 114
Creamy Pork, 120
Pork and Creamy Scallions Sauce, 133
Balsamic Radishes, 139

Balsamic Mushroom Mix, 151

GHEE
Cinnamon Toast, 13
Lemon Shrimp and Avocado Bowls, 30
Turmeric Brussels Sprouts, 148
Raisins Pudding, 154

GRAPES
Grapes Bowls, 154
Grapes and Rice Pudding, 154
Orange Bowls, 155
Figs and Grapes Compote, 161

GREEK YOGURT
Sweet Potato Mix, 28
Beef and Yogurt Mix, 42
Greek Rosemary Lamb Chops, 43
Pesto Dip, 82
Chicken and Yogurt Sauce, 115
Yogurt and Berries Pudding, 166
Strawberries and Ginger Cream, 167
Cinnamon Cream, 167

HARISSA
Harrisa Lamb Mix, 41

HONEY
Strawberry Bowls, 28
Apple Salad, 29
Balsamic Salmon Bites, 81
Garlic Chicken Bites, 82
Honey Cod, 93
Quinoa Pudding, 167

KALE
Kale, Sausage and Eggs, 24
Kale, Sausage and Eggs, 24
Green Beans, Kale and Eggs, 26
Mustard Salmon Mix, 32
Kale and Spring Onions Mix, 56
Lemon Greens Mix, 59
Mustard Greens, Olives and Kale Salad, 60
Jalapeno Greens Mix, 61
Chicken Salad, 77
Salmon and Kale, 99
Chicken with Tomato and Kale, 115
Turkey with Spinach and Kale, 119
Garlic Kale, 141
Spicy Cabbage with Kale, 147

LAMB
Lamb Rack and Cherry Tomatoes Mix, 35
Coriander Leg of Lamb, 36
Rack of Lamb and Baby Cauliflower Mix, 36

Lamb, Leeks and Mushroom Mix, 35
Lamb Fillets and Olives, 36
Garlic and Peppercorns Lamb Chops, 36
Lamb and Spinach Salad, 41
Harrisa Lamb Mix, 41
Lamb with Fennel and Tomatoes, 42
Greek Rosemary Lamb Chops, 43
Italian Lamb Chops, 120
Chives Lamb, 121
Basil Lamb, 122
Mint Lamb, 122
Lamb and Zucchini Mix, 122
Allspice Lamb, 124
Creamy Lamb, 124
Paprika Lamb, 125
Pesto Lamb, 125
Lamb and Potatoes, 126
Lamb and Corn, 127
Lamb and Avocado Mix, 128
Lamb and Cucumber Mix, 129
Ground Lamb and Carrots Mix, 129
Lamb and Capers, 129
Lamb and Savoy Cabbage Mix, 130
Orange Lamb, 131
Lamb with Ginger Artichokes, 132
Lamb and Broccoli, 134
Lamb and Radish Mix, 134
Citrus Lamb Mix, 135
Oregano and Chili Lamb, 137

LEEKS
Lamb, Leeks and Mushroom Mix, 35
Rack of Lamb and Baby Cauliflower Mix, 36
Chicken and Leeks, 112
Buttery Leeks, 138

LEMON
Lemony and Parsley Beef, 40
Lemony Okra, 53
Lemon Oysters, 70
Clams and Wine Sauce, 97
Lemon Chops and Peas, 127
Lemon Compote, 156
Black Currant Marmalade, 162
Smoked Salmon, Avocado and Eggs Mix, 17
Lemon Eggs, 19
Chickpeas Breakfast Spread, 29
Roasted Pork and Apples, 40
Chili and Paprika Pork, 42
Parsley Cauliflower, 52
Eggplant and Okra Mix, 53
Lemon Olives and Radish Mix, 57
Cauliflower and Chard Mix, 58
Ginger Green Beans, 63
Lemon Cod and Peas, 86

Lemon Trout and Cabbage, 90
Shrimp and Peas, 93
Sage Turkey and Olives, 106
Chicken with Tomato and Kale, 115
Pork and Mushrooms, 123
Nutmeg Pork Roast, 132
Lamb and Radish Mix, 134
Ground Beef with Beets and Radishes, 136
Parsley Artichokes, 140
Dill Tomatoes, 142
Lemon Cauliflower, 148
Apple Compote, 156
Nuts Custard, 159

LEMON JUICE
Berry Coconut Mix, 14
Smoked Salmon, Avocado and Eggs Mix, 17
Lemon Eggs, 19
Tomato Sausage Salad, 23
Chickpeas Breakfast Spread, 29
Mustard Salmon Steaks, 30
Shrimp Salad, 30
Mustard Salmon Mix, 32
Garlic and Peppercorns Lamb Chops, 36
Roasted Pork and Apples, 40
Lemony and Parsley Beef, 40
Turmeric Veggies and Rice, 44
Shrimp and Sweet Potato Bowls, 44
Eggplant Stew, 45
Spinach and Pear Salad, 48
Parsley Cauliflower, 52
Lemony Okra, 53
Coconut Endives and Radish, 56
Cabbage and Carrots Mix, 56
Lemon Olives and Radish Mix, 57
Cauliflower and Chard Mix, 58
Lemon Greens Mix, 59
Crab Dip, 67
Spinach Dip, 68
Shrimp Bites, 70
Lemon Oysters, 70
Lemon Mussels, 72
Squid Salad, 72
Octopus and Mango Salad, 73
Italian Shrimp Salad, 74
Apple and Shrimp Salsa, 74
Tuna Bites and Mint Sauce, 76
Lemon Salmon, 84
Shrimp and Tomatoes Mix, 84
Shrimp and Spinach, 85
Turmeric Tuna, 85
Shrimp and Corn, 86
Lemon Trout and Cabbage, 90
Garlic Mackerel, 92
Shrimp and Peas, 93

Basil Shrimp, 93
Shrimp and Quinoa, 95
Clams and Wine Sauce, 97
Tarragon Trout, 98
Turkey and Potatoes, 106
Sage Turkey and Olives, 106
Cumin Turkey, 110
Turkey with Mushrooms, 111
Chicken and Leeks, 112
Turkey with Chickpeas, 114
Cinnamon Chicken, 118
Garlic Pork Chops, 120
Beef and Artichokes, 123
Pork and Fennel, 124
Spiced Beef and Peppers, 126
Lemon Chops and Peas, 127
Pork and Olives, 128
Lamb and Capers, 129
Nutmeg Pork Roast, 132
Pork, Capers and Green Beans, 133
Lamb and Radish Mix, 134
Ground Beef with Beets and Radishes, 136
Green Beans and Capers, 138
Parsley Artichokes, 140
Garlic Brussels Sprouts, 140
Spicy Eggplant, 143
Paprika Okra, 144
Olives and Tomatoes, 145
Eggplant and Okra Mix, 146
Lemon Bok Choy, 146
Lemon Cauliflower, 148
Lemon Okra, 150
Walnuts Pudding, 153
Lemon Compote, 156
Apple Compote, 156
Avocado Cream, 157
Nuts Custard, 159
Black Currant Marmalade, 162
Peach Jelly, 164
Berry and Pumpkin Curd, 164
Lemon Shrimp and Avocado Bowls, 30
Turkey Hash, 45
Tomato and Mango Salsa, 55
Eggplant and Pearl Onion Mix, 55
Spicy Collards Greens, 59
Sprouts Salad, 61
Lemon Cod and Peas, 86
Shrimp and Pineapple Bowls, 87
Shrimp and Broccoli, 88
Cod and Carrots, 89
Lemon Sea Bass and Olives, 100
Nutmeg Fennel and Tomatoes, 149
Mascarpone and Plums Cream, 158

LENTILS (CANNED)
Lentils Stew, 43
Lentils and Quinoa Stew, 46
Spicy Lentils Bowls, 81
Turkey with Lentils, 112
Pork and Lentils Mix, 125

LIME
Herbed Pork and Sun dried Tomatoes, 33
Shrimp and Pico De Gallo, 75
Scallops and Radish Salad, 75
Lime Duck and Eggplant Mix, 101
Chicken with Endives, 107
Chicken and Lime Red Cabbage, 119
Turmeric Brussels Sprouts, 148
Coconut Broccoli Mix, 151
Coffee Cream, 153
Almond Cheesecake, 155
Strawberries Compote, 160
Peach Compote, 165
Lime Coconut Jars, 14
Lime Eggs, Tomato and Avocado Mix, 18
Beef and Yogurt Mix, 42
Italian Shrimp Salad, 74
Pesto Dip, 82
Garlic Sea Bass, 88
Shrimp and Mustard Sauce, 95
Shrimp and Rice, 95
Creamy Salmon Mix, 96
Shrimp, Crab and Avocado Bowls, 98
Mustard Chicken and Capers, 101
Turkey with Sauce, 102
Chicken with Brussels Sprouts Mix, 107
Coconut Turkey, 109
Spiced Chicken Wings, 111
Turkey with Lime Sauce, 111
Turmeric Duck, 112
Ground Chicken and Veggies Mix, 115
Duck and Plums Mix, 116
Turkey with Spinach and Kale, 119
Pork Chops and Green Beans, 121
Lamb and Broccoli, 134
Lime Fennel, 145
Turmeric and Lime Crème Brule, 153
Lime Jam, 163

LIME JUICE
Lime Coconut Jars, 14
Greens and Eggs, 22
Strawberry Bowls, 28
BBQ Cod Mix, 31
Calamari, Salmon and Shrimp Bowls, 31
Lime Lobster, 32
Herbed Pork and Sun dried Tomatoes, 33
Buttery Pork Tenderloin, 34

Garlic and Nutmeg Pork, 34
Thyme Pork Chops, 35
Coriander Leg Of Lamb, 36
Provence Chicken Breast, 37
Cranberry Beef, 40
Maple Pork Chops, 41
Pork Roast and Olives Salsa, 41
Beef and Yogurt Mix, 42
Curry and Coconut Pork Chops, 43
Chicken and Eggplants, 45
Turmeric Shrimp Mix, 46
Chickpeas Stew, 47
Green Beans Salad, 47
Cauliflower Salad, 48
Lime Brussels Sprouts, 49
Soy Mushrooms, 50
Thai Eggplant Mix, 50
Peppers and Seeds Mix, 51
Parsley Asparagus, 51
Tarragon Mushrooms, 51
Coriander Tomato and Spinach Mix, 54
Kale and Spring Onions Mix, 56
Simple Cabbage and Avocado Mix, 57
Apple and Zucchini Mix, 58
Spinach, Mango and Tomatoes, 60
Mustard Greens, Olives and Kale Salad, 60
Hot Cauliflower, 63
Dill Eggplant, 63
Dill Peas, 64
Thyme Shrimp Platter, 65
Parsley Calamari Bites, 71
Salmon Salsa, 71
Shrimp and Cucumber Salad, 72
Calamari and Radish Salad, 73
Clam Bowls, 73
Italian Shrimp Salad, 74
Cod Salsa, 74
Shrimp and Pico De Gallo, 75
Scallops and Radish Salad, 75
BBQ Chicken Meatballs, 76
Creamy Corn Dip, 76
Chicken Salad, 77
Duck and Spinach Salad, 77
Chicken Dip, 78
Radish Dip, 79
Beet Salsa, 80
Walnuts Bowls, 83
Cod and Green Beans, 85
Salmon and Avocado Mix, 85
Ginger Cod, 86
Chives Shrimp Mix, 87
Pesto Sea Bass, 87
Garlic Sea Bass, 88
Tuna and Brussels Sprouts, 88
Mackerel and Avocado Mix, 89

Chili Cod, 90
Balsamic Salmon and Beans, 90
Lime and Chili Mussels, 91
Tuna Bites with Pineapple, 91
Sea Bass and Avocado, 91
Smoked Salmon and Chives, 92
Italian Mackerel, 93
Honey Cod, 93
Curry Sea Bass, 94
Calamari and Mushrooms, 94
Coriander Shrimp Mix, 94
Parsley Cod, 96
Cod, Olives and Zucchinis, 96
Creamy Salmon Mix, 96
Trout and Capers Mix, 97
Creole Calamari, 97
Shrimp, Corn and Tomato Bowls, 98
Shrimp, Crab and Avocado Bowls, 98
Salmon and Kale, 99
Rosemary Calamari, 99
Lime Duck and Eggplant Mix, 101
Pesto Turkey, 101
Mustard Chicken and Capers, 101
Duck and Tomatoes, 103
Garlic Chicken Mix, 103
Chicken and Avocado, 104
Turkey and Tomato Sauce, 104
Chili Chicken, 105
Chicken and Mango Mi, 105
Ginger Turkey, 105
Chicken with Brussels Sprouts Mix, 107
Turkey and Fennel, 107
Chicken and Squash Mix, 108
Paprika Turkey Mix, 108
Chicken and Salsa, 109
Coconut Turkey, 109
Rosemary Chicken, 110
Spiced Chicken Wings, 111
Turkey with Lime Sauce, 111
Turmeric Duck, 112
Chicken and Cauliflower, 113
Duck and Plums Mix, 116
Chicken with Okra, 117
Turkey and Tomatoes, 119
Turkey with Spinach and Kale, 119
Chicken and Lime Red Cabbage, 119
Oregano Pork, 121
Pork Chops and Green Beans, 121
Hot Beef, 122
Lamb and Zucchini Mix, 122
Pork and Tomatoes, 123
Allspice Lamb, 124
Creamy Lamb, 124
Paprika Lamb, 125
Beef and Berries, 125

Pesto Lamb, 125
Lamb and Potatoes, 126
Lamb and Corn, 127
Parsley Pork, 127
Beef and Corn, 128
Pork with Tomatoes and Potatoes, 130
Lamb and Savoy Cabbage Mix, 130
Beef with Carrots and Cabbage, 131
Beef and Swiss Chard, 132
Lamb with Ginger Artichokes, 132
Pork and Creamy Scallions Sauce, 133
Lamb and Broccoli, 134
Citrus Lamb Mix, 135
Pork and Walnuts Mix, 135
Pork and Pumpkin Mix, 136
Lime Artichokes, 138
Basil Green Beans, 138
Buttery Leeks, 138
Green Beans and Corn, 139
Chives Radish, 141
Garlic Spinach, 142
Creamy Zucchini, 142
Cabbage Sauté, 143
Dill Endives, 145
Lime Fennel, 145
Paprika Olives Mix, 145
Balsamic Mushroom Mix, 151
Paprika Avocado and Mushrooms, 152
Lime Jam, 163
Peach Compote, 165
Lime and Chia Eggs, 21
Lamb and Spinach Salad, 41
Shrimp and Pineapple Bowls, 66
Peppers Salsa, 66
Radish Chips, 67
Fennel and Shrimp Salad, 80
Spicy Lentils Bowls, 81
Chickpeas Spread, 82
Pesto Dip, 82
Shrimp and Olives Bowls, 83
Mussels Bowls, 83
Tuna and Asparagus, 89
Chicken with Hot Red Chard, 113
Turkey with Pomegranate Mix, 114
Chives Lamb, 121
Mustard Asparagus, 139
Creamy Bell Peppers, 140
Cayenne Broccoli, 141
Ginger Bok Choy Mix, 146
Spicy Cabbage with Kale, 147
Mint Eggplant, 147
Balsamic Pearl Onions, 147
Coconut Cabbage, 148
Green Beans and Avocado Mix, 149
Peppers and Green Beans, 150

Ginger Radish and Spring Onions, 150
Broccoli and Rice, 151
Almond Cheesecake, 155
Strawberries Compote, 160
Pecan Plums Bowls, 162
Blackberry and Rhubarb Jam, 162

LOBSTER
Lime Lobster, 32

MACKEREL
Mackerel and Avocado Mix, 89
Garlic Mackerel, 92
Italian Mackerel, 93

MANGO
Tomato and Mango Salsa, 55
Spinach, Mango and Tomatoes, 60
Mango and Radishes Mix, 61
Octopus and Mango Salad, 73
Cod Salsa, 74
Chicken Salad, 77
Fennel and Shrimp Salad, 80
Chicken and Mango Mi, 105
Mango Bowls, 165
Fruit Salad, 166

MILK
Vanilla Pudding, 154

MUSHROOMS
Eggs, Green Beans and Mushrooms, 17
Ground Beef and Eggs Ramekins, 18
Shrimp, Eggs and Mushrooms, 24
Mushroom Oatmeal, 27
Lamb, Leeks and Mushroom Mix, 35
Pork Chops and Mushrooms, 40
Mushroom Dip, 78
Turkey with Mushrooms, 111
Mushroom and Tomatoes Sauté, 151

MUSHROOMS (BROWN)
Tarragon Mushrooms, 51
Calamari and Mushrooms, 94
Pork and Mushrooms, 123
Balsamic Mushroom Mix, 151

MUSHROOMS (CREMINI)
Mushroom Salad, 54

MUSHROOMS (WHITE)
Stuffed Mushrooms, 68
Bok Choy and Veggies Bowls, 22
Sausages and Mushrooms Mix, 23
Soy Mushrooms, 50

Mushroom and Broccoli Mix, 52
Paprika Avocado and Mushrooms, 152

MUSSELS
Lemon Mussels, 72
Mussels Bowls, 83
Lime and Chili Mussels, 91

MUSTARD (GREENS)
Mustard Greens, Olives and Kale Salad, 60
Greens and Shallots Mix, 60
Jalapeno Greens Mix, 61

NUTMEG
Coconut Eggs, 16
Banana Oatmeal, 27
Garlic and Nutmeg Pork, 34
Pork Chops and Mushrooms, 40
Creamy Garlic Spinach and Corn, 59
Spiced Chicken Wings, 111
Spiced Beef and Peppers, 126
Nutmeg Pork Roast, 132
Citrus Lamb Mix, 135
Nutmeg Brussels Sprouts, 141
Nutmeg Fennel and Tomatoes, 149
Cinnamon Apples, 153
Vanilla Pudding, 154
Grapes Bowls, 154
Almond Blueberries Ramekins, 158
Pears Jam, 160
Creamy Pears, 163

NUTS (MACADAMIA)
Nuts Custard, 159

OATS
Almond Oats, 19
Banana Oatmeal, 27
Mushroom Oatmeal, 27
Walnut and Berries Bowls, 28

OCTOPUS
Octopus and Mango Salad, 73

OKRA
Cumin Okra, 52
Eggplant and Okra Mix, 53
Lemony Okra, 53
Tomato and Okra Mix, 53
Spicy Beets and Okra, 55
Chicken with Okra, 117
Paprika Okra, 144
Eggplant and Okra Mix, 146
Lemon Okra, 150
Chili Okra and Radishes, 152

OLIVES (BLACK)
Lemon Olives and Radish Mix, 57
Mustard Greens, Olives and Kale Salad, 60
Greens and Shallots Mix, 60
Olives Balls, 68
Stuffed Mushrooms, 68
Shrimp and Cucumber Salad, 72
Octopus and Mango Salad, 73
Cod, Olives and Zucchinis, 96
Turkey Medley, 104
Chicken and Salsa, 109
Pork and Olives, 128
Olives and Tomatoes, 145
Beets and Olives, 146
Peppers and Green Beans, 150
Paprika Avocado and Mushrooms, 152

OLIVES (GREEN)
Cod Salsa, 74
Beet Salsa, 80
Lemon Sea Bass and Olives, 100
Olives and Tomatoes, 145

OLIVES (KALAMATA)
Simple Cabbage and Avocado Mix, 57
Lemon Olives and Radish Mix, 57
Mustard Greens, Olives and Kale Salad, 60
Peppers Salsa, 66
Olives Balls, 68
Squid Salad, 72
Calamari and Radish Salad, 73
Clam Bowls, 73
Scallops and Radish Salad, 75
Tuna Salad, 75
Chicken Salad, 77
Fennel and Shrimp Salad, 80
Shrimp and Olives Bowls, 83
Mussels Bowls, 83
Salmon and Olives, 86
Balsamic Sea Bass, 97
Lemon Sea Bass and Olives, 100
Paprika Olives Mix, 145
Beets and Olives, 146

ONION
Clam Bowls, 73
Sausages and Mushrooms Mix, 23

ONION (GREEN)
Apple and Zucchini Mix, 58
Creamy Radish and Corn Mix, 61
Green Beans and Avocado Mix, 149
Tuna Salad, 75

ONION (PEARL)
Eggplant and Pearl Onion Mix, 55
Pearl Onions Bowls, 65
Balsamic Pearl Onions, 147

ONION (RED)
Pepper Eggs Mix, 16
Eggs, Green Beans and Mushrooms, 17
Ginger Tomatoes Eggs, 21
Bok Choy and Veggies Bowls, 22
Eggs and Asparagus, 23
Kale, Sausage and Eggs, 24
Enchilada Eggs Mix, 25
Rack of Lamb and Baby Cauliflower Mix, 36
Beet Cream Soup, 38
Chicken Soup, 39
Tomato and Eggplant Stew, 43
Turmeric Veggies and Rice, 44
Turkey Hash, 45
Eggplant Stew, 45
Beef and Tomato Mix, 46
Peppers Stew, 47
Potato Stew, 47
Green Beans Salad, 47
Peppers and Eggplant Mix, 50
Cumin Okra, 52
Italian Tomatoes, 54
Tomato and Mango Salsa, 55
Cauliflower and Chard Mix, 58
Dill Eggplant, 63
Turkey Meatballs, 65
Stuffed Mushrooms, 68
Shrimp and Pico De Gallo, 75
Chicken Salad, 77
Duck and Spinach Salad, 77
Eggplant Dip, 81
Ginger Cod, 86
Shrimp and Broccoli, 88
Chili Cod, 90
Shrimp and Eggplant, 92
Curry Sea Bass, 94
Shrimp and Quinoa, 95
Shrimp and Rice, 95
Trout and Capers Mix, 97
Rosemary Calamari, 99
Lime Duck and Eggplant Mix, 101
Turkey with Sauce, 102
Chicken and Green Beans, 103
Turkey and Tomato Sauce, 104
Turkey and Potatoes, 106
Chicken with Endives, 107
Cumin Turkey, 110
Chicken and Red Beans, 110
Chicken and Cauliflower, 113
Chicken with Hot Red Chard, 113
Turkey with Chickpeas, 114
Cayenne Turkey and Green Beans, 116
Allspice Turkey, 117
Chicken with Okra, 117
Turkey Meatballs and Sauce, 118
Turmeric Pork Chops, 120
Chives Lamb, 121
Oregano Pork, 121
Basil Lamb, 122
Mint Lamb, 122
Lamb and Zucchini Mix, 122
Beef and Artichokes, 123
Pork and Mushrooms, 123
Pesto Lamb, 125
Rosemary Beef, 126
Sage Beef, 127
Beef and Corn, 128
Ground Lamb and Carrots Mix, 129
Lamb and Capers, 129
Beef and Spicy Zucchinis, 130
Pork with Tomatoes and Potatoes, 130
Beef with Carrots and Cabbage, 131
Lamb with Ginger Artichokes, 132
Beef and Beets, 134
Salmon Salsa, 71
Beet Salsa, 80
Pork and Red Onions Mix, 135

ONION (YELLOW)
Ground Beef and Eggs Ramekins, 18
Bacon and Radish Scramble, 20
Eggs, Cheese and Sun-dried Tomatoes Mix, 24
Chili Chicken, 38
Zucchini Cream, 39
Pork Bowls, 44
Lentils and Quinoa Stew, 46
Chickpeas Stew, 47
Cabbage and Carrots Mix, 56
Ginger Broccoli and Radish Mix, 58
Spicy Collards Greens, 59
Cauliflower Spread, 65
Stuffed Peppers, 77
Chicken Dip, 78
Creamy Salmon Mix, 96
Creamy Chicken, 113
Allspice Lamb, 124
Creamy Lamb, 124

ONIONS (SPRING)
Sausage Ramekins, 17
Smoked Salmon, Avocado and Eggs Mix, 17
Greens and Eggs, 22
Zucchini Bowls, 23
Shrimp, Eggs and Mushrooms, 24
Eggplant Bowls, 26

Cheddar Eggs, 27
Spinach Frittata, 27
Pesto Zucchini Ramekins, 29
Chickpeas Breakfast Spread, 29
Chicken, Shrimp and Rice, 32
Spring Onion and Soy Chicken, 38
Cauliflower Soup, 39
Pork Roast and Olives Salsa, 41
Lentils Stew, 43
Shrimp and Sweet Potato Bowls, 44
Chicken and Eggplants, 45
Turmeric Shrimp Mix, 46
Kale and Spring Onions Mix, 56
Creamy Corn, 62
Thyme Shrimp Platter, 65
Peppers Salsa, 66
Zucchini Salsa, 67
Crab Dip, 67
Stuffed Mushrooms, 68
Spicy Meatballs, 69
Artichoke Dip, 70
Cod Salsa, 74
Creamy Corn Dip, 76
Stuffed Peppers, 77
Mushroom Dip, 78
Shrimp and Olives Bowls, 83
Turmeric Tuna, 85
Lemon Cod and Peas, 86
Cod, Olives and Zucchinis, 96
Salmon and Sweet Potatoes, 99
Salmon with Quinoa and Rice, 100
Lemon Sea Bass and Olives, 10
Chicken and Squash Mix, 108
Chicken and Salsa, 109
Turkey and Quinoa, 111
Turkey with Lime Sauce, 111
Chicken and Leeks, 112
Turmeric Duck, 112
Turkey and Spring Onions, 119
Creamy Pork, 120
Pork and Mushrooms, 123
Pork and Tomatoes, 123
Pork and Lentils Mix, 125
Lamb and Savoy Cabbage Mix, 130
Ginger Pork, 131
Lamb and Broccoli, 134
Lamb and Radish Mix, 134
Citrus Lamb Mix, 135
Pork with Peppers and Avocado, 136
Green Beans Sauté, 142
Olives and Tomatoes, 145
Mint Eggplant, 147
Ginger Radish and Spring Onions, 150
Mushroom and Tomatoes Sauté, 151
Lamb and Pomegranate Mix, 35

Apple and Shrimp Salsa, 74

ORANGE
Orange Chicken Mix, 102
Citrus Lamb Mix, 135
Orange Pork and Veggies, 137
Orange Green Beans, 49
Orange Bowls, 155
Orange Jam, 157

Orange Lamb, 131
ORANGE JUICE
Lamb Fillets and Olives, 36
Orange Chicken Mix, 102
Citrus Lamb Mix, 135
Orange Pork and Veggies, 137
Orange Bowls, 155
Orange Lamb, 131
Orange Green Beans, 49

OYSTERS
Lemon Oysters, 70

PARSNIP
Ground Lamb and Carrots Mix, 129
Balsamic Carrots and Parsnips, 50

PASTE (CHILI)
Chili Okra and Radishes, 152

PASTE (CURRY)
Curry and Coconut Pork Chops, 43

PASTE (TAHINI)
Chickpeas Breakfast Spread, 29
Chickpeas Spread, 82

PASTE CURRY (GREEN)
Curry Trout and Green Beans, 94

PASTE CURRY (YELLOW)
Curry Chicken Thighs, 37
Curry Shrimp, 87

PEACHES
Peaches Bowls, 163
Peach Compote, 165
Plums and Peaches Bowls, 166

PEARS
Spinach and Pear Salad, 48
Pork and Pears Mix, 137
Pears Jam, 160
Peach Jelly, 164

PEAS
Lemon Cod and Peas, 86
Shrimp and Peas, 93
Lemon Chops and Peas, 127

PEAS (GREEN)
Dill Peas, 64

PECANS
Lamb and Spinach Salad, 41
Pecan Plums Bowls, 162
Nuts and Apples Bowls, 166

PEPPER (CAYENNE)
Pork and Blueberries Mix, 33
Chili and Paprika Pork, 42
Lime Brussels Sprouts, 49
Squid Salad, 72
Fennel and Shrimp Salad, 80
Cayenne Turkey and Green Beans, 116
Cayenne Broccoli, 141
Beef and Spicy Zucchinis, 130

PEPPER (CHILI)
Kale, Sausage and Eggs, 24
Hot Cauliflower, 63
Ginger Green Beans, 63
Spicy Lentils Bowls, 81
Lamb and Capers, 129
Salmon Salsa, 71
Chili Tuna, 84
Lime and Chili Mussels, 91
Italian Mackerel, 93

PEPPER (JALAPENO)
Shrimp and Pico De Gallo, 75
Creamy Corn Dip, 76
Jalapeno Greens Mix, 61

PEPPER (LEMON)
Lemony and Parsley Beef, 40

PEPPER CHILI (GREEN)
Turkey with Pomegranate Mix, 114
Lemon Sea Bass and Olives, 100
Chili Chicken, 105

PEPPER CHILI (RED)
Mushroom Oatmeal, 27
Chili Chicken, 38
Coconut Cheese Dip, 66
Turkey with Sauce, 102
Shrimp and Pineapple Bowls, 87
Chili Cod, 90
Spiced Chicken Wings, 111

Hot Beef, 122
Spicy Eggplant, 143
Chili Collard Greens, 144
Spicy Beets and Okra, 55
Spicy Collards Greens, 59
Chicken with Hot Red Chard, 113
Oregano and Chili Lamb, 137
Cilantro Hot Artichokes, 144

PEPPER FLAKES (RED)
Spinach Scramble, 15
Bok Choy and Veggies Bowls, 22
Eggs, Cheese and Sun-dried Tomatoes Mix, 24
Cod Salsa, 31
Turkey Hash, 45
Lentils and Quinoa Stew, 46
Spicy Collards Greens, 59
Hot Cauliflower, 63
Peppers Salsa, 66
Cod Salsa, 74
Sausage Bites, 79
Walnuts Bowls, 83
Shrimp and Spinach, 85
Lemon Cod and Peas, 86
Hot Beef, 122
Lamb and Capers, 129
Pork and Pears Mix, 137
Basil Green Beans, 138
Cilantro Hot Artichokes, 144
Balsamic Pearl Onions, 147

PINE NUTS
Peppers and Seeds Mix, 51
Tuna Bites and Mint Sauce, 76
Green Beans and Pine Nuts Mix, 149

PINEAPPLE
Balsamic Tomato and Pineapple Mix, 55
Shrimp and Pineapple Bowls, 66
Italian Shrimp Salad, 74
Shrimp and Pineapple Bowls, 87

PLUMS
Duck and Plums Mix, 116
Mascarpone and Plums Cream, 158
Maple and Plums Pudding, 158
Pecan Plums Bowls, 162
Plums and Peaches Bowls, 166

POMEGRANATE
Lamb and Pomegranate Mix, 35
Turkey with Pomegranate Mix, 114

POMEGRANATE JUICE
Lamb and Pomegranate Mix, 35

PORK
Pork and Blueberries Mix, 33
BBQ and Paprika Ribs, 33
Herbed Pork and Sun dried Tomatoes, 33
Buttery Pork Tenderloin, 34
Garlic and Nutmeg Pork, 34
Thyme Pork and Carrots, 34
Thyme Pork Chops, 35
Roasted Pork and Apples, 40
Pork Chops and Mushrooms, 40
Maple Pork Chops, 41
Pork Roast and Olives Salsa, 41
Chili and Paprika Pork, 42
Curry and Coconut Pork Chops, 43
Pork Bowls, 44
Turmeric Pork Chops, 120
Garlic Pork Chops, 120
Creamy Pork, 120
Oregano Pork, 121
Pork Chops and Green Beans, 121
Pork and Mushrooms, 123
Pork and Tomatoes, 123
Pork and Fennel, 124
Pork and Lentils Mix, 125
Lemon Chops and Peas, 127
Parsley Pork, 127
Pork and Olives, 128
Pork with Tomatoes and Potatoes, 130
Ginger Pork, 131
Nutmeg Pork Roast, 132
Balsamic Pork Chops, 133
Pork and Creamy Scallions Sauce, 133
Pork, Capers and Green Beans, 133
Pork and Red Onions Mix, 135
Pork and Walnuts Mix, 135
Pork and Pumpkin Mix, 136
Pork with Peppers and Avocado, 136
Orange Pork and Veggies, 137
Pork and Pears Mix, 137

POTATOES
Sweet Potato Mix, 28
Pork Bowls, 44
Shrimp and Sweet Potato Bowls, 44
Potato Stew, 47
Chives Potatoes, 64
Salmon and Sweet Potatoes, 99
Turkey and Potatoes, 106
Lamb and Potatoes, 126
Pork with Tomatoes and Potatoes, 130

PUMPKIN
Pork and Pumpkin Mix, 136
Sweet Pumpkin Bowls, 162
Berry and Pumpkin Curd, 164

Cinnamon Cream, 167

QUINOA
Quinoa and Berries Bowls, 26
Chives Avocado Quinoa, 28
Lentils and Quinoa Stew, 46
Shrimp and Quinoa, 95
Salmon with Quinoa and Rice, 100
Turkey and Quinoa, 111
Quinoa Pudding, 167
Avocado and Quinoa Bowls, 167

RADISHES
Bacon and Radish Scramble, 20
Ginger Broccoli and Radish Mix, 58
Coconut Endives and Radish, 56
Lemon Olives and Radish Mix, 57
Mango and Radishes Mix, 61
Creamy Radish and Corn Mix, 61
Radish Chips, 67
Calamari and Radish Salad, 73
Italian Shrimp Salad, 74
Cod Salsa, 74
Scallops and Radish Salad, 75
Radish Dip, 79
Pesto Radish and Corn Dip, 81
Lamb and Radish Mix, 134
Lamb and Radish Mix, 134
Ground Beef with Beets and Radishes, 136
Balsamic Radishes, 139
Chives Radish, 141
Beet and Radish Mix, 144
Ginger Radish and Spring Onions, 150
Balsamic Walnuts and Radish Mix, 152
Chili Okra and Radishes, 152

RAISINS
Walnut and Berries Bowls, 28
Raisins Pudding, 154

RASPBERRIES
Duck and Spinach Salad, 77
Coconut Raspberry Bowls, 157
Creamy Berries Bowls, 159
Berry and Pumpkin Curd, 164
Yogurt and Berries Pudding, 166

RHUBARB
Rhubarb Compote, 161
Blackberry and Rhubarb Jam, 162

RICE
Cinnamon Rice Pudding, 16
Turmeric Veggies and Rice, 44
Cardamom Pudding, 159

Grapes and Rice Pudding, 154
Raisins Pudding, 154
Carrot and Rice Pudding, 158

RICE (WILD)
Chicken, Shrimp and Rice, 32
Shrimp and Rice, 95
Broccoli and Rice, 151

SALAMI
Italian Squash and Olives Bowls, 25

SALMON
Smoked Salmon, Avocado and Eggs Mix, 17
Calamari, Salmon and Shrimp Bowls, 31
Salmon with Quinoa and Rice, 100
Mustard Salmon Steaks, 30
Mustard Salmon Mix, 32
Salmon Salsa, 71
Balsamic Salmon Bites, 81
Lemon Salmon, 84
Salmon and Avocado Mix, 85
Salmon and Olives, 86
Balsamic Salmon and Beans, 90
Smoked Salmon and Chives, 92
Creamy Salmon Mix, 96
Salmon and Kale, 99
Salmon and Sweet Potatoes, 99

SALSA
Cod Salsa, 31
Lentils Stew, 43

SAUCE (BBQ)
BBQ Cod Mix, 31
BBQ and Paprika Ribs, 33
BBQ Chicken Meatballs, 76
BBQ Chicken Wings, 109

SAUCE (CHILI)
Shrimp and Cucumber Salad, 72
Pork and Blueberries Mix, 33
Chili Chicken, 38
Chili and Paprika Pork, 42
Ground Chicken and Veggies Mix, 115

SAUCE (ENCHILADA)
Enchilada Eggs Mix, 25

SAUCE (HOT)
Mushroom Dip, 78

SAUCE (SRIRACHA)
Squid Salad, 72
Sriracha Turkey Bites, 80

SAUCE (WORCESTERSHIRE)
Bok Choy and Veggies Bowls, 22
Calamari and Radish Salad, 73

SAUSAGE
Sausage Ramekins, 17
Tomato Sausage Salad, 23

SAUSAGE (PORK)
Sausages and Mushrooms Mix, 23
Kale, Sausage and Eggs, 24

SAUSAGES (BEEF)
Sausage Bites, 79

SAVOY CABBAGE
Lamb and Savoy Cabbage Mix, 130

SCALLIONS
Parmesan Eggs, 14
Balsamic Calamari and Tomatoes, 30
Mustard Salmon Mix, 32
Maple Pork Chops, 41
Buttery Squash Mix, 49
Green Beans and Walnuts Mix, 57
Mustard Greens, Olives and Kale Salad, 60
Mango and Radishes Mix, 61
Rosemary Broccoli Mix, 62
Creamy Tomatoes, 62
BBQ Chicken Meatballs, 76
Chinese Beef Bites, 78
Shrimp Meatballs, 79
Radish Dip, 79
Eggplant Dip, 81
Chickpeas Spread, 82
Pesto Dip, 82
Mussels Bowls, 83
Salmon and Avocado Mix, 85
Shrimp and Corn, 86
Curry Shrimp, 87
Shrimp and Pineapple Bowls, 87
Tuna and Brussels Sprouts, 88
Mackerel and Avocado Mix, 89
Lemon Trout and Cabbage, 90
Smoked Salmon and Chives, 92
Calamari and Mushrooms, 94
Garlic Chicken Mix, 103
Chicken and Avocado, 104
Turkey Medley, 104
Ginger Turkey, 105
Paprika Turkey Mix, 108
Coconut Turkey, 109
Chicken and Peppers, 110
Masala Turkey, 114
Turkey with Pomegranate Mix, 114

Duck and Plums Mix, 116
Chicken Wings and Tomato Sauce, 116
Cinnamon Chicken, 118
Italian Lamb Chops, 120
Chives Lamb, 121
Lamb and Corn, 127
Parsley Pork, 127
Lamb and Avocado Mix, 128
Beef and Swiss Chard, 132
Pork and Creamy Scallions Sauce, 133
Pork, Capers and Green Beans, 133
Pork and Pumpkin Mix, 136
Mustard Chicken and Capers, 101
Scallops and Radish Salad, 75

SEA BASS
Pesto Sea Bass, 87
Garlic Sea Bass, 88
Sea Bass and Avocado, 91
Curry Sea Bass, 94
Balsamic Sea Bass, 97
Lemon Sea Bass and Olives, 100

SHALLOT
Calamari, Salmon and Shrimp Bowls, 31
Ginger and Shallot Duck, 37
Coconut Endives and Radish, 56
Beets and Olives, 146
Shallot Scramble, 13
Brussels Sprouts Salad, 20
Oregano Eggs, 26
Turkey Breast and Cranberries, 38
Greens and Shallots Mix, 60
Jalapeno Greens Mix, 61
Clam Bowls, 73
Broccoli and Tomatoes, 147
Broccoli and Rice, 151
Rack of Lamb and Baby Cauliflower Mix, 36

SHRIMP
Shrimp, Eggs and Mushrooms, 24
Lemon Shrimp and Avocado Bowls, 30
Shrimp Salad, 30
Calamari, Salmon and Shrimp Bowls, 31
Chicken, Shrimp and Rice, 32
Vanilla and Butter Shrimp, 33
Shrimp and Sweet Potato Bowls, 44
Turmeric Shrimp Mix, 46
Thyme Shrimp Platter, 65
Shrimp and Pineapple Bowls, 66
Shrimp Bites, 70
Shrimp and Cucumber Salad, 72
Italian Shrimp Salad, 74
Apple and Shrimp Salsa, 74
Shrimp and Pico De Gallo, 75

Shrimp Meatballs, 79
Fennel and Shrimp Salad, 80
Shrimp and Olives Bowls, 83
Shrimp and Tomatoes Mix, 84
Shrimp and Spinach, 85
Shrimp and Corn, 86
Curry Shrimp, 87
Chives Shrimp Mix, 87
Shrimp and Pineapple Bowls, 87
Shrimp and Broccoli, 88
Shrimp and Eggplant, 92
Shrimp and Peas, 93
Basil Shrimp, 93
Coriander Shrimp Mix, 94
Shrimp and Mustard Sauce, 95
Shrimp and Quinoa, 95
Shrimp and Rice, 95
Shrimp, Corn and Tomato Bowls, 98
Shrimp, Crab and Avocado Bowls, 98

SPINACH
Spinach Scramble, 15
Cream Cheese and Spinach Eggs, 17
Ground Beef and Eggs Ramekins, 18
Greens and Eggs, 22
Tomato Sausage Salad, 23
Sausages and Mushrooms Mix, 23
Spinach Frittata, 27
Shrimp Salad, 30
Mustard Salmon Mix, 32
Lamb and Spinach Salad, 41
Spinach and Pear Salad, 48
Creamy Spinach, 52
Coriander Tomato and Spinach Mix, 54
Creamy Garlic Spinach and Corn, 59
Lemon Greens Mix, 59
Spinach, Mango and Tomatoes, 60
Spinach Dip, 68
Duck and Spinach Salad, 77
Smoked Salmon and Chives, 92
Turkey with Spinach and Kale, 119
Pork with Peppers and Avocado, 136
Garlic Spinach, 142
Coconut Tomatoes and Spinach, 152
Eggplant Bowls, 26
Lemon Shrimp and Avocado Bowls, 30
Creamy Calamari, 32
Mushroom Salad, 54
Shrimp and Spinach, 85
Shrimp and Rice, 95

SQUID
Squid Salad, 72

STEVIA
Pork and Blueberries Mix, 33

STRAWBERRIES
Quinoa and Berries Bowls, 26
Strawberry Bowls, 28
Cocoa Strawberries Cream, 155
Avocado and Strawberries Bowls, 156
Sweet Coconut Mix, 159
Strawberries Compote, 160
Apples and Berries Compote, 161
Fruit Salad, 166
Strawberries and Ginger Cream, 167

SYRUP (CARAMEL)
Caramel Apples Mix, 155

SYRUP (MAPLE)
Maple Pork Chops, 41
Maple and Plums Pudding, 158

THAI CHILIES
Thai Eggplant Mix, 50

TOMATO PASSATA
Tomato and Eggplant Stew, 43
Pork Bowls, 44
Chicken and Eggplants, 45
Eggplant Stew, 45
Lentils and Quinoa Stew, 46
Chickpeas Stew, 47
Potato Stew, 47
Salmon and Olives, 86
Chicken and Green Beans, 103
Turkey and Tomato Sauce, 104
Beef and Artichokes, 123

TOMATO PASTE
Peppers Stew, 47

TOMATO SAUCE
Balsamic Calamari and Tomatoes, 30
Stuffed Peppers, 77
Sausage Bites, 79
Sriracha Turkey Bites, 80
Chicken and Red Beans, 110
Chicken Wings and Tomato Sauce, 116
Turkey Meatballs and Sauce, 118
Pork and Lentils Mix, 125
Bok Choy and Cauliflower Mix, 148

TOMATOES
Pesto Eggs, 15
Pepper Eggs Mix, 16
Chicken and Eggs, 21
Enchilada Eggs Mix, 25
Lime Eggs, Tomato and Avocado Mix, 18
Eggs, Cheese and Sun-dried Tomatoes Mix, 24
Italian Squash and Olives Bowls, 25
Herbed Pork and Sun dried Tomatoes, 33
Tomato and Eggplant Stew, 43
Italian Tomatoes, 54
Coriander Tomato and Spinach Mix, 54
Balsamic Tomato and Pineapple Mix, 55
Mustard Greens, Olives and Kale Salad, 60
Shrimp and Pico De Gallo, 75
Stuffed Peppers, 77
Shrimp and Quinoa, 95
Dill Tomatoes, 142
Tomato Jam, 165

TOMATOES (CANNED)
Lemon Okra, 150

TOMATOES (CHERRY)
Tomato Ramekins, 18
Brussels Sprouts Salad, 20
Ginger Tomatoes Eggs, 21
Bok Choy and Veggies Bowls, 22
Tomato Sausage Salad, 23
Sausages and Mushrooms Mix, 23
Balsamic Avocado and Tomato Salad, 29
Shrimp Salad, 30
Balsamic Calamari and Tomatoes, 30
Creamy Calamari, 32
Chicken, Shrimp and Rice, 32
Vanilla and Butter Shrimp, 33
Lamb Rack and Cherry Tomatoes Mix, 35
Lamb Fillets and Olives, 36
Pork Roast and Olives Salsa, 41
Lamb and Spinach Salad, 41
Lamb with Fennel and Tomatoes, 42
Turmeric Veggies and Rice, 44
Beef and Tomato Mix, 46
Peppers Stew, 47
Green Beans Salad, 47
Tomato and Okra Mix, 53
Mushroom Salad, 54
Tomato and Mango Salsa, 55
Simple Cabbage and Avocado Mix, 57
Spinach, Mango and Tomatoes, 60
Sprouts Salad, 61
Creamy Tomatoes, 62
Peppers Salsa, 66
Zucchini Salsa, 67
Salmon Salsa, 71
Squid Salad, 72
Octopus and Mango Salad, 73
Apple and Shrimp Salsa, 74
Scallops and Radish Salad, 75

Beet Salsa, 80
Mussels Bowls, 83
Shrimp and Tomatoes Mix, 84
Shrimp, Corn and Tomato Bowls, 98
Duck and Tomatoes, 103
Chicken and Salsa, 109
Chicken with Tomato and Kale, 115
Ground Chicken and Veggies Mix, 115
Turkey and Tomatoes, 119
Pork and Tomatoes, 123
Pork with Tomatoes and Potatoes, 130
Balsamic Tomatoes, 139
Pesto Tomato Mix, 143
Zucchini and Tomato Mix, 143
Olives and Tomatoes, 145
Ginger Bok Choy Mix, 146
Broccoli and Tomatoes, 147
Nutmeg Fennel and Tomatoes, 149
Mushroom and Tomatoes Sauté, 151
Coconut Tomatoes and Spinach, 152
Chili Okra and Radishes, 152
Greens and Shallots Mix, 60

TROUT
Lemon Trout and Cabbage, 90
Curry Trout and Green Beans, 94
Trout and Capers Mix, 97
Tarragon Trout, 98

TUNA
Chili Tuna, 84
Tuna Bites, 71
Tuna Salad, 75
Tuna Bites and Mint Sauce, 76
Turmeric Tuna, 85
Tuna and Brussels Sprouts, 88
Tuna and Asparagus, 89
Tuna Bites with Pineapple, 91

TURKEY
Sage Cajun Turkey, 37
Turkey Breast and Cranberries, 38
Turkey Hash, 45
Turkey Meatballs, 65
Sriracha Turkey Bites, 80
Pesto Turkey, 101
Turkey with Sauce, 102
Italian Turkey and Carrots, 102
Turkey and Tomato Sauce, 104
Turkey Medley, 104
Ginger Turkey, 105
Turkey and Potatoes, 106
Sage Turkey and Olives, 106
Turkey and Fennel, 107
Balsamic Turkey, 108

Paprika Turkey Mix, 108
Coconut Turkey, 109
Cumin Turkey, 110
Turkey and Quinoa, 111
Turkey with Mushrooms, 111
Turkey with Lime Sauce, 111
Turkey with Lentils, 112
Turkey with Chickpeas, 114
Masala Turkey, 114
Turkey with Pomegranate Mix, 114
Cayenne Turkey and Green Beans, 116
Oregano Turkey, 117
Allspice Turkey, 117
Turkey Meatballs and Sauce, 118
Turkey and Tomatoes, 119
Turkey with Spinach and Kale, 119
Turkey and Spring Onions, 119

WALNUTS
Walnut and Berries Bowls, 28
Spinach and Pear Salad, 48
Balsamic Beet Salad, 48
Duck and Spinach Salad, 77
Fennel and Shrimp Salad, 80
Walnuts Bowls, 83
Pork and Walnuts Mix, 135
Balsamic Walnuts and Radish Mix, 152
Walnuts Pudding, 153
Almond Blueberries Ramekins, 158
Nuts Custard, 159
Creamy Berries Bowls, 159
Nuts and Apples Bowls, 166

WINE (RED)
Thyme Pork and Carrots, 34
Turkey Breast and Cranberries, 38
Roasted Pork and Apples, 40
Pork Chops and Mushrooms, 40
Mushroom Salad, 54
Rosemary Calamari, 99
Turmeric Pork Chops, 120
Italian Lamb Chops, 120
Chives Lamb, 121
Oregano Pork, 121
Basil Lamb, 122
Mint Lamb, 122
Allspice Lamb, 124
Pork and Fennel, 124
Pork and Olives, 128
Ground Lamb and Carrots Mix, 129
Nutmeg Pork Roast, 132
Balsamic Pork Chops, 133
Pork and Pears Mix, 137
Mushroom and Tomatoes Sauté, 151
Allspice Turkey, 117

Sage Beef, 127

WINE (WHITE)
Mussels Bowls, 83
Paprika Cod, 84
Chives Shrimp Mix, 87
Tuna and Asparagus, 89
Lime and Chili Mussels, 91
Chives Cod, 91
Calamari and Mushrooms, 94
Coriander Shrimp Mix, 94
Trout and Capers Mix, 97
Creole Calamari, 97
Clams and Wine Sauce, 97
Lemon Sea Bass and Olives, 100
Turkey Medley, 104
Chicken with Endives, 107
Cayenne Turkey and Green Beans, 116
Oregano Turkey, 117
Turkey with Spinach and Kale, 119
Turkey and Spring Onions, 119
Parsley Pork, 127

ZUCCHINIS
Turmeric Veggies and Rice, 44
Lentils and Quinoa Stew, 46
Ground Chicken and Veggies Mix, 115
Orange Pork and Veggies, 137
Zucchini and Eggs, 18
Zucchini Bowls, 23
Prosciutto and Zucchini Eggs, 25
Pesto Zucchini Ramekins, 29
Zucchini Cream, 39
Apple and Zucchini Mix, 58
Zucchini Salsa, 67
Squid Salad, 72
Cod, Olives and Zucchinis, 96
Creamy Cod and Zucchinis, 99
Lamb and Zucchini Mix, 122
Beef and Spicy Zucchinis, 130
Balsamic Zucchini Mix, 140
Creamy Zucchini, 142
Zucchini and Tomato Mix, 143
Broccoli and Zucchini Mix, 150

Copyright 2019 by Nicole Coleman All rights reserved.

All rights Reserved. No part of this publication or the information in it may be quoted from or reproduced in any form by means such as printing, scanning, photocopying or otherwise without prior written permission of the copyright holder.

Disclaimer and Terms of Use: Effort has been made to ensure that the information in this book is accurate and complete, however, the author and the publisher do not warrant the accuracy of the information, text and graphics contained within the book due to the rapidly changing nature of science, research, known and unknown facts and internet. The Author and the publisher do not hold any responsibility for errors, omissions or contrary interpretation of the subject matter herein. This book is presented solely for motivational and informational purposes only.

Made in the USA
Middletown, DE
16 December 2019